WHERE THE RIVER ROARED: THE WISHOM TALES

I. "Spearing Salmon-Wishham." Special Collections Division, Univ. of Washington Libraries. Edward S. Curtis, c. 1909, photo NAI209

For Judy McWhorter Goodwin and
Richard McWhorter, "Big Foot's" grandchildren

WHERE THE RIVER ROARED:
THE WISHOM TALES

by
Donald M. Hines

Great Eagle Publishing®
Issaquah, Washington U.S.A.

WHERE THE RIVER ROARED:
THE WISHOM TALES

by Donald M. Hines

Great Eagle Publishing, Inc.
Published by: 3020 Issaquah-Pine Lake Rd SE
STE 481
Issaquah WA 98029 7255 U.S.A.

PUBLISHERS CATALOGING IN PUBLICATION
(Provided by Quality Books, Inc.)
Hines, Donald Merrill, 1931-
        Where the river roared: The Wishom tales/ by Donald M. Hines. -- 1st ed.
        p. cm.
        Includes bibliographical references.
        ISBN 0-9629539-6-2

        1. Tlakluit Indians--Mythology. 2. Tlakluit Indians--Folklore. 3. Coyote (Legendary character) I. Title.

E99.T58H56 1998   398.2'0899741
                         QB198-586

Library of Congress Catalog Card Number: 98-92829

CONTENTS

PART TWO.
THE TRADITIONAL TALES OF
THE WISHOMS

I. MYTHIC TALES OF THE ORIGIN
OF MAN, OF ANIMALS, PLANTS,
PHENOMENA

IV. COYOTE AS TRICKSTER

V. TALES OF CONFLICTS AND ADVENTURES

VI. TALES OF MONSTERS AND OGRES

VII. TALES COMPARABLE WITH EUROPEAN *MÄRCHEN*

VII. TWO ORAL TRADITIONAL HISTORIES OF BRAVE DEEDS AND DARING

PART THREE.
APPENDICES

ILLUSTRATIONS

PART ONE.
INTRODUCTION

I. A CULTURAL OVERVIEW
OF THE WISHOM NATION

A. LOCALE OF THE WISHOMS

G one now are the Indian villages from beside the Columbia River at Celilo, with the river's roaring rapids always in ear. Gone too are tribal fishing platforms and the racks with slabs of salmon air-drying against the long winter. Gone too are the smokes of many cooking fires, and the sounds of village families at work and play.

Now change rules: the Wishom Indians[1] were long ago removed from beside the river to the Yakama Reservation, Central Washington. And the Columbia River level, raised by numerous great hydroelectric dams, inundates where formerly the tribe lived, fished. And over tribal lands where silence and solitude were common now din with the sounds of another people: the freeway racket of cars or trucks, the throb and clatter of diesel locomotives, trains. How sad, now, that the Wishoms' heritage, their traditional tribal way of life, may be disappearing not only from view, but also from memory.

The Wishom Indian tribe[2] dwelt originally about

the dalles, or Five Miles Rapids on the north bank of the Columbia River where it begins its cut through the Cascades Range. No large tribe, they may have numbered only 1000 to 1500 in all. Their village sites were located approximately from the White Salmon River to Celilo Falls, along the Washington side, nearly opposite modern The Dalles, Oregon. If their permanent village sites were directly on the river, they hunted, or sought vegetable foodstuffs on the higher country considerably back from the river, even to the vicinity of modern Mount Adams. The tribespeople called themselves *i'tcxluit* [i.e., *Tlakluit*], and in all probability were the *"Echeloot"* met by the Lewis and Clark expedition. The Wishom were known by their Yakama and Klikitat tribal neighbors as *Wuy'cxam*, which is anglicized today as "Wishram," or "Wisham." Their principal settlement was *nixlu'idix* at Spedis, and Spier lists a total of perhaps 19 dwelling sites in 1850 which may have included fishing sites plus winter villages wherein up to 200 people might have dwelt. The name "Wishram" is preserved today in names on the land: the town of Wishram, Washington; and the huge Burlington Northern railroad yards nearby.[3]

B. GEOGRAPHIC LOCALE
THE COLUMBIA RIVER

The dominating natural feature of the Wishoms' tribal area, the Columbia River originates in British Columbia and flows a distance of 1900 km to the Pacific Ocean, its drainage area covering over 640,000 sq km. A large, and fast-flowing river, the Columbia is subject to annual flooding during spring and summer due to snow melt run-off from the mountains in its drainage area. Occasionally high flood levels occur, such as those of the flood of 1894, even of 1948.[4] But during fall and early winter, water levels are low. Even at low and medium stages of water level, river currents reach 8 to 10 km per hour--over short distances currents of 8 to 16 km per hour have been gauged, certain death to the unwary Indian canoer who risked being caught up and swept through the rapids, or over Celilo Falls.

Because its channel consists of a series of rapids in the vicinity of the Wishom and Wasco villages, the river once provided a unique fishery where migrating fish could be taken in a relatively easy manner. But recently the Columbia River's water levels were altered--the dynamic white water coursing in anguish over rapids and Celilo Falls has disappeared. In 1957, with the closing of the flood gates behind The Dalles Hydroelectric Dam, the water level of Lake Celilo behind the dam was raised 110 feet, and the river depth was fixed at 48.8 m. Now the character of the river has been changed, and old tribal dwelling sites, prime archaeological digs, have been inundated--lost.

LANDFORMS SURROUNDING THE WISHOMS

The second dominating natural feature of the Wishom's tribal territory is the deep chasm or "the dalles"[5] through which the Columbia River flows. This chasm is bounded on the north [Washington side of the Columbia River] by steep-sloped, rough hinterlands. To the south [the Oregon side of the Columbia River] stretches an up-land, the Deschutes-Umatilla Plateau. Opposite the Wishom tribal area, the John Day and the Deschutes Rivers rise far to the south, and flow in generally direct northerly channels to the Columbia River. Along the Washington side few streams or tributaries join the Columbia River until approximately Pasco and Kennewick, Washington.

The Columbia River canyon is remarkable for its north wall, which features steep inclines often characterized by a series of parallel basaltic cliffs thinly covered with soil. This northerly wall is approximately 2700 feet high, while across the river on the Oregon side, the southerly basaltic rim is perhaps 900 feet in height. The river canyon varies between three to eight kilometers in width. The canyon's south shore includes a narrow flood plain of rock shelves mantled with sand. Other low areas reveal basaltic scabland surfaces. Mid-river islands display basaltic outcroppings covered by alluvial and loessial silts and sands. Indeed, the canyon reveals strong geological evidence of the events that shaped it: during an earlier ice age, catastrophic flooding deposited silts and sands; wind action deposited loess and sands; and in more recent millenia volcanic eruptions resulted in ash beds.

CLIMATE

The climate within the Columbia River Canyon comprises an arid to semi-arid zone characterized by low precipitation, warm to hot dry summers, and relatively cold winters. The area's climate is affected by the Cascade Mountains, a barrier to moisture-rich winds from off the Pacific Ocean's Japanese Current; and by the Columbia Gorge or Canyon, which serves as a channel or conduit for changing weather systems. Temperatures at The Dalles vary from ca. -31°F to 114°F. Annual precipitation is perhaps nine to ten inches of moisture, with rain or snow falling mostly November to March. Harsh blowing winds and sand are common, as in Wishram Tale 8 "The East Wind and the West Wind." And severe winter snowstorms occur, fierce enough to close modern freeways.[7]

FLORA

In the Wishoms' reaches of the Columbia River Canyon, thanks to the harsh climate, and poor and thin soils, only sparse plant life survives. Lichens and mosses cover the soils at the lower levels, and elsewhere some perennial grasses survive plus shrubs such as sagebrush. Except perhaps for willows growing at the river's edge, no trees occur: not on the river bottoms; not on the sideslopes; indeed, not for many miles back from the Columbia River canyon slopes. And wood for fires by which to cook food, or to warm the winter long houses; or for manufacture of eating bowls or of dugout canoes was difficult to obtain. Indeed, as the tales give hint, driftwood was gathered for cooking or other fires.[8]

FAUNA

Animal life hunted by the Wishoms included such large hoofed animals as deer (*Odocoileus sp.*), elk (*Cervus elaphus*), and pronghorn antelope (*Antilocapra Americana*). Some other animals might have been found near the river: wolves, foxes, badgers, and even bears. But for lack of forage, game animals were hunted at a considerable distance from the riverside villages. Second, migratory flocks of ducks and geese were hunted on the river bottoms near where they nested, rested, or wintered over. But third, the seasonal runs of anadromous fish which made their way past the Wishoms' villages to upriver spawning grounds were the Wishoms most important resources, either for tribal subsistence or for trade. Varieties of salmon taken included the chinook salmon (*Oncorhynchus tshawytscha*), the coho salmon (*Oncorhynchus kisutch*), the sockeye salmon (*Oncorhynchus nerka*), and steelhead trout (*Salmo gairdneri*). Still other migrating fish taken by the Wishoms included the American shad (*Alo sapidissima*), and lamprey eel (*Entosphenus tridentatus*).

The fishing cycle extended from perhaps late February or early March until May for spring chinook salmon--from June to September for Coho or silver salmon--from late June to mid-July for sockeye or blueback. The main run of steelhead occurred during summer, with a secondary run occurring during winter. Shad were fished from mid-June to the end of July, and an early fall chinook salmon run occurred during September into October. Other fish caught by the Indians included white sturgeon (*Acipenser transmontanus*), smallmouth bass *(Micropterus dolomievi)*, suckers (*Catostomu* sp.), and rainbow trout (*Salmo gairdneri*).[9]

C. SUBSISTENCE AND FISHING TECHNIQUES

Seemingly a sedentary people, the Wishoms were a "salmon culture," and were blessed with great stores of easily obtained edibles and no threat of famine. Indeed, salmon permeated their culture, appearing in their art, and traditional narratives. Primarily fishers, the Wishoms netted or speared the teeming spring and autumn runs of salmon, taking them close by their villages from platforms which jutted out at the systems of rapids near Celilo Falls. Also in season they fished for the mammoth sturgeon, also suckers and eels. While the men fished, the women carried great loads of fish to the villages, where each fish was split open and laid out to air-dry. Later, the dried salmon was pulverized and stored in baskets for winter-time use or trade. Indeed, the Wishoms' stores of dried fish were greatly sought after, as when during mid-September 1855 a group of Yakamas was "on its way to The Dalles to get dried salmon,"[10] met up with, and murdered Yakama Indian Agent Andrew Bolon near present-day Goldendale, Washington.

To a lesser extent, the Wishom women harvested edible roots and berries which were dried for winter use. Least important for the Wishoms was the hunt for game animals. The tales make little or no mention of the horse which was needed for the long trek up and out of the river canyon, and thence to likely hunting areas.

II. CULTURE FORMS AND HISTORY

Based in part on Edward Sapir's notes made during his collecting trip to the reservation in 1905, and enlarged by collecting trips made during 1924 and 1925, Leslie Spier published *Wishram Ethnography* in 1930.[11] Of great importance, the volume is the most detailed description extant of a Southern Plateau Indian culture. Indeed, Spier's work details Wishom Linguistic Relationships and Territory; Material Culture including Fishing and Hunting Techniques; Cooking and Meals; Manufacture of Canoes; Manufacture of Tools and other Articles; Houses; Dress and Personal Adornment; the Wishom Calendar, Colors, Directions, and Gestures; Social Organization including Caste, Chiefs and Councils, Marriage, Slaves, Trade, Warfare; Religious Practices and Beliefs, including the Shaman; Particulars about the Individual and more. Readers interested in further information on traditional Wishom culture and material forms are directed to Spier's *Wishram Ethnography*. In 1855 the Wishoms were removed from their riverside villages to the Yakama Reservation where they dwell today. Some Wishom peoples may yet reside today in the riverside town of Wishram, Washington.

A. THE WISHOM LANGUAGE

Sapir's *Wishram Tales*, published in 1909, contains both a construction in written form of the Wishom tongue, an oral language, and an English translation of the traditional narratives. The Wishom Indians spoke an Upper Chinook dialect, and were the easternmost Chinookan tribe on the Columbia River. According to Sapir, "the language spoken by them is, to all intents and purposes, the same as that of the Wasco on the other side of the river and of the White Salmon and Hood (or Dog) River Indians further down the stream."[12] Still, the Wishoms, like the Wascos, dwelt more than 170 miles upstream from Chinook-speaking coastal tribes. Travel was arduous enough, and the physical effort to secure sufficient food supplies against the winter was taxing enough so as to leave little energy for travel for all but an adventurous few. What's more, the Wishoms habitat, milieu, and perhaps culture could not have differed more from those of the coastal tribes. Still, the reader interested in the Wishom language should study Sapir's *Wishram Texts*.

B. TRADITIONAL LITERATURE OF THE WISHOMS

The oral traditional literature of the Wishoms was taken down at differing times by three individuals. First, during July and August 1905 **Edward Sapir** traveled to the Yakama Reservation, and there he recorded a substantial body of tales, mostly heard from informant Louis Simpson, also Pete McGuff. Second, about 1903 **Lucullus V. McWhorter** moved from the Midwest to Yakima, Washington, and the vicinity of the Yakama Reservation. A rancher and cattle trader, over a lifetime he collected a great store of Indian tribal tales and legends, including many given by the Wishoms. Third, in 1924 and 1925 University of Washington Anthropology Professor **Leslie Spier** made several trips to the Yakama Reservation where he sought out ethnographic details from Wishoms in order that he might add to and round out the ethnographic information which Sapir had first collected. Spier also obtained some additional Wishom tales. Spier relates that neither he nor Sapir had actually traveled to the Columbia River and the site of the Wishom villages, *more than 30 difficult miles south* of the Yakama Reservation.[13]

The importance of traditional narratives in Wishom culture are evident in Pete McGuff's recounting of "Winter Bathing," which appears in *Wishram Texts*, pp. 188-191. "Myths" were told to youths by the old men--and McGuff was fond of listening to them. But more than entertaining, the traditional narratives were instructional, were so very important that the youthful listeners were directed to stay awake, to pay attention--*or else*.

"A long while ago, when I was a boy, the old men would tell myths in winter. Now there I was listening to them. I would be told: 'If you fall asleep before it is finished, straightway you will have to go and bathe. If you do not fall asleep, you will not go and bathe.' Now I was fond of myths when I was a boy, so I would be satisfied with the things that I was told and would listen to them. If I fell asleep too early, (when) it was all finished, they would wake me up. An old man would say to me: 'Go in bathing!' I would try to refuse, but in vain, so I just had to go. I was undressed entirely naked where he knew there was lots of ice (on the Columbia River?) or also where it was pressed together tight.

"He would give me an ax for chopping up the ice. He would say to me: 'You will chop right through it, you will dive under water, you will stick your head out, you will turn around, you will look to the rising sun, you will cry out '*wa!*', you will shout. You will duck down under water, you will stick your head out, you will look across this way (i.e., *north*), straightway you will again shout '*wa!*' You will duck down under water, you will stick your head out, again you will shout as before, you will look across yonder (i.e., *south*). You will duck down under water, you will stick your head out, you will look to the setting sun, you will shout '*wa!*' You will duck down under water for the fifth time, you will stick your head out, you will look up to the sky. Then enough; you will return home."

-usw-

The Wishoms' tribal narratives are remarkable for their imaginative power and wide-ranging scope, frequently extending from the heavens earthward; from the mythic and the legendary to the secular; from the apparently complex to the simpler version; from the better to the lesser narrative.

III. INTENT OF THIS WORK

This work presents the comprehensive edition and collection of traditional narratives of the Wishom tribe. We have searched out and compiled what we believe is the largest, the most complete body of traditional narratives for the Wishom people. What bibliographical search plus luck have discovered is all here. Here are *primary sources*, narratives taken directly from the lips of Wishom narrators, texts of inestimable value. More remarkable for this late date, the texts found herein derive from memories of tribal informants who were alive at the time of or shortly after the tribe's assignment to the Yakama Indian Reservation, when tribal memories of cultural details and language skills were active and robust. Second, these tale texts are as complete and as authentic as possible. They have not been rewritten or edited for "literary excellence." Indeed, the likelihood of discovery of more *traditional* and *authentic* told Wishom narratives is, we believe, remote. Third, bibliographic annotation from collections of Plateau and North American oral narratives from outside the Wishom tribe only emphasizes the traditionality, the authenticity of these Wishom tales: 1) as deriving out of an oral milieu, 2) as vital narrative forms, 3) as an inimical part of the tribal culture. Finally, we would plead that the modern reader of these tales should 'listen with his eyes.' By this we mean that while reading the reader should imagine a narrator's voice, hear vocal devices which create characters, and sense the varied pace of a spoken narration which finally brings the tale to its conclusion.

The narrative texts in this volume derive from three sources:

1. **Thirty-six** Wishom tales collected by Edward Sapir and which appeared first in his *Wishram Texts, Together with Wasco Tales and Myths...* .

2. **Four** Wishom texts which first appeared in Leslie Spier & Edward Sapir's *Wishram Ethnography*.

3. **Fourteen** Wishom texts collected by L.V. McWhorter and which were extracted from the McWhorter Papers, Holland Library, Washington State University, Pullman Washington.[14] These narratives have not appeared previously in print, and are used here with permission.

Awarded a research grant from the National Endowment for the Humanities in 1973, I set about to compile a descriptive listing of primary resource materials concerning the Inland Pacific Northwest frontier. But just across the street from my English Department office at Washington State University I found an extraordinary lode--the "Papers of Lucullus Virgil McWhorter." The collection consists of several hundred thousand items: books, clippings, journals, letters, photographs, notes, manuscripts, manuscript fragments, and mementos, occupying at least twenty-five shelf feet. With the kind permission of Dr. Earle Connette and his staff, and his successor, Prof. John Guido, Head, Manuscripts, Archives and Special Collections, Holland Library, Washington State University, I turned over the fading, written-in-pencil pages of the McWhorter Collection, awestruck at the riches at my fingertips. Then, with photocopies of McWhorter's original texts supplied me by the WSU library staff, I spent a considerable period of time becoming familiar with the texts, and puzzling how best to make them available to a wide readership. Accordingly, this latest volume of Wishom tales not only brings into print what has appeared previously, but rounds out the collection with McWhorter's considerable addition. More, the tales herein have been arranged and annotated so as to make these Wishom oral narratives of greatest, widest use, preserving the past for the sake of future generations. I have made only minimal changes of spelling or direct discourse to maximize reader understanding. These tales have not been rewritten, but preserve the oral sense of their original narration.

Following nearly a century after Sapir's collecting efforts, this work constitutes the definitive canon of known traditional narratives and genres for the Wishom Indian nation. In order to demonstrate the traditional nature of the varieties of narratives here, the tales have been grouped into categories (e.g. myths, legends, tales) which may or may not have been evident to the original tribal raconteurs, but which the modern reader and scholar require now for a more complete understanding of the tribal lore. In creating this work we have especially relied on Laurits Bødker's *Folk Literature (Germanic)*.[15] And we have freely consulted Stith Thompson's *The Folktale*;[16] also his *Tales of the North American Indians*.[17] Here are primary texts told or translated by tribal members plus their interpretation of the lore. We believe the authenticity of the tales is high, even though they were taken down during the early twentieth century, at least 50 years or more following the culturally destructive move of many Columbia River tribes and bands onto the same reservation. Here is an extensive record of the mental life of the Wishom tribe to inform the modern reader who is now far removed from our Pacific Northwest past. These collected tales enable study of Wishom narrative stylistics, even the belief systems of the tribe. Particularly possible now is comparative study of the oral literature of the Wishoms with that of neighboring tribes, and neighboring culture areas, something previously impossible to do.

A. ENGLISH LANGUAGE AND TRADITIONAL WISHOM NARRATIVES

The English language versions of these Wishom narratives have posed no small amount of anguish. To be *like the original*--to attempt to reproduce pristine, pre-1855 Wishom language forms--or to be *readable to moderns*? We have opted for the latter--**wide readability**. Sapir's notes about the Wishoms are frustrating to the modern researcher, and often less than reliable. First, Sapir's comments predate the great works of collecting and of scholarship directed to American Indian oral literature. Indeed, Sapir's views derive from his acquaintance with the available, but relatively scant body of known American

Indian traditions of his time, especially relating to the Yakama Reservation where he spent but a single five-week collecting tour. As a result, because extensive comparative scholarship wasn't possible for him, his perceptions and pronouncements are not always reliable.

B. ORGANIZATION AND SUBSTANCE OF THE WORK

The traditional narratives in this work have been grouped into categories after the scholarly example and folkloric scholarship in Stith Thompson's *Tales of the North American Indians*. Within each category of Wishom oral literature, each narrative bears a descriptive title, given by the Indian raconteur or by the original collector/editor. Then, each narrative has been assigned a number which marks its place in the canon of Wishom traditional narratives and variants. And narrative variants are listed, from the complex to the simple. Details describing the informant from whom the tale was obtained, along with the time of the original narration plus other details about the tale, are given in the List of Informants at the end of this volume. Finally, the complete tale itself appears in the form of its first telling.

MYTHS: TALES OF THE ORIGIN OF MAN, ANIMALS AND PLANTS, PHENOMENA

Mythic tales of the Wishrams are likely set in an earlier time, especially a time before the coming of the people: when divine beings or culture heroes were seen, especially the "animal people" who comported themselves, conceptualized, walked upright as humans; when the origination of many celestial and earthly phenomena occurred. These narratives tend to be imaginative enough, (but are concrete/tangible in substance; are not symbol-ladden but purposive, instructive in character).

1. Tales tell of the origination of man, and of tribal characteristics among the Indians which result from dismembered parts of a swallowing monster which are thrown over a wide region: 1A "Coyote at Lapwai, Idaho," and 1B "Coyote and *Itc!e'xyan*."

2. The origination of man and his characteristics occurs also when *Is-tam-ma*, Chief of the Beavers, is slain; his body dismembered; and the parts thrown over the land: 2. "*Is-tam-ma*, Chief of the Beavers."

3. Coyote's visit to the Land of the Dead, and his misadventures resulting in death for the world of mankind are recounted: 3. "The Visit to the World of Ghosts."

4. Coyote's ineptness results in the destruction of the trail between earth and the upperworld (man may not longer go and mingle with the spirit people): 4. "How Coyote Destroyed the Trail to the Upper World."

5. Three mythic explanations are recalled for the salmon runs, in particular the suddenness of the coming and of the amount of fish, even of the heralding swallows which precede them, in the lower Columbia River or somewhere in the Cascades: 5A "Coyote and the Five Sisters of the *N-Che-Wana*;" 5B "The Origin of Fish in the Columbia;" 5C "How Coyote Destroyed the Fish Dam at the Cascades, Distributing Salmon in the Rivers."

6. Origins of the characteristic stripes on the back and tail of raccoon are recounted: 6A "The Raccoon Story;" 6B "Raccoon and his Grandmother." A variant version explains the origin of stripes on Chipmunk: 10 "Chipmunk's Stripes."

LEGENDARY TALES

Legendary narratives describe extraordinary

events actually believed to have happened, perhaps close to modern 'historical time.' Legends give explanations for the origination of specific places, the quality of weather, of names and naming on the land.

1. The present existence, also strength of the West Wind is explained: 7 "Coyote Enslaves the West Wind."

2. Wintery weather, formerly extremely cold; but now cold only a short time of year due to the wrestling victory of West Wind over East Wind, is explained: 8 "The East Wind and the West Wind."

3. Two versions of the same tale, told by Wishom brothers who were Sapir's informants, recount how a) several lewd women were transformed into birds; b) or how several lewd women were transformed into rocks or place marks: 9A "Coyote and the Mischievous Women;" 9B "Coyote and the Mischievous Women (Second Version)."

4. The origination of a specific place-name, "Dried Salmon," or "White Salmon Landing" (*lmuyaqso'qu*), is recounted: 10 "Coyote Eats Dried Salmon."

5. Two tales recount how Coyote originated ways of taking the salmon: 11 "Coyote Makes a Fishtrap;" and 12 "Coyote Spears Fish."

6. Two narrative accounts relate of the separation of the Wishom tribe, of a portion traveling northward to live: 13A "The Wishom Tribe; A Story of their Division and Separation;" also 13B "A Quarrel of the Wishram."

7. The mass slaying and then restoration to life of the Wishom, and an explanation of their name (*ila'xluit*) are given: 14 "Why the Wishram are called *Ia'xluit*."

8. How Coyote rendered the Wishram's Sahaptian neighbors inferior is given: 15 "Coyote in *Sk!in*."

9. How Coyote provided mouths, the means to eat fish, to a man (and men) who had no mouth (a possible explanation why the Indians who formerly resided at

Castle Rock reputedly had very large mouths) is related:
16 "Coyote and the Mouthless Man."
        10. Two visionary narratives foretell of the coming
of the white man or recount of an extensive famine: 17 "A
Famine at the Cascades;" and 18 "A Prophecy of the
Coming of the Whites."
        11. Three tales recount of a monster serpent who
either devours an infant, or pursues two hunters who
manage to slay it: 19 "the *Gy-u-boo-kum* (I);" 20 "the *Gy-
u-boo-kum* (II);" and 21 "The *Gy-u-boo-kum* of the
Wishoms." {the great serpent is also mentioned in 41
"Eagle and Weasel};

TALES OF MAGIC AND THE MARVELOUS
        These Wishom narratives relate of supernatural
adversaries, supernatural helpers, of magic powers, and
marvelous objects and happenings. Marvelous creatures
are commonplace; the physical laws of the universe are
commonly set aside wonderfully; and travel between the
upper world and the world of man occurs with ease.
        1. An account of wish-fulfilment, several girls,
while sleeping out at night, wish that stars seen overhead
might come to earth as husbands for them. Widely recorded from Indian tribes across North America as the
"Star Husband" tale--alas, bad choices equal bad (too old)
husbands: 22 "Star Husband."
        2. A marvelous, shining, magic-empowering rock
[i.e., a meteorite?] is discovered in 23 "The Star-Rock of
Riches."
        3. A shamanistic dance ceremony displays
participants' magic powers (or Coyote's lack thereof): 24
"Coyote's People Sing."
        4. Coyote's children and Antelope's sons vie at
"shinny ball," and the death of Coyote's children is recounted: 25 "Coyote and Antelope."

5. The widely told North American Indian tale of the Bungling Host is recounted: 26 "Coyote and Deer."

TALES OF COYOTE AS TRICKSTER

Trickster tales detail how Coyote, an animal often endowed with human characteristics, dupes his dull-minded adversaries with his sly wit, commits incest with his daughter, even tricks his foes into slaying themselves horribly. Second, Coyote assumes other character roles, such as the fool who is done in by his own efforts, or the fool who seeks wisdom by talking to his dung. Third, Coyote even assumes a background role in which he does or says little at all. Fourth, few in number, some narratives depict Coyote as demi-god or culture-hero (or, as used by Sapir, "transformer"--perhaps an unfortunate term.)

1. Coyote's encounter with the fearsome ogress, *At!At!A'lia* is related in two narratives. Duping the dull-witted ogress into smearing herself with pitch, trapping her in a sweathouse, all supposedly to make her attractive, etc., then Coyote sets her afire: 27A "Coyote and *At!At!A'lia*;" also 27B "Coyote and *Tah-Tah Kle-ah*."

2. Coyote's sly ruse is revealed whereby he "dies," returns as another, and marries his own daughter: 28 "Coyote and His Daughter."

3. When Coyote traveled to the upper world, became the slave [understudy?] of the Sun, he was rejected, would not do--he tattled loudly of the many seen faults of the people: 29 "Coyote and Sun."

4. The unsavory partnership between Coyote and Skunk is described, where Skunk pretends to be dead, and assorted animals are assembled to sing/drum the funeral rites. But then Skunk "comes to life," "sprays" and slays them all--the slain animals provide meat for the duo: 30 "Coyote and Skunk."

5. The marriage of Coyote's daughter is recounted,

of how she gives birth to a son but abandons him, of the son's growth to manhood and his ultimate revenge against her: 31 "Eagle's Son and Coyote's Son-In-Law."

6. Clever, helpful Coyote shows a truly ignorant man how copulation is correctly done--impregnates the wife: 32 "Coyote and the Pregnant Woman."

7. Coyote pretends to "doctor" a girl he has previously "caused to be sick." As the drummers drum, she complains bitterly to her mother that Coyote is copulating with her. But the mother tells her to never mind--a cure is a cure: 33 "Coyote as Medicine Man."

8. Coyote commits an obscenity [upon himself], the story of which was supposedly confined to a mountain near modern Mosier, Oregon, thereby naming "*Idwo'tea*" or "story" mountain: 34 "The Story Concerning Coyote."

TALES OF CONFLICTS AND ADVENTURES

In these narratives occur enmities, struggles between fathers and sons, husbands and wives. The solutions to these conflicts undoubtedly posed useful lessons to the Wishram.

1. A Wishom retelling of the ancient tale of "Oedipus" recalls a chieftain, a giant with prodigious feet, who slays his many infant sons except one--this survivor grows up, returns to slay his father: 35 "A Cascade Indian Legend."

2. The sons of a Chief exact revenge for their father's death by a treacherous Chief who loved gambling, who murdered those who lost to him while gambling "at the bones:" 36 "How Young Eagle Killed *Pah-He-Nuxt-Twy*."

3. The revenge of the son of Salmon against the five Wolves for the death of his father, for their taking [marriage] of his mother (Salmon), and for her subsequent abandonment is recounted: 37A "The Salmon Story;" 37B

"Salmon Myth."

4. In a tale of magic, Eagle and his four brothers (Blue Jay and Beaver, Sparrow Hawk and Chicken Hawk) spear a seal. Dragged down river, they land, are fed ghoulish food--attempts are made to murder them. But Eagle's magic is too powerful--he is too strong in single-combat, so they escape: 38 "The Adventures of Eagle and His Four Brothers."

5. The five East-wind Brothers travel one by one to the East "where the people are assembled"--but the four older brothers are slain. The youngest brother (with Coyote) arrives at the house of the five Thunder brothers, and demonstrates the greater strength of his shamanistic powers: 39 "The Five East-Wind Brothers and the Five Thunder Brothers."

6. Taken to a remote site, an incorrigible is abandoned, cast away by his people. Helped by his grandmothers, he survives and then exacts a deadly revenge against his people: 40A "The Deserted Boy (I);" 40B "The Deserted Boy (II)."

TALES OF MONSTERS AND OGRES

Tales of ogres and bugbears occur in some number. Seldom are these particular monsters all-powerful, for wily or well-behaved youths may outwit them, escape their clutches.

1. When Weasel seizes a woman, the wife of a *Gayaba'xem*, that alligator-like monster pursues them, and must be killed: 41 "Eagle and Weasel."

2. An ogress, "Tuh-tan-nah," abducts two boys. While carrying them home to devour, she is deceived into believing her children are endangered, and runs off. As a result, the two boys escape: 42 "*Tuh-tan-nah*."

3. A youth is taken by an *At!At!A'lia* to her home not as prey but to keep "for herself." But the youth suc-

cessfully escapes: 43 "The Boy That Was Stolen by
At!At!A'lia."

4. Abducted by an *At!At!A'lia,* a brother and sister
deceive the ogress into running off so that they can escape:
44 "The Cannibal Woman."

TALES COMPARABLE WITH EUROPEAN MÄRCHEN

The Wishom narrative placed here conforms most
closely to the one hundred or so folktales familiar over
Northern Europe and found within North American Indian
oral tradition. How strong the power, the tenacity of Native
American oral tradition is obvious in that tales such as
these, which travel on great currents of oral tradition
across many oceans, over great spans of time, are absorbed
essentially intact into the Indians' culture where unique
changes, if small, are made to assure "cultural fit."

1. A single *märchen,* a Wishom variant of the
"Jack and the Beanstalk" story, occurs as 45 "A Wishom
Legend." No legend, the tale contains most of the elements
of the *märchen:* A-T 328 except there is no magic beanstalk, certainly not present among the *flora* near the
Wishoms. There is neither magic harp nor magic hen
which Jack might steal, for neither stringed instruments
nor kept chickens were likely familiar to the tribe. Instead,
Jack, simply known as "a boy," blazes or marks a horizon-
tal trail "toward the sunrise," using arrows stuck into the
ground that he can find his way back. He succeeds in
winning the young daughter's support, and with her help he
is hidden from the violent father (apparently a bad man
and a cannibal, but no giant). The youth creates plenty for
all by demonstrating how to hunt wild birds and animals,
and how to cook and thereby to eat game, not people.

C. ORAL AUTOBIOGRAPHIES, ORAL TRADITIONAL HISTORIES

Two extraordinary accounts provide detailed "told autobiographies" as well as "Oral Traditional History"[18] from two Wishom Indians. First, during July and August 1905 Louis Simpson related his "A Personal Narrative of the Paiute War"[19] to Edward Sapir. Second, beginning in 1911 and continuing intermittently for 15 years, *Che-Pos To-Cos* (Owl Child), whose English name was Alec McCoy, related his "Autobiography" to L. V. McWhorter.[20] Both accounts provide a point-of-view, much like a mirror held up from within Wishom culture, that we might observe much reflected therein of tribal beliefs, and practices, especially warfare.

Owl Child's "Autobiography" in the McWhorter Papers consisted of approximately fifty pages of varied manuscript plus notes.[21] Owl Child's recollections detail his youth and parents, also his training for acquisition of *Tahmahnawis* later when a teenager. Owl Child's penchant for travel coincided with work as a ranch hand in Montana, and breaking horses for the "English Army" in Canada. Of no small interest, Owl Child recalls the difficulty of travel from his village of birth to Portland, and how that "village" appeared in very early days. Owl Child's life among the Piegan Blackfeet of Montana is recounted: of his "Montana" wife and daughter, of his buffalo hunts; of his war exploits with the Piegans: scars from tribal wars against the Crow Indians, of near death while warring against the Sioux Indians, of escape from capture by seven Flatheads and Nez Perce Indians. Owl Child also detailed his witnessing of the massacre of several hundred cavalry troopers and the suicide of their leader in Southern Montana at a place where two rivers met. Finally, Owl Child recounts

his service as a mercenary with the U.S. army against
Captain Jack in the Modoc War, 1873.

Narrated to Sapir sometime during July or August
of 1905, Louis Simpson recounts his service as a mercenary for the U.S. Army during the Paiute or Snake Indian
War, 1866-1868. Simpson details how he and his Indian
cohorts warred against the Paiute Indians. And from the
Indian perspective, the tactics, the hardships, the sufferings
of war, and, finally, victory are recounted.

Unlike the eye-glazing, mind-numbing accounts of
"oral history," the rambling and lengthy tape-recorded
accounts by political or pop-cultural "big shots" of one sort
or another, "Oral Traditional History" consists of the told
accounts of deeds of brave action which figure in the
collective memory of a tribe's history. Flourishing by word
of mouth and living in memory, Oral Traditional History
accounts are related by peoples who lack a capability or
the practice of written records. Unique to Oral Traditional
History, "told historical accounts" are often related by the
doer(s) of the brave deeds. As a result, an *omniscient* and
entirely *detached* view of the conduct of battle is not
possible. Instead, history is told, perspective gained at the
battle line of the thrill, the danger, the terror along with the
horrendous, screams of the injured and dying and the
nightmares which may last for decades. Oral Traditional
History recounts with each telling exemplary actions--
deeds which are fit models for future generations to
emulate. Most important, as related by skilled raconteurs,
tribal oral history is related within oral narrative modes,
which essentially obey the form and substance of folk
narrative.

D. IMPORTANT APPENDICES

Concluding this volume are appendices of explanatory

matter of considerable interest and use to the reader. First,
NOTES TO THE NARRATIVES are included. Sapir and
especially McWhorter asked often after explanations for
cultural details in the narratives which they recorded.
Given by the original taleteller or else supplied by the
collector, these notes provide very important background
details and explanations crucial for a more complete
understanding of each narrative. Each note can be identi-
fied according to initials of its author: ES = Edward Sapir;
LVM = Lucullus V. McWhorter; LS = Leslie Spier; DH =
Donald Hines.

Second, an **INDEX OF MOTIFS** lists the folkloric motifs extant in each narrative. First, in the Wishom
narratives we have sought to locate and to catalog the
numerous details of character, plot, and background of
each narrative. These narrative particulars or motifs aid
our understanding of subtle details of narrative and of
cultural context which we might otherwise miss. For
example, the motifs underscore the widespread presence of
magic which pervades this oral literature, even Wishom
culture. Second, the motifs have been helpful in assigning
a text to a particular category of narrative, whether myth,
legend, or tale. Third, motifs help assure us that the tales
are authentic Indian lore, that each narrative lives as an
oral and traditional tale. By comparison, a written "short
story" would fail to survive in an oral milieu, would fail to
conform to the particulars of "told literature" found in the
scholarly indexes. Indeed, for the Wishom narratives we
have employed Stith Thompson's *Motif-Index of Folk-
Literature*, also Thompson's *Tales of North American
Indians.*[22] In this manner, we have sought to note details of
character, plot, or background which exist and mark
Wishom oral literature.

Third, **COMPARATIVE NOTES TO OTHER
PLATEAU INDIAN TALES** are included. To begin

with, the told tales of the Wishoms are quite unique, differ considerably from their artful cousins which live only in the printed pages of a book--"written fiction e.g. short stories"--for example, Charles Dickens' *Christmas Carol.* For most of us, if we were forced to **tell** the Dickens story to another person (could not read it from the book), we might relate stumblingly of a hard-hearted rich man, a bank clerk with perpetual cold fingers and a handicapped son, and Christmas hobgoblins. Our "telling" would be very brief, likely chaotic in structure, and perhaps, mercifully, easily forgotten. By contrast, an oral tale lives best by word of mouth, its characters and form and substance seem naturally shaped to the tongue, springs easily to life with the telling of the tale. (Still, an oral narrative can fit, however awkwardly, onto pages of a book such as the accounts of the voyage of Odysseus, told long ago by Homer.) Still more, that each Wishom tale resembles the *form* of the tales told by nearby tribes helps assure us of authenticity of the Wishom lore. And that the Wishom narratives parallel the *characters*, and *plots* and many *background details* found in nearby tribes' collections of tales further assures us of the authenticity of these Wishom texts. Indeed, the traditionality and the authenticity of these Wishom oral narratives are assured by the great number of comparable versions which are told among the other tribes over the Plateau Region. Finally, cited here from an extensive list of collected oral narratives from 12 Plateau Indian tribes found northward from the Columbia River through Central British Columbia, and northward are listings of extra-tribal versions of each Wishom narrative. A listing of the tribes, the collections of tribal tales, and the short titles used in compiling the Comparative Notes appear in Appendix Three.

Fourth, a **LIST OF INFORMANTS** contains biographical data, if available, on taletellers, and details of their tribal life. A further assurance of authenticity, these Wishom narratives were written down at or following a tale-telling session with real tribesmen and women as narrator.

Fifth, a **SELECTED LIST OF READINGS** is included which provides the inquiring reader with a list of useful works for further study of the tribal life and lore of the Wishoms and their immediate neighbors. Finally, **ACKNOWLEDGMENTS** of sources and of individuals for whose help I am indebted concludes this work.

Donald M. Hines
Issaquah, Washington

II. "Preparing Salmon-Wishham," Special Collections Division, Univ. of Washington Libraries. Edward S. Curtis, c. 1909, NAI182

III. "Wishham Basket Worker," Special Collections
Division, Univ. of Washington Libraries.
Edward S. Curtis, c. 1909, NAI167

PART TWO.
THE TRADITIONAL TALES
OF THE WISHOMS

I. TALES OF THE ORIGIN OF MAN, OF ANIMALS, PLANTS, PHENOMENA

1A. COYOTE AT LAPWAI, IDAHO[23, 24]

Now Coyote goes toward the uplands, and he approaches truly a bad place, the land of the mountain monster.[25] Anything with wings would try to fly overhead, but still the monster would swallow it without difficulty. Should it try to go by underneath, the monster would swallow it likewise. Then Coyote thought: "What shall I do?" He saw a hill and thought: "I shall make a hazelbush rope."

Then Coyote made it and tied it onto the hill; then he tied it about himself also. Now he saw the monster lying down, lying with face and belly down. He tied some hazelbush ropes all together and made a long rope. Then he went up to him; his rope ran out, falling somewhat short.

Again he made another rope. Again he went up to him and came a little nearer, yet fell short. Again he made a rope; again he went up to him and fell short. Thus he kept doing, and at the fifth time reached close enough, about five steps off.

Then Coyote said: "O mountain monster! I am challenging you that we two swallow each other." The mountain monster lay silent. He did not say anything at all. Again Coyote spoke to him; it was the fifth time before the monster looked up at him.

The monster said "Yes" to him, although Coyote was tied to the hill by means of his rope.

Now the mountain monster drew in his breath-- "*fu2*."[26] The rope was stretched out somewhat forcibly. In a little while he let it come to rest.

Then Coyote also drew in his breath-- "*fu2*."

The mountain monster became somewhat shaky. Again he also tried to draw him to himself-- "*fu2*."

The fifth time the two did thus. The mountain monster went at it with great force. Oh, dear! Coyote became uneasy. Somehow he kept rising straightway. Coyote kept getting higher and higher, and his rope almost snapped. Now the hill was worn far in at that part which had the rope tied to it. Long the monster tried to draw him to himself --"*fu4*" for quite some time before he let him come to rest.

Now Coyote, in his turn, drew in his breath-- "*fu4*," also for quite some time.

Then the mountain monster was heard groaning: "*A'rna, a'rna, Bu'xu*," he was heard. Then his belly burst, and his guts went out of him. It is for this reason that he was always lying down, lying down on his belly. If he were to be turned over, his belly would straightway burst.

And then Coyote tried to draw him to himself-- "*fu.*'" Straightway he turned over. And that monster's guts were spilt out. Thus was his character.

And then Coyote skinned him. Then he made people out of that same monster's flesh. He cut off a

little, threw it away: one village came into being. In this
way he made people. Then he discovered that he had no
more flesh; yet he had not yet made the Wishram people.
There was only the tongue lying down.

"Well, then I shall make the Wishom people out
of it." And indeed Coyote made the flat-headed Wishom
people out of the tongue. Therefore the people dwelling
farther up say that the Wishoms' heads are like a tongue,
flat.

Again Coyote looked around. Behold! As yet he
had not made any people belonging to that place, to
Lapwai. But there was nothing left at all. And then he felt
sorry. There was only blood on his hands. Then he
plucked some grass, wiped his hands with it, and threw
it away. He said: "Out of that you have become the Nez
Perces people." Thus do men say: "Nez Perces are brave
warriors, a people made out of blood. They are a dangerous people of warriors."[27]

1B. COYOTE AND *ITC!E'XYAN*[28]

And then Coyote went on again. Straightway he
arrived at another place. Coyote heard that the Merman[29]
was always swallowing people. Wheresoever a canoe
went, straightway the Merman seized it. Everyone he
swallowed.

"Now let him swallow me also," thought Coyote.
And then Coyote went and got a big tree. Then he came
into view. The Merman caught hold of him, and he was
swallowed down.

Straightway Coyote fell down under the water
(apparently) to the bottom. And then he saw many
people; many canoes were piled together there under the
water.

Then Coyote caught sight of the Merman's heart hanging. And then Coyote was told: "That is the Merman's heart." Then he cut it off; the Merman's heart was cut off.[30] And then everything floated up to the surface-- all the canoes and the people and Coyote.

And then Coyote said: "By what right, perchance, do you alone, Merman, do thus to the people? This day you will have had enough of doing thus to the people. I, Coyote, have told you. Soon the people will come into this land, and then they shall say, 'Thus did Coyote transform the Merman.' And then you, the Merman, will do no harm."

2. *IS-TAM-MA*, CHIEF OF THE BEAVERS[31, 32]

The story is an old one, from far back towards the beginning. It was here where the city of Yakima now stands. All was a lake, water over all the level land. *Pahqu-ti-koot*, the Gap, was all closed up. This lake was full of beaver, beaver in all the water.

There lived here a boy and his sister, who was younger than he. We call this sister *Che-an-no* [fish gills inside the salmon's head. It is rough when dry and stands out separate like hair if not oiled.] That was the girl's name. Her brother had a hard time. He killed birds and everything to get oil for his sister's hair. None was good. Her head hurt her all the time. When her hair was dry, her head was in pain. The boy thought, "I will try for the beaver!"

The boy made a bone spear, a strong spear. He speared one beaver, took it out from the lake. He heated rocks and cooked the beaver. The tail was fat. It would smooth his sister's hair. He thought that oil was the best; so he speared beaver every day. He speared them for the tail-oil for his sister's hair.

Finally the boy speared all the beaver in the lake, got all that he saw. He looked around. All were gone but one, a very little one deep down in the water. He did not want to spear it; it was so small. But there were no others. He thought, "There are no other beavers. I will get the little one for my sister's hair, now all dry and standing out from her head."

So the boy speared the last beaver, speared the little beaver deep in the lake. When the spear struck that little beaver, it became big. Large and mighty, it jerked the boy into the water. It was too strong for him. But the boy would not let go of his spear. This Beaver was *Is-tam-ma*, greatest of all beavers. He was from the ocean, but the boy did not know. *Is-tam-ma* had horns, was Chief of all *Wish-pooch*.[33] But the boy did not know.

There was a big struggle. *Is-tam-ma* took the boy fast over the lake. He broke through the mountain at *Pah-qu-ti-koot*, letting all the water loose. The boy would not let go of the spear, and the beaver took him and the water. All along the course, the boy grabbed willows and trees to hold him back. He caught at everything. The willows stayed him a little, then gave way; the roots were torn from the ground. They reached the *n-Che-wana*, going down to the ocean. At the Cascades [mountains] the boy caught pine trees. The pine trees stopped him a little, then broke off. The *Is-tam-ma* took the boy along. When the girl found that her brother was gone, taken by the great *Is-tam-ma*, she mourned from sunrise to sunrise. Night and sunshine she cried for her brother, for oil for her hair.

In the meantime, the boy was carried on the *n-Che-wana*. *Schegue-schegue* [variety of bulrush] called to the boy, "Grandson! Why not hold onto me? I will save you." But the boy did not pay attention. They were now

near the ocean. The old man called again, "My Grandson! You will die! The ocean is near to swallow you up!
Hold onto me."

The ocean was not far away. The boy caught the
old man as a last chance for his life. He held tight; the
old man did not come from the ground. The boy stayed
tight there. For a long time he held, until the old man was
nearly torn from the ground. Then the old man called to
him, "Catch hold of another *Schegue-schegue*! I am
nearly off!"

The boy did so; he held good and fast. This
second old man was strong. He did not come from the
ground. The boy was stopped from going farther. The
beaver was dying and could not pull so heavy. It was now
that the boy saw the big *Is-tam-ma* with great horns roll
over in the water. He then knew that it was the mighty
Chief of all the beavers that he had fought. *Is-tam-ma* was
dead.

The young man took the beaver and cut him into
small pieces. There was a big pile of pieces. The boy
studied after cutting *Is-tam-ma* to pieces. He studied
about it. Then he threw a piece over the land of Klamath
and said, "There will a people grow!" He took a bone
and threw it to the land of the *Wahk-puch-pal* and said,
"There will grow the strongest, the meanest people--
always mad! They will be the enemy of all the tribes,
fighting those who come near them. None will like them.
As the *Wahk-puch*, they will have no friends."[34]

Thus the tribes were planted. The boy threw all
the pieces but the liver. This he cast to the Kittitas and
Wenatchee country. From the liver the people grew short
and dark of skin. Because they grew from the liver, they
are this color. Only the tail of *Is-tam-ma* was left. That
was for the boy's sister.

The boy was now a great man. He carried the

tail, leaving the mountain like a saddle.[35] Water came out. This is Canyon Creek, on our own Yakama Reservation. We call this stream *Pouen-kute*. The boy came on, brought the beaver tail to his sister. The girl sat crying, her hair all standing out. She was crying for her brother, crying for oil for her hair. Her brother brought oil for her hair. As soon as he arrived, he heated rocks and baked the oil for her hair. She was crying, almost dying. The brother oiled his sister's hair, and she became well. This girl is *Che-an-no*, in the salmon's head. *Che-an-no* is the same as lungs but breathes water-air.

The boy now looked around everywhere. The land was all dry with only a small stream passing through. The gap is there where *Is-tam-ma* passed, dragging him through the broken mountain. Out from there the waters of the lake had gone down to the ocean.

After the boy had oiled his sister's hair, she was glad. He said to her, "A new people are coming, and this land will be for them. They will come soon, a different people from us. This is my work. I have made this land for them."

This is all of the story as I heard it when a little boy, told me by the older people. I guess the new people for whom this land was made dry was the *Sho-yah-poo* [white people]. The whites have taken nearly all the land.

3. THE VISIT TO THE WORLD OF GHOSTS[36]

Coyote's wife died and also his two sons died. And also Eagle's wife died and Eagle's two sons died. Now then Coyote said: "It is not well. I, Coyote, am thinking of whither my wife and my son[37] have gone."

And then Eagle said to him: "I know whither

your wife has gone. If you wish to have her, let us two go to bring both of them back--my wife and your wife, also your son and my son. I know where the two of them are."

And then both of them, Coyote and Eagle, did go. They went to fetch their wives. Straight on and on they went and arrived at a great river. There was no land in sight, water alone was all there was. And then Eagle took a flute. And then Eagle blew into the flute and said to Coyote: "It is good, O Coyote, that you should look. You shall not look at me. Look across yonder. You will behold the ghost people." And then Coyote looked over to the other side. He (?) blew into the flute, Eagle sang.

And then Eagle said to him: "Did you see anything on the other side?"

"I saw nothing at all."

Eagle said to him: "Indeed you, O Coyote, would not see any person. But truly people are dwelling there."

He said to him: "I think perchance Coyote is not strong, but truly I, Eagle, am strong. Now we two have come here. On the other side, O Coyote, on the other side is your wife, she who has died. She has come to right across from here. Also your son and my, Eagle's, wife and son, so that no one would take us two across to where the people are dwelling.

"Now look! I have blown into the flute; you Coyote did not see anyone. Now there we are. It is just good that you Coyote will think,[38] that 'Now we have arrived.' Now just close your eyes; then I shall take hold of you and you will hang on to me."

Eagle said to him: "You shall not look in any direction. If you do, we two shall die, we shall be drowned." And then he took hold of him. And then the two of them stood up. Now then Eagle stepped across to the other side of the water. And then Coyote looked and they both fell into the water. They struck the water at their feet and legs. They came to a stand on the ground and Coyote was thrown off.

Eagle said to him: "It is not well, Coyote, that we two should now be [nearly] drowned. I said to you, 'You shall not look; we must come to a stand on the land before you look.' Thus I said to you."

Eagle said to him: "Just you remain quiet, Coyote. Now we two have arrived. Now you shall listen. Soon you will see the people. Soon you will see your wife and your son. Likewise I, Eagle, shall see my wife. Soon you will see them."

And then it became dark. Just then people came together, in truth the dead. And then the moon came down to the ground; straightway it became somewhat light. And then a certain person came forward and got hold of the moon. And then the person swallowed the moon.

Now then Coyote heard someone speak of his wife. And then the person said: "This here is Coyote's wife; this here is Eagle's wife." Now then both of them listened and they recognized their wives.

Coyote thought: "Truly just here is my wife, also Eagle's wife." Then Coyote thought: "I shall kill this person here soon;" but Eagle remained quiet.

And then the two of them slept overnight. They passed another night; they passed still another night. And then Coyote killed the person. He gradually skinned him. And then he put that skin down over himself and said to Eagle: "Come look at me!"

So Eagle went and then came to look at him. He saw now that Coyote had something strange on himself and became afraid of him. And then Eagle said to him: "It is well you have slain her whose name is *Nikciamtca'c*.[39] She would kill people. You have slain her, so people's spirits would no longer come here to this place."

And then it became dark. The people assembled together, truly those were the dead. The people entered and they arrived to assemble; that is where they assembled. Truly when anyone died, straightway his spirit went there.

And then Coyote put down over himself the skin of her whom he had killed. Now then Coyote sat down where the moon was descending to the ground. Then Coyote jumped, there he landed. And then he got hold of the moon and swallowed it.

Coyote landed somewhat too short. And then the people said: "It is another person."

Some of the old men said: "Truly that is Coyote. Truly he killed her before."

And then Eagle took hold of his wife and hid her [i.e., in a box]. And he took hold of his son; he hid him also. And Coyote took hold of his wife; he hid also her. And Coyote hid also his son. Eagle closed the box; inside were his wife and his son and Coyote's wife and Coyote's son. And then Coyote spit out the moon; he threw her away.

Now then the two of them went and started homewards. Eagle carried the box on his back. They passed the night; they passed another night; they passed another night; they passed another night.

And then Coyote heard the people talking among themselves. The people were laughing among themselves behind his back. On the fourth day they passed another night. And then they went on. Now the people were again talking excitedly among themselves. Truly Coyote's wife and Eagle's wife and Eagle's son were there.

And then on the fifth day Coyote said to him: "Now I will carry that box on my back, I, Coyote. It is

not well that you should carry it; You are a chief, Eagle.
I, Coyote, I shall carry it on my back."
Then Eagle said: "No! Never mind. I am carrying
it on my back."
Then Coyote said to him: "Now I, Coyote, shall
carry it on my back."
And then Eagle said: "No!" Eagle was afraid. He
thought: "He will open the box."
Now here, back of the two of them they are
talking among themselves, they are laughing among
themselves. And then Eagle freed himself of his burden.
And then it was given to Coyote; so then Coyote carried
it on his back. And then Eagle said, "Just don't you go
far ahead; both of us will go." Now it seemed just as if
the sun were near.[40]
And then Eagle said to him: "Now I will defecate."
But then Coyote said to him: "No! You are a
chief. Go a little farther." So then Eagle went farther on.
And then Coyote relieved himself of the burden
and opened the box. And then Coyote saw his wife, and
he saw his son, and Eagle's wife and son. Now then
Coyote slowly opened the box. And then Coyote's wife
escaped from the box, also Eagle's wife. Both of them
got out; Coyote saw the two. So the two escaped. In vain
he seated himself upon the lid; he threw the lid away.
Coyote fell some distance away.
Then Coyote cried and Eagle spoke. Eagle said
to him: "I for my part was thinking that you wanted your
wife and your son, and I, Eagle, my wife and my son.
Now this day you have made a mistake in regard to them.
You shall never see them again. Now they have died for
all time. If we should all have passed through this day,
they would have returned to life and we would all of us
go together, we, the two women and the two boys. But

you made a mistake in regard to them. If any person dies, he will die for all time. This day you, Coyote, have brought it about thus. We should have brought those people[41] with us. We should all have gone homewards. And then Indians would always be doing thus, but then you made a mistake in regard to them. Whenever a person died, he would have come back home for the fall and the spring, but you made a mistake in regard to them. Never again will a person do thus; he is to die for all time and will never again be seen. Thus, Coyote, have you brought it about. Thus people will say, 'Coyote and Eagle went, went to fetch their wives. And then Coyote made a mistake in regard to them. Thus Coyote did; badly he did.'" Thus the myth.

4. HOW COYOTE DESTROYED THE TRAIL TO THE UPPER WORLD[42]

Two brothers lived on this earth, Coyote [*Paht-paht*] and Red Fox. Fox was the younger, Coyote the older brother. Fox told his brother, "I am going to have a feast of deer, berries and roots. That is where I am going."

Coyote thought, "I wonder where he is going. I wonder where they are going to have that feast. I will ask my brother."

He asked him, and the brother answered, "I am going up, away up high, to the good Spirit Land. There I will have the feast."

Coyote said, "I was up there when I was young, and I know all about it." Coyote did not know what the place looked like, but he had a smart idea and told his brother that he knew the place.

The younger brother said to him, "You are not fit

enough to go where I am going."

Coyote told him, "I am all right to go. I was there when I was young."

Red Fox told him, "I will take you up; and whatever I tell you to do, you must do."

Coyote made reply, "All right! I will do that, my youngest brother."

So they went up, these two brothers. It was the morning before *Sapalwit* [Sunday]. They arrived in the Spirit Land as the sun was setting. The Long House was already built, filled with Indians. They went around the house three times and then walked in through the doorway. Fox was in the lead; Coyote came behind. They had all kinds of grass to perfume their bodies, also flowers. The head man of the Long House took the two brothers close to the drum. The people started to dance that night the *pum-pum* dance. Coyote danced hard, enjoyed himself. He went half an arrow-length in the air. His brother told him, "You must not dance so hard. You will tire yourself out."

Coyote made reply, "I understand this *pum-pum* dance. You must not say anything to me. I told you I knew this place before you came here."

The sun came up *Sapalwit* morning. The people picked out seven men and seven women. The women went to pick huckleberries and dig fresh roots. The seven men went to kill deer, grouse, rabbits, and all different kinds of game. They used bows and arrows, and all Indians were dressed in buckskins. The manager said to them, "You are going for five days. You will bring in the game and berries and roots the day before *Sapalwit*."

All the fourteen people, men and women, stood in front of him, and he asked them questions, "Are you following your religion of the Great Spirit, and will you do right?"

All lifted their right hands and said, "Yes."

The fourteen were gone the five days and then brought in game, roots and the fruits. All at the Long House danced the *pum-pum* dance day and night, all the week. They did not stop to eat or drink. Coyote danced three days and three nights, the hardest dance he ever made. His brother said, "Do not dance so hard. Take it easy."

Coyote answered a reply, "This is my dancing. I will do as I like to do."

The middle of the third night, Coyote was tired. He lay down to sleep.

There was a night watcher who found a man sleeping. He wanted to know who it was, so turned him over. He saw that it was Coyote. He stopped the singers and dancers and told them to be still awhile. He said to them, "Coyote must have got here without us knowing. He lies sleeping while others are dancing. This is the way something comes round to cheat us without us knowing."

The manager still spoke, "If a crooked man is here, he must be sent down on the earth. All crooked work must be done down there, not up here. If there is a crooked man living on earth, he must not come up here. That is the law of the Great Spirit."

So they got hold of Coyote, opened the door, and threw him down to the earth. Then that *Sapalwit* morning they had the feast. Fox was the only one to stay there from the earth. Next morning at sunrise Fox came back home. He came to the lodge. His brother had not gone there. Coyote still lay dead where he had fallen. But Coyote finally woke up. He came back to himself. He came back home and said to his brother, "Did you have a good feast?"

Fox answered his brother, "Yes, a good feast."

Coyote got bad feelings. He said, "I have the

laws of the Great Spirit. Why did they throw me down to earth?"

That is what he asked his brother, Red Fox. Red Fox said, "The people you saw up there were not alive. They were spirits."

Coyote said, "That has got to be stopped! They will have no more feasts up there. All game, all different kinds of roots, different kinds of berries will come down to earth."

Coyote then closed the trail[43] that led up to the Spirit World. When a man dies, his spirit is all that goes up. His body stays here on earth. Coyote ruled, "Indians shall not go up where the spirit people are having a good time. That law shall not be any more."

After that time, Indians have had the feast here early in the spring, here on earth. When they bring all the fresh roots of different kinds, berries, and game to the Long House, if a human being has straight thoughts and mind, if he is a straight man, he goes in and eats. When you eat that food, it is just like you make petition; and when you die, you will see where they held the feast before, where Coyote was thrown out to earth.

That is the law Coyote made, that if each human being goes right, he will see the Spirit Land when he dies. That has been the law from that time to this day. All we Indians know about that law. This is the end of the story of the *Pum-pum* religion. This is the end of my story, the story told you by myself, *Ye-mow-wit,* the Wishom. It was the faith of *Colwas,* Chief of the Wishoms--who would not fight the white man. Because of this faith, he did not want war. He was my grandfather.

5A. COYOTE AND THE FIVE SISTERS
OF THE *N-CHE-WANA*[44]

It was on a stream entering the *n-Che-wana*
[Columbia River], somewhere in the upper country, that
Coyote [*Speel-yi*] had his residence. There were several
people in the lodge, some of them young. One young
man was the mightiest of *yah-mas* [mule deer] hunters.
No one could equal him as a hunter of the deer.

One day this young hunter killed a deer. He
dressed it there in the woods where he killed it. He
decided to play a trick on Coyote, who was greatest of all
tricksters. He would make a good trick on Coyote.

The hunter fixed everything ready for Coyote to
carry the deer home. He took out the entrails, made rope
of them, and tied the deer into a pack for carrying. He
then left it, going to the lodge without any game. He said
to Coyote, "I left the deer there for you! You better go
bring it home. It is all tied, ready for packing."

Coyote went for the deer where the hunter told
him. He found it and started home with it on his back.
Why the young man tied it with guts was to bother
Coyote for a time. The rope broke. Coyote did not know
that this rope was guts. It might be buckskin!

In the meantime the young man made the rain to
come. He possessed the same power over the rain as did
Coyote. The rain fell fast. It rained and made the streams
high. It kept on raining hard. The gut-rope, now wet,
broke often. Soon Coyote could hardly cross the creeks
in places. The hunter was watching. He thought, "Coyote
will go down and drown!" He wanted to get rid of him.

Coyote crossed in several places, but at last he
came where he could not cross. He tried, but the water
took him downstream. Rain was still falling, pouring
down on all the earth. Coyote floated into the *n-Che-*

wana. He floated quite a ways, when he thought, "I may as well go on down and see what I can find."

He went still further. Then he got ashore and gathered some tules [reed]. He gathered enough to make a baby basket, a cradle-basket. After making the cradle, he got on it, packed in like a baby. He could get in and out of it as he pleased. Coyote fixed himself as a baby in the basket and shoved from the shore, pushed out on the water. He floated down the river, down the *n-Che-wana*, and out onto the ocean. Then he floated towards the South.

There were five Sisters living at the oceanside. These girls had control of all kinds of fish. No other person could catch fish. They had all the fish stored in a lake. Anytime they wanted fish, they could get them; only they got fish. Coyote in his basket floated round to these five Sisters. The Sisters happened to be at the ocean side and heard the child crying in the cradle. The oldest Sister said, "Somebody got drowned! A child has floated down this way! We better catch him and raise him as our brother."

The youngest Sister said, "No! It is not a baby! It is Coyote! We better not have anything to do with him!"

One of the Sisters said, "We better raise him up! He will be a help to us!"

The youngest Sister said no more. She let them have their way. The oldest girl took the child from the cradle. He was small, and the Sisters thought, "Maybe we cannot raise him!"

After they took him into their lodge, they put the tail of the eel to his mouth. He began nursing at it. This is why the eel's tail is pointed to this day. It has no tail like other fish. The older Sisters thought, "He is old enough to eat! We can raise him! He will grow up to be our brother."

They cared for the baby, for Coyote, keeping him in their lodge. Every morning the Sisters went to dig roots; they were gone all day. Then Coyote would leave his cradle to look where the fish were kept.

He studied how to get them loose. The girls had five horn spoons, or bowls. Coyote sized up everything. He made five wooden diggers. He would make a canal, draw the lake, and let the fish go. It took five days to get things ready to begin work. At night there was a baby in the cradle for the Sisters to care for. In the daytime, this baby was a man, working at the canal.

On the day to draw the lake, Coyote took the five horn spoons. He fitted them over his head. He thought, "I will not be able to complete this work before the Sisters come home and find me."

Everything was ready to dig the last of the canal. Coyote dug all day, dug hard. He had about finished, when one of the women broke her digging stick. She said to her Sisters, "Something is wrong at home! We must go see about it right now!"

They started home, hurried all the way. They found the baby was not in the cradle-basket, was not in the lodge. They did not know where he had gone. The youngest Sister said, "We better go to the Lake! It may be Coyote! I told you not to have anything to do with him. Better to have let him alone!"

The Sisters hurried fast to the lake. Yes! Coyote was there. He was digging hard to draw all the water out. The Sisters said, "We will have to club him!"

Each of the Sisters had a club, the kind used in clubbing the salmon when caught. Coyote had the five horn spoons with him. He saw the Sisters coming. He knew that they would kill him if they could. He had the five horn spoons ready! He put them on his head.

The oldest girl struck him on the head and broke

one of the spoons. She did not hurt Coyote. He kept on working hard.

The next oldest Sister struck him; another spoon broke. Coyote paid no attention, kept on digging.

The next oldest girl struck him; she broke another spoon. Coyote was not hurt in the least. He kept digging, digging fast.

The fourth Sister struck him, struck him on the head, and the fourth spoon was broken. Coyote now had but one spoon left to protect his head.

There was also but one club still unused, held by the youngest Sister. She struck hard and broke the last spoon just as Coyote finished his work. The water and the fish went into the ocean.

Coyote hallooed; he called aloud, "All little fish go upstream! Big fish stay in the ocean!" The fish began to do as told. Coyote called again, "I made a mistake! All big fish go upstream! Little fish stay in the ocean!" But it was too late. The first order could not be changed. All small fish, salmon, sturgeon, eels and others went up the streams, while larger fish and whales remained in the ocean. Had Coyote made no mistake, big fish and whales would now be in the streams for the use of Indians while fish now in streams would be in the ocean.

After Coyote had given these orders, he hurried to leave. He first said to the Sisters, "No use for you to keep and kill all the fish. Other people are coming. We might as well have fish for them. This is why I came, why I drew the water from your lake. Here is the rule, the law I now make: You can go with the fish only as they travel up the *n-Che-wana*. Go along the shore, a little ahead of the salmon, as they travel. When people see you, they will know that salmon are coming in the river. Soon they will learn to watch for you, to know when fish are coming.[45]

You will control the fish no more, only as I am telling you. I will make fishing grounds up the *n-Che-wana* and other streams. Indians can always find plenty of these fishing places."

Coyote now left, followed his fish up the *n-Che-wana*. After going for a time, he got hungry. He said to himself, "I have fish in the ocean and in the *wana* [river], traveling for everybody. No use for me to go hungry. I will make a fishery here on the oceanside." Coyote looked; he saw smooth water everywhere. He studied how he could make a good fishery there. He then made this rule, this law: "When people come to this place and are hungry, this they must do: Call these words, halloo loudly, 'Fish must come ashore as my make!'"

Coyote then called out the command of his own ruling. The fish came ashore, but Coyote had made a mistake. It was a gravelly place at the water's edge, too slippery for him to hold. The big salmon got back in the water. Then Coyote said, "I will counsel with my five Sisters."

He did so, but his Sisters said, "We will not help you! Whenever we tell you what to do, you always say, 'I made a mistake! I knew that before!'"

Coyote threatened to bring rain to destroy the Sisters. This scared them. They agreed to instruct him what to do. They said, "You have a club ready to kill the fish. Hit him on the head! You must call the salmon out of the water where there is sand. You can then hold him. You cannot hold him on the rocks--too slippery."

Coyote made reply, "Yes! I knew that, but I forgot. I made a mistake."

Coyote traveled on. He found a sandy place sloping down to the water. He hallooed, "Fish must come to shore as my make!" A big fish came out of the water, rolling in the sand. Coyote could hold him good. He had a club ready, as his Sisters had directed. He struck the salmon on the head and killed him. He carried the fish away from the water and cut him open. He placed him on a stick to bake before the fire. While the fish was roasting, Coyote was very tired. He lay down to rest.

There were five Wolves who knew that Coyote was cooking fish. They wished him asleep. While he was sleeping, they sneaked up and ate nearly all the fish. They left only a little end of the tail for Coyote. They oiled his lips and his hands, rubbing bones of salmon over them. Then they left him soundly sleeping.

Coyote awoke; he stretched himself. He thought, "Well! I must have slept! My fish is all gone! I must have eaten it." He found the oil on his lips, on his hands. The bones and split-stick were lying by his knee. He said, "Yes! I must have eaten the fish, but I am hungry! I left only a little piece of the tail. I will finish that."

Then Coyote ate the rest of the salmon, the small tail-end left by the Wolves. He was still hungry! He wondered how it was and decided to consult his five Sisters again. He said to them, "What became of the salmon? It is gone and I am still hungry."

The Sisters replied, "We will not tell you! You would say, 'I know all about the salmon!'" But when Coyote was bringing the rain, they told him, "The five Wolves ate the salmon while you slept. But you can do the same to them sometime. They catch all kinds of duck and waterfowl eggs."

Coyote was cunning. He said, "I know all about that salmon. I know all about the Wolves, how they cook eggs with hot rocks baked on the ground."

Coyote had the same power as the Wolves. He could wish them asleep while eggs were cooking. He found where they were cooking eggs in the brush. He wished them asleep, then ate all their eggs but five, one for each Wolf. He rubbed egg on their mouths and ruffled up the hair on their necks to make them ugly. Then he placed one egg by the side of each Wolf as he slept.

After completing this work, Coyote left the Wolves and followed on up the river. At every stream entering the *n-Che-wana*, he made some kind of fishery. He ordered certain kinds of fish for each stream and a certain way to fish in each stream. In some streams, fish would only run when about ready to spawn; they would then run up from the *n-Che-wana*. In some, Chinook salmon would run before being ready to spawn. Coyote went up each stream and made fisheries, made falls or some kind of trap. He came to the top of Cascade Falls. He said, "No Chinook will run up *Ho-ho-lah-me*,[46] only *um-to-li*."

Coyote came on up the *n-Che-wana*. It was between [place and incident forgotten by narrator]. He came to the Little White Salmon River and said, "Nothing but *to-las* will come to this place. I will drive the *to-las* to this place. It will take a good man to spear them." This is so. You see the salmon's back in the water, but you miss him. You cannot spear him. But there is a way to catch the salmon. It takes two men to catch them, two men to be there. Traps of sticks must be placed. The two men must stop there all night. No other men must go there at night. Salmon only run here at night; they go into the lake in daytime. All the salmon come down the stream. The men close the trap with sticks and the fish cannot go back upstream to the lake. Clubs only must be used. Indians kill with these clubs and divide the salmon among themselves. In drying at this place, salmon never spoils. It can be dried either by fire or no fire. Hang it on bushes or trees and it dries without tainting. This was the law made by Coyote to rule this and the fisheries on *Ho-ho-*

lah-me.

Coyote fixed all these fisheries there and again traveled up the *n-Che-wana.* He came to the *Lou-lo pol-me.*[47] Nothing but *um-to-li* were to come up this stream. No trapping was done, only spearing in the *Lou-lo pol-me,* not much fancy fishing. All the salmon here were to be dried by fire. This was the law made by Coyote to rule the fisheries of *Lou-lo pol-me.*

Coyote came on up the Big-river where he ran among some women he was afraid of. They were Fleas. Fleas got all over him and nearly ate him up. Coyote said, "I cannot go through here!---" [part of story forgotten by narrator]. Coyote came a ways and made a place in the rocks to hang his robes, his clothing. This place can still be seen in a bluff. You hang your clothes there in the sun and fleas all jump off and leave them. Coyote got rid of all the Flea women and came on up to *Why-phot.*[48] He said, "This river [Klickitat] will belong to one big tribe. I will make chinook salmon and eels to go up its waters. I will make good fishing grounds for the people who will live here."

Coyote made the *Klah-ti-hut* ["dropping over"].[49] He made everything nice at this place. He made a place to sit, and a place to brace the foot. He made a place a short ways above the falls where the salmon was to be ground, a solid rock hollowed out. Coyote tried the grinding, to see how it would work. There is a great smooth rock where the half-cooked salmon was spread to dry, to become brittle in the sun so it could be ground. He tried it once, then gave it up and did not finish it good. He gave up the grinding. Salmon would come, but could not be ground; they could only be dried. Coyote did this for the Klickitat Indians, a big tribe that was to come.

Below [what is now] Fort Casteel on the *Klah-ti-*

hut, Coyote created a fishery where salmon are to be speared only. If a fish escapes the spear man, there is no use trying more that day. If he does wait, it will be a long time before another fish comes for him to try his spear. That was a rule laid down by Coyote when he made the fishery. He also formed a "basket" in the rocks where the salmon can be placed when caught.

Finishing up on the *Klah-ti-hut*, Coyote continued up the *n-Che-wana*. He made another fishery at *Soon-me* ["big-eddies"], below [what is now] The Dalles. Here the fish could be seined only. Coyote continued up the *n-Che-wana* and made a fishery between Tumwater and [what is now] Celilo. Then he went up to *Y-Yum*.[50] There he made all kinds of fisheries. He made *Skein* Island. Coyote said, "There will be an island fishery here. Anytime the people want good fishing, if they work it as I make the rule, they will have the best of fishing. When the fish begin to come up the *n-Che-wana*, one man, only one, must go to the island. He must strip naked, roll in the sand, run about and do all sorts of fun-tricks. He must do this one whole day. If this is not done, then there will be no good fishing. Fish will not come.[51] But if he does my ruling, fish will come. After the man has done this thing, the people can go to the island and stay there, catching and drying fish. This fishery is for all people."

Completing his work at *Skein*, Coyote traveled on up the *n-Che-wana* making various fisheries for the tribes that were to come. He made them up the many streams, fisheries of different rulings. Everywhere he fixed fish traps for the use of the tribes. Somewhere in the Umatilla country, he made a place where, if the person stands in exactly the right place on the bank of the *n-Che-wana* and calls the command loudly, "Salmon must come to shore as my make! [i.e., mate?]" the salmon will have to come out for the use of the caller. One salmon only will come.

This was the rule of Coyote.

Coyote made fisheries up the Snake River and all its streams. Many of these are unknown to the Yakamas. He made seining and spearing fisheries all along the *n-Che-wana*, above the mouth of the Snake River, and above [what is now] Pasco. For these fisheries, he made a North Wind to blow. Dry and cooling, this wind blows during all the fishing season, that the people may dry their catch. No fire is needed. This wind begins about mid-sun and continues during the afternoon and evening. It always comes as ordered by Coyote.[52]

When Coyote passed a certain gap in the hills above [what is now] White Bluffs, he wanted the *n-Che-wana* to run in a different direction. But there was too much sage. The fish did not like the smell, so he let it go in its present channel. The trace where he wanted the river to go can still be seen. All about are the fish-traps Coyote prepared, bundles of standing rocks.[53] Coyote abandoned this incomplete fishery because of the smell of sage. He traveled on up the *n-Che-wana*, leaving at various places fisheries for Indians who were to inhabit that region. He went to the Wenatchee River. He made some riffles, the same as he had abandoned in [other] places before completed. In these, the Indians must set scaffolding, triangular-formed posts, across the river. Then poles are lashed reaching from post to post. Against these poles, willow sticks are placed up and down so the fish cannot pass. Then the fish can be speared. It is a successful fishery.

Coyote then went up the Wenatchee and made the Wenatchee Falls. This was the big fishery for all the tribes. The chinooks, the "bluebacks," and all the good fish are there. Coyote ruled that spears and gaff-hooks were to be used at this fishery. If a fish tore loose from spear or hook, he made a place below the fishery where the wounded fish would float out to the shore and die. The Indians could get these fish and use them while still fresh and good. None were wasted. This was Coyote's own work, to save all the fish.

The Wenatchee tribe had the west side of the river; the tribes east of the river had that side of the stream. In the middle of the river, the middle of the falls, sits Coyote's daughter, a big rock. At this place the salmon jump, and she rules. If any Indian caught a big salmon, if he was about to be pulled in, he was to yell loudly. Then he would not be pulled into the water. Coyote ruled that Indians come there for a big time, and all must halloo when fish were caught. This was done. Salmon could be air-dried without fire.

Coyote planted all kinds of roots on the Wenatchee side, camas and other roots among the rocks on the sides of a hill. He planted serviceberries on the steep bluffs on the Wenatchee side. These berries were for the benefit of young people. The rule was that young women could go there to pick berries, and any young man could come and talk to them. The girl could not run away nor hide. If agreeable, they would agree to marry and go away as man and wife. This was an Indian custom, Indian law. It was good to do so.[54]

Coyote also ruled that no matter how many Indians came to the Wenatchee fishery to camp, all camps must be set adjoining, continuously, one opening into the other with the trail running directly through the tepees. Persons traveling on this trail, either on foot, horseback, or pack-train must pass through the tepees. Fires must be on one side of the trail so people could pass. The trail must always be kept clear for travelers. This trail was on the Wenatchee side of the river, where bluffs are close and narrow.

Coyote further ruled that any Indian, man or

woman, coming from a distance to this fishery, if they had arranged to stay only one sun, maybe two suns, they would always stay longer. Coyote's daughter would attract them and they would never leave under four or five suns. This was the law and ruling of Coyote. Something always occurred to detain travelers overtime.

Coyote traveled on up the *n-Che-wana*, making fisheries of various kinds. He created the "High Falls" [Kettle Falls] in the Okanogan country, and many others. But the Yakamas and Klickitats do not know about these; they do not understand the mode of catching the fish and drying them there. Our tribes have not seen fisheries of those countries.[55, 56]

5B. THE ORIGIN OF FISH IN THE COLUMBIA[57]

Coyote[58] heard about two women who had fish preserved in a pond. Then he went to them as they were collecting driftwood from the river. He turned himself into a piece of wood trying to get them to pick him up. He drifted along. But then they did not get hold of him. He went ashore, ran off to way yonder up river, and transformed himself into a boy. He put himself into a cradle, threw himself into the river, and again drifted along.

The two women caught sight of him wailing. They thought: "Some people have capsized, and this child is drifting towards us."

The younger one thought: "Let us get hold of it." But the older woman did not want to have the child. Now it was drifting along.

The older one thought: "That is Coyote." Nevertheless the younger woman took the child and put it in a canoe.

The two women started home towards their house. The child was wailing, and they arrived home with it. They took off the cradle from it and looked closely at it. As it turned out, the child was a boy.

The younger one said: "A boy is better than driftwood." And then she went and cut an eel and put its tail in his mouth. Then straightway he sucked at it and ate it all up. She gave him another eel, and again he sucked at it, eating up only half. Then he fell asleep, and half the eel was lying in his mouth.

The two women said: "He is asleep. Now let us go for some more wood."

And then they went far away. He arose and saw them going far off. Then he made himself loose and seized their food. He roasted the fish on a spit; when it was done, he ate. He caught sight of the fish, which were their food, in a lake. Then he examined the lake carefully, and discovered a spot where it would be easy to make an outlet from it to the river.

"Here I shall make the fish break out from the lake, and then they will go to the Great River."[59] He made five digging sticks, made them out of young oak. And then he put them down in that place. He started back home towards their house. Again, just as before, he put himself into the cradle. Again there in his mouth lay the eel's tail. Again he fell asleep.

Now the two women arrived. "The boy is sleeping," they said; "very good is the boy, being a great sleeper." And then they retired for the night.

Daylight came, the boy was sleeping. Again they went for wood. Again he saw them going far away. Then he got up and took their food. He roasted it on a spit and ate it all up. Then straightway he went to where his digging sticks were. He took hold of one of his digging sticks. Then he stuck his digger into the ground. He pulled it out, and the earth was all loosened up; but his digging stick broke. He took hold of another one and again stuck it into the ground. Then he loosened up the earth, and his digger was all broken to pieces. He took hold of another one of his digging sticks. Again he stuck it into the ground; he loosened the earth all up, and his third digger was all broken to pieces. He took hold of the fourth one; again his digger broke. Now at last he took hold of the fifth and stuck it into the ground; he loosened the earth all up. And then the fish slid over into the Great River.

Now then the older woman bethought herself. She said to her companion: "You said, 'The child is good.' I myself thought, 'That is Coyote.' Now this day Coyote has treated us two badly. I told you, 'Let us not take the child, that is Coyote.' Now we have become poor. Coyote has made us so." Then they went to their house, and he too went to them to their house.

He said to them: "Now by what right, perchance, would you two keep the fish to yourselves? You two are birds, and I shall tell you something. Soon now people will come into this land. Listen!" And the people could be heard "*du'lululu*" (like thunder rumbling afar). "Now they will come into this land; those fish will be the people's food. Whenever a fish will be caught, you two will come. Your name has become Swallows. Now this day I have done with you. Thus I shall call you, 'Swallows.' When the people will come, they will catch fish; and then you two will come and it will be said of you, 'The swallows have come; Coyote called them so.'[60] Thus will the people say: 'From these two did Coyote take away their fish preserved in a pond; now they have come.'" Thus did Coyote call those two.

5C. HOW COYOTE DESTROYED THE FISH DAM AT THE CASCADES, DISTRIBUTING SALMON IN THE RIVERS[61]

The Five Sisters lived at the Cascades of the *n-Che-wana*. The youngest sister was smartest of them all. They had a dam in the river and headed off the salmon from the upper waters. This was bad. Coyote [*Paht-paht*] said, "This must not be done! Fish must be free for all the people."

Coyote sat and studied a long time. He would go see the Five Sisters. But if he went as a man, they would not have him, would not let him come there. Coyote knew what he would do. He would be as a baby. He took tules, the same as the old women use in weaving mats, and made matting. He made a basket. Coyote said, "I will be a baby in the basket!"

He put the basket in the *n-Che-wana*. He got in the basket, crying like a baby every evening. One of the girls went down to the river to get water, where she heard the baby crying. She called to her Sisters, "A little baby has come down the river! Somebody has drowned!"

All the women but the youngest came and saw the baby. They said, "We must take the baby and care for it!"

The youngest Sister knew something was wrong. She did not go. The other Sisters rushed and got the baby, took him in the lodge. They gave him a little fish to eat. He liked it. The Sisters said, "He will grow quick, grow big quick!"

The youngest Sister told them, "Yes! Your baby will grow big quick!"

The next morning the Sisters all went to dig roots. They left the baby in the lodge, tied about the waist to a stake. They gave him a fish to eat, a small fish. He ate it. The Youngest Sister knew all about it, what was going to be done.

As soon as the Sisters left him alone, Coyote untied himself. He commenced making wooden hats. He made five wooden hats.[62] He also made five root-digging sticks. He made all these in one day, preparing for a big work. Coyote thought, "This will not do. I must open the dam and let fish go by for all people."

Coyote now commenced to dig open the big dam so the fish could get through. He knew when the Sisters would be home, when he must be back in the lodge again as a baby, only a little stronger. He stayed that night in the lodge. Next morning when the Sisters went to dig roots, he worked at tearing out the dam. For three days he did this, going back to be a baby in the lodge each night. Every day he was growing a little bigger, a little stronger. The older Sisters would say, "Our baby gets stronger every day."

Coyote worked again on the fourth day. He worked all the time with the root-digging sticks. The baby appeared stronger, and the Sisters were glad. But the youngest Sister knew what would happen.

On the fifth day the Sisters again went to dig roots, leaving the baby in the lodge tied to the stake. On this last day Coyote unhitched himself and put the five wooden hats on his head. On this day he had the dam nearly opened when the Sisters returned home. They said, "*Eh*! Our baby is gone!"

The youngest Sister told them, "Yes! Your baby has the dam nearly out."

They ran to the river, saw Coyote working. They fought him with clubs. They struck him on the head. The first wooden hat broke. They struck him again; the second hat was broken. They struck him again; the third hat was broken. They struck him again; the fourth hat was broken. The fifth time they struck him on the head; the fifth wooden hat was broken. All the time Coyote was digging hard. When the fifth hat broke, the dam gave way. The water rushed by, and the fish went upstream in big herds. The *n-Che-wana* was alive with them. Coyote was glad. He yelled, "*Ha-a-a-aha*! The new people will come, and all will have fish. You cannot keep the salmon this way. Salmon must be free for all."

The Sisters could not say anything. Coyote had destroyed the great dam. He said, "I will make this a big fishing place. Indians will camp here and have good times. They will study out all about high water and low water, and how is the best way to catch fish." Coyote made a good fishing place at the ruined dam of the Cascades.

Coyote brought the salmon up the *n-Che-wana*. He traveled along, got hungry. He wanted salmon, but did not know how to catch it. He asked his Five Sisters how to get salmon. They said, "We will not tell you. You always say: 'Yes, that is as I thought.'"

Coyote said, "You better do it."

The Sisters answered, "No! We will not tell you."

The Sisters were afraid of rain, and Coyote said, "*A-ow*! I will make it rain." He threw back his head, blew rain from his mouth, "*Ch-ch-ch-ch-chu*."[63] The Sisters were scared. They said, "Oh quit! We will tell you." Coyote quit making rain, and the Sisters said, "You go to the edge of the river and call: 'Come up, my make [i.e., mate?]; I am hungry.'"

Coyote said, "Yes, yes! I thought so."

He did as they told him. The fish came up on the rocks, "*C-c-c-r-c*!" Coyote grabbed a fish, but it got back in the water. He could not hold it. He did not know how to catch the salmon. Coyote said, "Well Sisters! How is this? I called, 'Come up, my work;' but they go back again."

The Sisters would not tell him. Coyote said, "All right! I will make it rain." He threw back his head and blew the rain, "*Ch-ch-ch-ch-chu.*"

The Sisters were scared and said, "Quit! We will tell you. Go call the fish out on the sand. You can hold them there."

Coyote said, "Yes! That is what I thought."

He went to a sandy place and called, "Come up, my make! I am hungry!" The fish came up on the sand, "*C-c-c-r-c.*" This time Coyote caught a salmon and held him. He hit him on the head with a club, killed him. Coyote made a fire. Split the salmon, stuck it on sticks to roast before the fire. It smelled good, for Coyote was hungry. It was about roasted; Coyote had his salmon nearly done. He soon would eat it. He watched it and felt good.

There were five Wolves living away off from the river. They said, "Coyote is roasting his fish. We better make him sleep. We better go eat his fish now."

Coyote went to sleep, just as his salmon was done. The Wolves came. They took his salmon, ate it all up. They greased Coyote's face and fingers good, while he was sleeping. The Wolves then went away. Coyote woke up and looked for his fish. It was gone. He said, "I roasted him! When did I eat him? My fingers, my face are greasy. I am hungry, but I ate my fish."

He went on again, still hungry. He could not stand the hunger. He stopped at a sandy place and called, "My make, come up! I am hungry."

The fish came up on the sand, "*C-c-c-r-c!*" Coyote caught one and clubbed it on the head, killed it. He cleaned it, put it on sticks to roast by a fire he built. It was about done when the Wolves put him to sleep again. They took the hot salmon. They ate it all up. They greased Coyote's mouth and fingers good, then ran away.

Coyote woke up to find his salmon gone. He said, "I ate him. My fingers and face are greasy. I am hungry, but I ate my fish. I cannot understand."

Coyote then went on a distance up the river. He was too hungry. He came to a sandy place at the water's edge and called, "Come up, my make. I am hungry."

The salmon came up, "*C-c-c-r-c!*" Coyote caught a fish, cleaned him, split him. He built a fire, put his salmon on sticks to roast. It was about done. The Wolves put him to sleep. They came and ate all the roasted salmon. They greased Coyote's fingers, his face, then went back home. Coyote woke up. He looked for his salmon; it was gone. He felt hungry. He found his face and fingers all greasy and said, "I ate my fish, but I am hungry. I cannot understand why I am so hungry when I ate my fish. I am awfully hungry."

Coyote went on again, suffering with hunger. Soon he came to a sandy place and called, "Come up, my make! I am hungry!"

The fish came up, "*C-c-c-r-c!*" Coyote caught one, hit it on the head with a club, killed it. He cleaned it, split it open and put it on sticks to roast at a fire he built. It was about done when the Wolves put a sleep on him, took his fish and ate it all up. They greased his mouth good, then went back home. Coyote woke up. He looked for his fish, but it was not there. He felt his fingers, his face--all greasy. He said, "How is this? I ate my fish, but I am still hungry. I will ask my Sisters."

He called, "How is this, my Sisters? I ate my salmon, but I am still hungry. Five times I have eaten a whole salmon. I am more hungry than at first. I am awfully hungry. Tell me about it."

But the Sisters said, "No, we will not tell you. You always know anyhow."

Coyote said, "All right! I will make it rain." He threw back his head; he blew rain from his mouth, "*Ch-ch-ch-ch-chu.*"

The Sisters did not want to get wet. They cried, "Oh wait! Do not make it rain. We will tell you all about when you roast fish." Coyote then quit making rain. The Sisters said, "Five Wolves live in the mountains. They put sleep on you, came and ate your salmon. They greased your mouth, your fingers. They did this five times."

Coyote said, "Oh yes, yes! That is what I thought."

The Sisters said, "We will tell you now what you must do. The Wolves gather all kinds of eggs and roast them. They get duck eggs, pheasant eggs, any kind they find. You go over there where they are now roasting their eggs. You put them to sleep and eat their eggs. When you are through, put egg on their mouths, their fingers. They will think that they ate the eggs."

Coyote said, "Yes! That is what I thought to do!"

Coyote then went to where the Wolves were roasting eggs. He put sleep on them and ate all their eggs. He rubbed egg on their fingers, about their mouths, then went away. Soon the Wolves woke up. They saw their eggs were all gone, but they were hungry. They looked at each other, saw egg on their faces. They said, "You ate the eggs."

"No, you ate all the eggs; it is on your mouth." This is the way they quarreled among themselves about who ate the eggs.

The Wolves gathered more eggs, built a fire and began roasting them. Coyote sneaked up, came near. He put a sleep on the Wolves, ate their eggs. He stuck egg on their fingers, on their mouths. He placed shells near each of them. Then he hurried away. The Wolves woke up, found the eggs all gone. They thought, "How is this? The eggs are gone, but I am hungry."

They saw egg on each other's faces. They got mad and quarreled about it. "You ate the eggs. The most shells are with you!"

"No! You ate all the eggs. It is on your mouth, and I am hungry. I did not get any eggs!" This was a big quarrel among themselves.

The Wolves hunted more eggs after awhile, built a fire to roast them. Coyote was watching. He put a sleep on them, then came and ate all the eggs. He played a trick on them again, rubbing egg on their fingers and mouths. The Wolves woke up, found no eggs. The shells were with them, egg was on their hands and mouths, but they were very hungry. They looked around, then looked at each other. They began to quarrel, "You ate all the eggs! It is on your mouth! The most shells are with you."

"No! You ate them! I am hungry! I got no eggs! You ate them all! There are shells near you."

The Wolves quarreled like that, then went to hunt more eggs. When they had a lot of eggs, they built a fire and began roasting them. Coyote came. He put a big sleep on them. Then he ate all their eggs again. He put egg on their fingers and mouths, then ran away. The Wolves woke up and found no eggs. They were awfully hungry this time. They got mad, because they thought the other one was tricking them. They quarreled hard, "You ate all the eggs! There are the shells with you."

"You ate the eggs! It is on your mouth. I got no eggs! I am hungry!"

They quarreled a long time and then went hunting more eggs. When they found many, they came and built a fire to roast them. When they were nearly cooked, Coyote made a sleep to come over the Wolves, then came and began eating their eggs. He smeared egg on their mouths, on their fingers. They woke up, saw Coyote eating the last of their eggs. There was nobody to tell them this. The only way to know it was seeing him eating the eggs. They saw him getting even with them. They now knew who had eaten all their eggs. They sneaked away ashamed. Coyote laughed at them.

Coyote came to The Dalles. Here [i.e., opposite, on the Washington shore?] the Wishoms would be. The falls would be heard far away. Coyote put the rocks in place and made a great fishing grounds. Coyote then came to *Y-yum*.[64] Here would be different Indians, a different language. But they would understand each other. They would be not far apart. The fishing would be good. Coyote ruled that they make different nets, different spears. Coyote came above Celilo, making a different fishing grounds. Here he fixed it for canoes, for different nets.

He came on again, making places for fishing the same way, all different kinds. He came to the Yakima River. He reached *Top-tut*. Coyote said, "This is far from *Y-yum*. I will make a good fishing place. They will catch fish from both sides of the river [Yakima River]. The people will come from above to fish here." Coyote made the *Top-tut* falls, good fishing. He made three holes [triangular] clear across the river, below the falls. In these, posts can be set and tied together for scaffolding. These posts can be worked in high water, from both sides.

Coyote came up on where Mabton [i.e., one of several towns or places in Washington cited here] now is. He was going to make a fishing place there, but it was too close to one he made at Prosser. He made the *Tom-man-cha-tah-nee-kohpt* [falls of the fish trap] in the Satus River. He made a rule that salmon must be caught a certain way at this trap. He ruled that salmon could not go above there. They could go up the other way, up Dry Creek, *Pawen-kute-copa* [tule weeds, or swamp tule], but not to the head of the Satus River. No salmon could go up Toppenish Creek. Coyote wanted a wife from the Yakamas. They would not give him a woman; so he let no fish go up that stream. The water in it is too bad for salmon.

Coyote came on up and started to make a fishing place near [what is now] Chief Sluskin's, below *Pah-qy-ti-koot*, but it was too close to *Top-tut*. He tore it out. It shows some. He left it so a few fish can be caught there.[65] Coyote then went to Wenatchee. He made the fishing grounds there. They are good. He then went to Spokane, made the falls in that river for other people. He stopped there and said, "Salmon can go on up above these falls. People can catch them anywhere."

Here Coyote was tired. He quit.[66]

6A. THE RACCOON STORY[67]

Raccoon and his paternal grandmother, an old woman, were living together. Whenever it was summer, then they used to gather acorns. Now finally Raccoon got to be lazy in picking them; the sun made him so. And then he became angry; he gathered only acorns with worm-holes. She used to tell him, but in vain: "Keep picking only the good ones!"

"No!" And he got angrier than ever and picked none at all.

Winter came on and he was hungry. Yonder he sat back in the house; silent he sat, saying nothing. Then his paternal grandmother said to him: "Why do you sit silent, grandson? Are you hungry?"

"Yes," he answered her.

"What, pray, shall I give you?" She showed him all sorts of things, but to no purpose.

"No!" he said.

Then she said to him: "How would it be if I gave you acorns?"

"Yes, grandmother, give them to me."

She said to him: "You shall go to our cache."

"Yes," he said to her. He took their basket and went on to their cache; he went to get acorns. They had five caches. He arrived there. Then he uncovered one of them, the first; immediately he ate up all there was in the first cache.

Again he uncovered one of them; again he ate and ate all there was. Only the shells and the worm-eaten acorns he always threw away. He ate up everything. The shells and worm-eaten acorns he swept back down into the cache. Again he uncovered one, the third; also that he uncovered. Again, as before, he chewed and ate up all of the acorns. Again, as before, he swept the shells and worm-eaten acorns down into the cache. He uncovered the fourth.

Then a certain person shouted: "Raccoon is stealing! Ho!" He listened. After a short while he heard him shout again, as before: "Raccoon is stealing!" and he looked about carefully.

Then he caught sight of Crow coming towards him. He said to her: "No! I am not stealing. My paternal grandmother told me to get acorns, that's why I came." He uncovered the fifth cache.

Then he called Crow: "You too come!" So she went up to him, approached him.

He said to her: "Now there you have come far enough. Do not come right up to the cache. I'll just throw you acorns from a distance."

"Yes," Crow said to him. And then he ate; those

which were bad, those he always threw to her. Those that were worm-eaten he would throw in her direction. And thus the two of them ate.

Then he said to her: "Don't you tell on me."

"Yes," Crow said to him. Again, as before, he swept their shells down into the cache. A few acorns were left over; those he packed into the cache.

He went home.

Then a long time elapsed, and his paternal grandmother also went to their cache. She arrived there. She uncovered the first cache. Alas! There were only shells and worm-eaten acorns. Similarly in another one. Similarly all five were uncovered. She went home. She arrived there. Raccoon was nowhere to be seen. In truth, he had already concealed himself in the rear of the house.

She seized him there, where he was sitting, looking up smilingly at his paternal grandmother. She took hold of a stick and whipped him on his nose. He cried, ran off, ran out of the house. Once more she whipped him, and, as before, she thus kept whipping him. She followed him, and at last he got quite outside. She whipped him at the tip of his tail. That is why today Raccoon's back is black in places; it is like that wherever she whipped him.

Then Raccoon said to himself: "Now I shall go away for good. Never again shall my paternal grandmother see me." Then he cried. Thus he said: "My paternal grandmother whipped me!" And thus he went on.

He approached people who were assembled together, gambling at shinny. They said to him: "You shall come;" they shouted to him. He did not look at them at all; he went straight ahead, wailing.

"Ha, ha, ha!" they all laughed, "Oh, yes! Raccoon has been stealing, that is why he is crying."

Again he said:

"My paternal grandmother whipped me!
My paternal grandmother whipped me!
        You people, indeed, are happy;
But as for me--my paternal grandmother
        whipped me!"

Straight on he went. Again he approached some people. There were many people again. Again as before, they shouted to him: "You shall come."

Again, as before, he said:

"My paternal grandmother whipped me!
My paternal grandmother whipped me!"

"Ha, ha, ha! Raccoon has been stealing. His paternal grandmother killed him," the people made fun of him.

Again, as before, he said:

"You people, indeed, are happy,
But as for me--my paternal grandmother
        whipped me."

Now he passed by them, a little farther ahead. He went straight on until he came to trees on which all sorts of food were growing. There he sat down and remained quiet for a short time. Then he climbed up on a berry bush.[68] Then he ate the berries.

Now his paternal grandmother, for her part, became sad. She thought: "I don't know why I treated my grandson in that way. Now I shall go and look for him." Then she got ready to go.

And then she went. She cried (wept):

"Oh, my grandson! grandson, my grandson!
I know not why I whipped my grandson.
        He killed a fawn; a breech-clout I

made of it,
thus with its hoofs on.

Grandson, my grandson!
He brought me a fawn; a breech-clout I
made of it,
just that way, with its hoofs on."[69]

Raccoon was perched on top, eating the berries.
Then he turned to look, and saw her coming. Quietly he
was sitting above, saying nothing.

Whenever a bird flew, whirring its wings, she
would shout: "Is that you, grandson?" She would turn to
look; it was not a person at all. Again she wailed.

He thought to himself: "Now I shall talk to her."

Then again he thought: "Never mind! I shall not
talk to her. I shall just kill her."

Then again he thought: "I shall just associate
kindly with her."

Now she reached him. She said to him: "Is that
you, grandson?" He was perched on top of the tree,
saying nothing; he said nothing at all to her.

In vain she said to him: "Is that you, grandson?"
He did not speak to her at all.

Then she said to him: "Let me also have some
berries!" Then he picked them until his hand was full. He
stuck thorns into the berries.

He said to her: "Open your mouth wide and I
shall give you some." Then she did thus. He threw them
at her so as to just fill her mouth. She choked; she tried
to tell him to get water, but in vain. He did not go for it.
And then she rolled about. Then he ran after her, but in
vain, as she had already become different. A short time
elapsed and she flew: *du'lulu*.

Raccoon burst out crying. He kept running after

her, but in vain. He tried to seize her, but without success. She kept flying about: *du'du.*

In vain he called to her: "Grandmother, come now! Not again shall I do thus to you. Let us now go home." He kept following her about, but in vain. Now she just uttered: "*Pe'spesps.*"[70] That same paternal grandmother of Raccoon, in truth, had become Pheasant.

So then he remained alone. Then he went on. Straightway he came to Coyote. Now they two lived together alone.

Then Coyote said to him: "Do not go far away: perhaps a *'wala'lap'* will meet you--they are wicked beings."[71]

And then Raccoon went on again and came to Grizzly Bear. "What did you do to yourself so as to be striped black on your nose?"

"I sharpened an adz. And then I hit myself with it, then poured black pitch and urine on myself."

"You shall do thus to me too, younger brother!"

"If indeed you are nervy, then I shall do thus to you."

Then Grizzly Bear said: "You shall do thus to me."

"All right," said Raccoon. And then the two of them sharpened Grizzly-Bear's adz, sharpened it perfectly. Then they prepared the black pitch very hurriedly. Then Grizzly Bear lay down; then Raccoon hit him on the nose with the adze. Immediately he poured the black pitch and urine on him. Then he ran out and left him.

Then he went on and on. Straightway he came to Coyote. Then he said to him: "Grizzly Bear is following me. I hit him with an adze." Then Coyote hid him.

Then Coyote took a grasshopper and just made him black on his nose. Then Coyote started a fire and made it blaze near the grasshoppers. He magically transformed them, so that they appeared to be children.

Then Grizzly Bear pursued Raccoon. Straightway he came upon Coyote. He said to him: "Did a boy come past you? He made a scar on me right here."

"*Tc!i'tqxala, tc!i'tqxala,*"[72] said Coyote.

Again he asked him: "Did not a boy come past you?"

"*Tc!i'tqxala, tc!i'tqxala.*"

"Ha, ha! I, for my part, do not speak Molale,[73] younger brother!" Indeed, Coyote had already swallowed the grasshopper; he had just made his nose black to make him look like Racoon.

"I'll tell you--perhaps I swallowed him some time ago."

"Let's see, then! Vomit!" said Grizzly Bear.

Then Coyote vomited; a person came out of him whose nose was black.

Then, surely, Grizzly Bear recognized this person as him. Then Grizzly Bear said: "Just what did you do to yourself that you are thus small?"

"If, indeed, you are nervy, then I could do thus to you too, just like me."

"Surely, you shall now do thus to me too, younger brother!" And then the two of them went and heated some stones.

Then Coyote went and cut off an elder-bush [i.e., Alder? Elderberry?] limb. Then he bored it all through and hung it inside of himself in his belly. And then he went and threw down five hot rocks into himself, one by one.

Grizzly Bear said to him: "Thus I should like to do."

Coyote swallowed five rocks one after another. Then he drank water and they boiled in his belly. He rubbed himself. Then he sang: "I am clean, clean." Then he said to his elder brother: "In this way I became clean and small."

Grizzly Bear said: "Thus you shall do to me, younger brother!"

Coyote said: "If, indeed, you are nervy, then I shall do thus to you." Coyote stood up and the rocks just went pouring out of him from his tube. And then Grizzly Bear sat down.

Coyote said to him: "Shut your eyes." Then he dropped the rocks down into him. His belly all burned up. He began to die.

Coyote kept telling him: "Do you too say, 'Clean, clean,' just as I kept saying." He died. Coyote took off his skin from him; then he ate him.

6B. RACCOON AND HIS GRANDMOTHER[74]

There were Raccoon and his paternal grandmother.[75] And then he stole the acorns. Now then his paternal grandmother went to the cache. And then she too went to get acorns. She arrived; there were no acorns in the cache. And then she went to the house. And then his paternal grandmother whipped him on his nose; and again he whipped him on his nose a little above; and again she whipped him on his forehead; then she whipped him twice on his tail.

IV. "Wishham Bride." Special Collections
Division, Univ. of Washington Libraries.
Edward S. Curtis, c. 1909, photo NAI214.

II. LEGENDARY TALES

7. HOW COYOTE ENSLAVED
THE WEST WIND[76]

The people went and Coyote went. And then they
fought with one another. That Coyote captured someone
and made him a slave. In truth he had caught a flea where
the people were fighting. And again he captured a child
and took him. In truth that was the West Wind, whom
Coyote made a slave. And then the people stopped
fighting.

And then they sat in the canoes, and the people
started out for home. They sat down on Coyote's slave,
so that his body became mashed to pieces. In truth that
was the flea. They also sat down on *Ap!a'lali*[77] so that she
became mashed to pieces. She whose name is *Ap!a'lali*
nowadays is small; and Chub is also that same one's
name.

And then they arrived home and got out of the
canoes. Coyote's slave was taken hold of, he whose body
was mashed to pieces. And then the people said: "This
one is Coyote's slave." Then he took him in into the
house--both of his slaves he took into the house--and set
him down.

And then Coyote saw that his older slave [i.e.,
West Wind?] was all swollen in his eyes and in his ears
and that his body had become all covered over with
swellings. So then Coyote said: "My slave has become
sick." And then Coyote told the people: "He will die."

Now then in the middle of the night the slave breathed and Coyote's house became loosened. Coyote awoke; his slave was not to be seen. Coyote went to where he had left him. His slave was not to be seen. And then Coyote looked for him, went about everywhere, but did not find him.

And then Coyote defecated out his two younger sisters. He said to them: "You two tell me what has become of that one."

And then they said to him: "Now you yourself will say, 'Just so did I think.' That is not a child, that is the West Wind." His two feces spoke thus to him and told him what to do. Always his two younger sisters would tell him.

And then they said to him: "If you wish to get him, then you must set a trap for him." And then the two jumped up into him. The one threw him down senseless, while the other one jumped up into his belly quietly.

The two said to him: "You will set a trap in the mountains and there you will catch that slave of yours. When snow will fall, black[78] will be the land in the mountains. And then you will lay a trap for him and there you will catch your slave. He will be caught by your trap."

And then Coyote looked over the land in the mountains and then set a trap for him. West Wind was caught in Coyote's trap.

Now the next morning Coyote went into the mountains, went to look for him. He saw him sitting; he was bound fast at his feet. And then Coyote seized him and recognized him. He took his slave with him to the house.

And again it happened to the boy as before; his body swelled all up. And again Coyote saw how he was. And again Coyote said: "Perhaps he will die." Again it was night. And again he escaped. In this way he escaped four times. Truly Coyote caught the West Wind for the fifth time. And again he escaped.

And then Coyote's two younger sisters said to him: "Now you will not catch that West Wind. This time he has escaped from you for all time. If you had killed him, there would be no west wind. But you did not kill him, so there will always be a west wind. Whenever a west wind will come, then the people will say, 'Coyote made a mistake about the West Wind.' Thus will the people say. So that there will always be a west wind as long as people will be in this land." Thus is the tale.

8. THE EAST WIND AND THE WEST WIND[79]

The West Wind and the East Wind (Wallawalla wind) wrestled with each other. And then the West Wind poured out grease when the two took hold of each other. Now then that one, the East Wind, caused ice to be spread out. The East Wind was thrown down; he was laid low. Then the two again took hold of each other. The West Wind threw down the East Wind. Then the two again took hold of each other.

Now the West Wind again poured out grease. The East Wind was thrown down. Again the two wrestled with each other. Again the East Wind was thrown down. Again the two wrestled with each other. Again the East Wind was thrown down.

The East Wind was addressed by the West Wind: "You aren't strong, East Wind! Thus shall the people say, 'The West Wind and the East Wind wrestled with each other.' For all time to come have I become strong."

The people said: "The West Wind is strong for all time to come. The East Wind is not strong."[80] Thus is the tale which was made by ancient men. Nowadays there are not such.

9A. COYOTE AND THE MISCHIEVOUS WOMEN[81]

Then Coyote traveled up the river. He went and went, and arrived at a certain land. He caught sight of two women across the river. And then each shouted out to him from across the river: "How fond I am of you!" Thus the women spoke to Coyote.

Then he thought: "Well, now, I should like to have the women." He threw himself into the river and dived under. He came to land where he had seen the two of them. He looked about; there was nothing to be seen.

He turned about to where he had thrown himself into the river. There they were still. Again he threw himself into the river and dived under the water.

He thought: "Truly, they like me; but I for my part have left behind a fish-line."[82] He put his head above water; there was nothing to be seen.

Across yonder were the two women where he had first caught sight of them. He thought: "Truly, they make me crazy." Now he felt cold. He thought: "How now! They are really two birds, but they make me crazy."

He thought: "Never mind, now!" and called out to them: "Now you two there have for all time become birds in the water.[83] People will say, 'These two have made Coyote crazy, so he called them birds.' For all time you two shall be birds in the lake."

9B. COYOTE AND THE MISCHIEVOUS WOMEN (Second Version)[84, 85]

Coyote went along until he came to open country. He caught sight of two women dancing on the other side of the river. They called out to him: "Come, Coyote! We love you."

And then he thought: "I shall deceive them by pretending that my wife has died." So then he burst out crying. He said to them: "Not long ago my wife died."

And again they said to him: "Come, we love you." And then he swam up close. He was under water. He stuck his head out, but did not see them across from where he had started. He turned around and saw them on the other side.

Then again he swam, swam towards the two women. Again he approached them; again he was under water. He stuck his head out, but again he did not see them. Then again he turned about, and again saw them on the other side.

And then he thought: "Now I shall take them home." So he took them home. He said in his heart, he thought: "Now the Indians will come, but you two shall not make the people crazy." So then they were turned into rocks.[86]

10. COYOTE EATS DRIED SALMON[87]

And then he went on. Over there he saw in the trail some dried salmon. And then he ate it. Then he fell asleep and died. The salmon went out of him through his nostrils, his mouth, and at his ears. In truth, it was a flea which Coyote had swallowed. It had killed him, so that he fell asleep.

And then he named the land. He said: "Now the name of this land shall be Dried Salmon.[88] Now forever shall you people call its name Dried Salmon." Thus is its name: *Lmuyaqso'qu*.[89]

11. COYOTE MAKES A FISHTRAP[90]

Then Coyote went on; straight on he went. He saw white salmon in the water. Then he thought: "How shall I catch them?" And then he thought: "I shall make a fishtrap." He saw the white salmon jumping along, and made a fishtrap. And then he tied[91] the fishtrap, tied it onto the string. He jumped straightway right into the fishtrap.

And then Coyote said to the fishtrap: "If, fishtrap, you become filled, if your mouth becomes filled with white salmon, then you shall cry out, '*U'4,* I am full.' You shall cry out, 'Now the fishtrap is quite full of white salmon.'"

And then it cried out: "*U'4*, I, the fishtrap, am full."

Coyote shouted: "*U'4*." And then Coyote went and saw that it was full now. Then he unloosened the fishtrap.

Then Coyote said: "For all time shall you people catch salmon thus. Thus did Coyote do." (The name of this land is *Skalxe'lEmax* or *Sq!E'ldalpl*.)[92]

12. COYOTE SPEARS FISH[93]

And then again he went on. He went and went until he arrived at a certain place. And then he said: "Now I am extremely thirsty for water."

They said to him: "There is no water."

Then he saw the river, and said: "I desire some of the water." And then a woman went for the water. She dipped down the bucket and lost hold of it.

Coyote saw that she was crying. And then Coyote went and got hold of the bucket. He went to the water and dipped it down. And then he took some water along with him to the house. Then it was drunk without the knowledge of the other people.

He saw white salmon with their mouths agape. And then Coyote made a salmon spear. He said to an old woman: "Give me a string; I am going to prepare a salmon spear." And then she gave him some large beads. He did not want them. So then he went and cut up some wild cherry bark in thin strips. He wound it around on the salmon spear.

And then he speared a white salmon. Then he brought it to the house and steamed it. Then it was done, and they ate a side of split fish. They ate it without the knowledge of the other people.

And then Coyote said: "Thus shall you people get white salmon in this land."

"Now you shall get a woman."

Coyote said: "I do not want any woman. Never mind! I'll not take her."

13A. THE WISHOM TRIBE: A STORY OF THEIR DIVISION AND SEPARATION[94]

"Wishram" is a very poor corruption of a truly poetic appellation. According to an intelligent member of this practically extinct tribe, *Wish'-hum*, or *Wish'-hoom*, is descriptive of the deep, rumbling roar of the swirling, tumbling cataract of the Tumwater [of the Columbia River] near which they lived. "*Wish-h-h-u-u-u-m-m-m*" is the manner in which this tribesman put it when explaining the significance of the name. *Tum-water* he interpreted as pertaining to the same element; thus, *T-u-u-u-m-m-m-water* is a "tumming" roar of falling or rapid waters [the horrendous miles-long stretch of rapids on the Columbia River from approximately Celilo down to near Hood River]. The Wascos called the Wishoms *E-Chahliut*, pertaining to a place or home, a people of a "different talk."

The story of a division of the Wishom tribe in no remote times was told me by Jobe Colwash, known as Jobe Charley, of the Yakamas; it is as follows.

Coyote's son traveled down the big river, the Columbia to the ocean. He had sick eyes, and he made a sweathouse where he sweated and nearly died. Two ducks found him lying in the sweathouse almost dead. They came to the Wishoms and said, "We found Coyote's son away down at the ocean. He was nearly dead. Maybe he is dead now. We will go back and see, and come back and tell you. If he is alive, we will make the noise, '*W-i-s w-i-s w-i-s w-i-s w-i-s*!' But if we come making no noise, say nothing to us. He will be dead."

The next morning the ducks came back. They were flying low. The Indians heard the noise which told them that the son of Coyote was living. Coyote [*paht-paht*] went with his canoe and brought his son. But the people quarreled about how the ducks made the noise heard. Some said that the ducks made the noise with their mouths. But no, others replied, the ducks would grow tired thus creating the noise. It was done by the two longest feathers of the wing, the wind fluttering through between these feathers. This would not cause the ducks to grow tired.

The people divided up, joining the two disputing sides. Finally they fought. Then one faction left. Traveling towards the snow-land, they passed into what is now Canada where they still remain. Members of this northern branch have been met by their Southern cousins, and conversation carried on without trouble. But the rancor of the old feud still remains with them both, and all because of the mystery noise created by ducks in flight.

13B. A QUARREL OF THE WISHRAM[95, 96]

The Wishram were dwelling at *Wa'q!Emap*.[97] Some of them were dwelling at *Wa'q!Emap*; some of them were dwelling at the village *Nixlu'idix*. Now then a duck flew over their heads. And then they heard it. It made a noise: *shu'lulululu*.[98]

Now then one man said: "It made the noise with its beak."

Another said: "It made the noise with its nostrils."

Still another said: "It made the noise with its wings."

So then they got to arguing. And then they seized their bows and arrows. Then indeed they fought. Both parties killed each other. They fought and fought until they ceased.

And then whenever anyone fished with a dip-net, two men with bows and quivers of arrows remained near their friend, kept watch over him. While he, the dipnet fisherman, caught salmon, his two friends stayed near him.

Three years passed by, and they dwelt there. There they continued to fight until at last they ceased.

And then one group of the Wishom said: "Because we have been disgraced, let us now go off somewheres. We have been disgraced before our friends. Let us go look for another country."

So then they took up cedar planks and then set off. Far they went--among the Wallawalla. They went on past *AcnE'm*. They went on past *NuL!a'-ik*. They went straight on past *NuL!a'nuL!a*. They went straight on past *Sts!E'mtsi*. They went straight on past *Wisu'm*. They went straight on past *Ta'malan*. They went straight on past *Txa'iauna*. Straight on they went to a small river.[99] They went straight on to *Po'uwankiut*. They went straight on past *Xit!a'i*. They went straight on past a dried-up small river. They went straight on past *SA'tAs*. They went straight on past *I!Lu'mEni*. They went straight on to *Pala'xi*.[100]

Now there they remained. And then they caught Chinook salmon, blueback salmon, eels, and suckers. They ate them. And then they said: "Behold! The country is small. Now let us go off yonder. Let us look for another country."

They went straight on to *Patixkwi'ut*. Now today white people call it "The Gap."[101] There they remained. Only at night do people catch salmon there. They fish with dipnets. The name of that same country is *IxElExtgi'dix*.[102] And again they said: "Behold! The country is small."

And again they went on, went to seek another country. To this day I can see where those Wishom used to live long ago. Among the rocks their cedar boards are standing. That is how I know that they took cedar boards with them. I think those are the cedar boards of those Wishom. Perhaps some may have died there.

And again they went on, went to look for another country. They moved. They thought to themselves: "We will get lots of salmon. Far away somewheres there is a good country, and there we will dwell."

They went straight on to Wenatchee.[103] There the Wishom arrived. And there they dwelt, dwelt a long time. And then they said: "Now let us all move."

And then again they moved. They took a country for themselves where there were lots of salmon and lots of deer. To this day they dwell there and they are just nothing but Wishom. If I should go off, should travel until I came to those Wishom, they would recognize me. Straightway they would kill me. To this day these Wishom hold the the land where there are many salmon and mainly deer. But we people (the river Wishom) have not [ever?] seen them. Thus the Wishom believe.

14. WHY THE WISHRAM ARE CALLED *ILAXLUIT*[104, 105]

Once there were lots of people at this village [i.e., *nixlu'idix*?]. There came a monster of a woman, called *Akxa'qusa* (for whom an arrow was later named), who ate all the people of the village.

Soon after East Wind's daughter came with the wind blowing over the village and saw it was destroyed. There were only pieces of clothing and small bits of bodies lying around.

She gathered the pieces together in five piles and sprinkled them with paint. She stepped over these piles east and west, north and south, five times. Then the piles formed into five people. Now she named them *idaxa'luit*.

She said to them:

'imca'lq	*ixlu'it*	*imca'lxam*
"Your flesh	coming together	your land

iya'xliu   *nixlu'ia"*
    (his) name pertaining to   drew together."

The name *nixlu'idix* means 'at once it (your flesh) came
together'.[106]

15. COYOTE IN *SK!IN*[107]

And then Coyote went on. He traveled up the
river. Straightway he arrived at *Sk!in.*[108] In *Sk!in* he
urinated[109] on the people.

Coyote went across to the Falls. He went thither
by means of a round-pointed canoe. He shouted. And
then he said: "Mind, now, that you always do thus; you
shall shout.

Whenever you cross over, then you shall shout.
You are the *Ilka'imamt.*[110] Thus I have named you."

16. COYOTE AND THE MOUTHLESS MAN[111]

Again Coyote traveled up the river. In the water
he saw the canoe of a certain person, as it turned out, a
man. He saw how the man dived into the water. He came
up out of the water, his hands holding one sturgeon on
that side and one sturgeon on this. He put the sturgeons
down in the canoe. Then Coyote looked on and saw him
count them with his finger, pointing about in the canoe.

Coyote thought: "When he dives, I shall take hold
of and steal from him one of his sturgeons. Let us see
what he'll do."

The person dived under water. And then Coyote
swam towards his canoe. He seized one of his sturgeons.
He took the person's sturgeon with him, and hid it in the

bushes. And then Coyote seated himself there and hid. Then the person came up out of the water into his canoe. He put his sturgeons down in the canoe, again one and one. And then he counted them; again he counted them. Quite silently he counted them. There was only one sturgeon in his canoe.

And then he pointed his finger out, first up high, then a little lower, again a little lower still, finally a little lower still on the ground. There he pointed, where Coyote was sitting. Quite silently he held his finger there.

Coyote tried to move to one side. There again was the man's finger. No matter which way Coyote moved, there was the man's finger pointing at him, Coyote.

Where his finger was pointed to, there he went straight up to him. Straightway he went to meet Coyote. Straightway he came quite close to him.

The man kept pointing at him; Coyote kept dodging from side to side. The person kept him well in eye. And Coyote also looked at the person. The person was strange in appearance. As it turned out, he had no mouth. He had only a nose and eyes and ears. He spoke to Coyote with his nose, but Coyote did not hear him. Just deep down in his nose could be heard: "*Den dEn dEn dEn.*" In fact he was scolding Coyote in this way.

Thus he said to him with his nose: "You are not good."

Thus the person kept telling him. His heart was dark within him.

"But perhaps now this man desires the sturgeon back. Perhaps he is going to kill me," thought Coyote.

And then the person went back to his canoe. Coyote made a fire when he had gone. He gathered some stones and heated them in the fire. And then they all became heated up. He cut the sturgeon in two, cut it all

up, and carefully made ready the stones. He laid the
sturgeon out on the stones and steamed it. Soon it was
entirely done. And then he removed it and laid it down.
Then that same man who had no mouth came back to
him. He met Coyote as he was eating.

And then he[112] took hold of that good well-done
sturgeon. Then thought Coyote: "Wonder what he'll do
with it!" He looked at him;[113] he took the good sturgeon.
He just sniffed at the sturgeon, then threw it away.

And then Coyote thought: "It is not well." He
went and brought the sturgeon back and brushed it clean.

Now Coyote is thinking: "What is he going to do
with it?" Once again he[114] took hold of it and did with it
again as before.

Coyote went up to him and looked at him closely.
And then he thought: "I don't know what I shall do to
make him a mouth." Secretly he took a flint and chipped
it on one side. It became just like a sharp knife. And then
he went to him with the flint secretly in hand and looked
at him closely. In vain the man tried to dodge from side
to side.

Now Coyote put the flint down over his mouth.
He sliced it open and his blood flowed out.

The man breathed: "*Ha4 ha4.*"[115] Coyote said to
him: "Go to the river and wash yourself." When he had
come up out of the water, he stopped and spoke to
Coyote.

Coyote was spoken to thusly: "You do not seem
to have steamed a large sturgeon."

And then Coyote said: "Well, you would have
killed me. You wanted the sturgeon for yourself. You got
after me for the sturgeon."

Now the people told one another: "There is a
man whose mouth has been made for him." In truth, all
the people of that same one village[116] were without

mouths. And then they betook themselves to him. Coyote made mouths for all the people of that same one village. He called that same land *Nimicxa'ya*.

They said to him: "We will give you a woman."

He said: "No! I should not care for a woman. I'll not take one."

17. A FAMINE AT THE CASCADES[117]

Long ago, I believe, the people suffered severe hunger. Many of them died. They tell about a man who sent his wife to get food. "Now it is good that you go to my elder sister. She will give you some food for our children to eat."

"That is good," his wife said to him. "I shall go." Then she set out.

She gave her sister-in-law a seashell for a necklace, a large seashell. Then her sister-in-law cut up some dried, pounded salmon and dry fishskin. The man's wife brought it home.

Her husband said: "You will not give it to our children. You will put it away in some hidden place."

"Yes," she said to him. Then she put it away. He had many slaves. All of them were hungry.

Now springtime was near at hand. In the morning he went off to the river. He constructed a fishtrap at the falls when no one saw him. Very early in the morning he always went. Finally, he caught two suckers.

Again, he went off in the morning. As before he kept catching suckers which he always put away. The fish got to be numerous which he brought to their house.

He said to his wife, "You shall cook these suckers carefully. You shall give our children just a little bit, so that it will not make them sick."

"Yes," she said to him.

To his slaves she also gave each two suckers. Indeed, they were all hungry now. But the suckers were not yet cooked. As a result, some who ate of them died.

It became quite warm and the husband caught a little more. Finally now he began to catch Chinook salmon. Now they were all living prosperously.

His elder sister's children came to them, and one of them had a seashell necklace around her neck. The man's wife told her about it. The girl took it off of herself, and gave it to her aunt. The girl was told: "I shall put the dried fishskin and the dried pounded salmon of you people around your neck."

The girl arrived back at their house. Her mother recognized their fish, and she was ashamed. All the people talked about her [i.e., the man's wife?] being stingy. Many people then died of hunger. Everywhere there was much snow and ice in the river.

18. A PROPHECY OF THE COMING OF THE WHITES[118]

Long ago, I believe, the people learned that whites would soon come. One old man, I believe, learned of it at night. Then he dreamt. He saw strange people, and they spoke to him, showed him everything. And he heard something like three or four Indian[119] songs.[120]

In the morning he spoke to all the people. And then everybody gathered to hear him-- women, men, children, old men-- everybody. He told the people what he had seen in his sleep at night. And then they who were gathered together heard him, and danced every day and every night. They were made glad because of his story [i.e., revelation].

He said: "Soon all sorts of strange things will come. No longer will things be as before. No longer shall we use these things [traditional Indian gear and ways] of ours. The whites will bring to us everything strange. They will bring to us something which you just have to point at anything moving way yonder, and that something will fall right down and die." As it turned out, it was the gun of which he spoke.

"There will be brought to us a bucket for boiling purposes. No longer will you use your old-fashioned bucket made out of stone." As it turned out, they really brought to us what he told the people of [i.e., metal cooking pots].

"No longer will you make fire by drilling with sticks as before." Still more were the people made glad, and they danced with energy. "Certain small pieces of wood will be brought to us with which you will make a fire." As it turned out, it was matches whereof he spoke.

For days and nights they danced. They were not at all hungry. Truly they did their best in dancing. Everything they saw [i.e., *envisioned*]: ax, hatchet, knife, stove.

Strange people will bring us such things. White people with mustaches on their faces will come from the east. Do you people be careful!" Then indeed they would again jump up and down. They did their best strongly.

And truly things are just so today. Now surely the old man dreamt just that way. Up to that time there were no cattle at all. Presently white people brought them, only farther up [i.e., in Montana] there were buffaloes. Nor were there any horses either, only dogs. Thus long ago did it happen to the people dwelling along the river.

19. THE *GY-U-BOO'-KUM*[121] (I)

It was at Grand Dalles, on the *n-Che-wana,* that this I am telling you happened. My ancestors saw it as I am giving it to you.

A girl went from the village to dig camas and took her sister's little papoose with her. Arriving at the camas patch, she placed the sleeping baby, wrapped in a buckskin robe, by the side of her big basket. Taking her digging stick and small basket, she went a distance of about two bow-shots and began digging camas. She filled the small basket and went to empty it in the big one. When she got there, she found the baby gone. All about where it had been sleeping were marks as if a log had been dragged. The big basket had not been moved. The girl was scared! She ran crying to the village, calling to her people. The Indians saw her running, heard her crying, and said to her, "Why do you run crying? What is wrong with you?"

The girl told them about the missing baby and what she had seen in the dust where she had left it sleeping. The mother of the papoose heard her sister and began wailing for her lost baby. All the people felt bad.

The men hurried. They armed with bows and arrows and ran to the place. It was as the girl had told them. The papoose was gone, but the big burden-basket was there undisturbed. They saw the broad trace in the dust, saw where the trail led towards a cliff some distance away. They followed it. It brought them to a dark hole in the rocks. They saw where it had gone into this hole. It must be some kind of a *puch* [snake]. They talked and counseled how to get the Thing out to kill it. The rocks could not be torn away. They were too strong and heavy in place. Finally they thought to try fire. Maybe smoke would kill the Thing, whatever it was. Or maybe the smoke would drive it out from its rock-house, where they could kill it.

Then the Indians brought *goom*-stick [pitchwood] and built a big fire in the mouth of the cavern. This was about midday, and the fire was kept burning till next morning. All that day and all the next night that fire blazed. It did not burn low at any time. The rocks were hot. The smoke went deep into the crevices of the cliff.

On the third morning, the men killed the fire. They waited till the rocks cooled. Nothing came from the den. No life came from the rock-house, and they again counseled what to do. They talked and finally decided. There was a Snake Indian slave boy in the village. He could go into the rock-hole. If he were killed, it would make no difference. He was only a slave.

They tied a hair rope around the slave's waist, gave him an Indian hemp rope, and made him crawl into the smoke-blackened hole. The men held the rope tied to the slave. They measured it out as he went far under the cliff. *Eh*! Suddenly the slave stopped, was still. Soon they felt him jerk on the rope, making signals. They pulled him out. He told them that he had found a dead body in there, had tied the hemp rope to it. The men pulled on the rope. It dragged heavy at the other end. They pulled hard. Whatever it was, it was coming slowly. More men took hold of the rope, and soon a terrible-looking form came into sight. The Indians hurried with the rope. They brought the Thing out from the cavern, out into the light. It did not move; it was dead. The men came close to it. The women came to look at the Thing that had swallowed the little baby. It was as long as a lodgepole, and big around as a man's body. Its mouth was under its head, like that of a sturgeon. On its tail were rattles of the *wahk-puch*, only larger. They were the size of the eagle's wing. Its skin was like the *puch*, and it smelled bad. It was the dreaded *Gy-u-boo'-kum* ["terrible noise"].

The Indians cut the monster open, found the smothered baby and buried it. This was the last *Gy-u-boo'-kum* ever seen in that country. None ever bothered the Wishoms afterwards.

Some of the Wishoms give a prelude to the foregoing legend. On the morning of the tragedy at the camas patch, some men were passing near the cliff where the reptile subsequently took refuge, when they were pursued by the *Gy-u-boo'-kum*. The men fled over a neighboring bluff, or ridge. Descending into a canyon, they crossed to the opposite side. The reptile continued on their trail, giving vent to a chirping bleat not unlike that of a fawn when disturbed or lost from its dame. But finally the creature abandoned the chase and was seen to go off in the direction where it later developed that the camas digger and papoose were. The girl busy digging roots heard the monster, heard its terrifying, fear-producing noise. Startled, she looked and saw the reptile coming, head in the air. She saw it seize and swallow the baby, then go to its "house" in the rocks. Frightened, she sped to the village and alarmed the people.

Lame Sam, a Wishom, often told the story of two men being chased near The Dalles by a lizard-like serpent which they could not shake from their trail. Gaining on them, it opened its enormous mouth to take one of them in when they destroyed it by throwing large stones down its throat. Removing its hide, they startled their tribesmen who had gathered for a social time by suddenly appearing in their midst with the skin of the reptile thrown over them, emulating its crawling motion. The consternation and scattering of that assembly ended in general rejoicing when it was learned that the dreaded man-eating Terror had at last been killed.[122]

20. THE *GY-U-BOO'-KUM*[123] (II)

There was another one of those bad animals. It was near The Dalles, on the *n-Che-wana*. Two young warriors were hunting on the mountainside. They crossed a canyon and sat down to rest. They were not thinking of trouble in that place. Soon they heard a distant noise, some kind of voice back on their trail. They listened! They heard it again, a little louder! It was coming along the same way they had just traveled! They did not know what it was, never heard anything like it before! *Eh*! It was coming closer! But the young men did not run. They were not afraid! They were used to fighting.

The strange noise grew louder. The young warriors stood up, listening! They looked but saw nothing. But something was traveling fast on their trail. Its barking-scream could be heard a long ways. It had a rattling bark, not like the Indian dog, coyote, or mountain wolf. It was something not understood. That sound was bad, not good to hear. It echoed down the canyon where they had crossed. It approached the top of the ridge, just off from where they were standing. The hunters watched sharp, bows and arrows ready. They saw a head, an ugly head, come in sight above the canyon's rim! The head was followed by a long, thick body, crawling on the ground. A big noise came from its mouth, a rattling like a thousand maddened *wah'k-puch* shook the air as the monster came straight for them. The warriors could see its eyes! They thought, "We cannot stand before this Thing!"

Then they ran, fleeing up the mountain for their lives. That *Wah'k-puch*-animal did not stop. It gained on the hunters. They knew that they must do something quickly! They would soon be caught! Maybe one could escape. There was a bunch of elders, only a few big

bushes. One of the men said to the other, "Run behind
the bush! He may not see you! I will go up the mountain!"

The Indian made answer, "No! I will do as you
say, but not to escape. I know what I will do!"

That was the answer of the warrior to his friend
who would die for him. He dodged behind the bush and
drew his bow. He sent an arrow into the *Puch*-thing as it
passed. It turned and came at the man. He yelled to his
friend to look back! The Indian did so and sent an arrow
into the turning monster. That caused it to halt, and the
ambushed hunter sent his second arrow to its side. As it
again whirled, the man on the hillside drove another shaft
into its vitals. Thus the fight went on. The arrows were
poisoned and the Thing grew weak. It could no longer
move swiftly. Other war-poisoned arrows struck it. The
monster ceased to turn, ceased to come at the men. It lay
on the ground, twisting and writhing. Its rattles, larger
than the spread hands of two men, still clashed in the air.
The squirming became fainter and finally ceased. The
Thing was dead.

The two hunters now returned to the village and
reported what they had done. In two days the people went
to see the strange animal. They found that it was the *Gy-
u-boo'-kum*. It was all bloated up. Many magpie-birds lay
about it dead. They had eaten of the poisoned body. No
other such monster was ever seen by the Wishoms. My
grandfather got the story from one man who saw the dead
Gy-u-boo'-kum.

21. THE *GY-U-BOO'-KUM*
OF THE WISHOMS[124]

There were two brothers of the Wishom tribe.

The Wishoms used to cross the mountain to the Klickitat country and, on passing the crest of the ridge, were often met by a terrible *Gy-u-boo'-kum* with great horns. It was a bad animal, big-mouthed, and many Indians were swallowed by it. They could not escape by running. The snake-like creature always overtook them and would devour them, swallow them whole.

There were two brothers among the Wishoms, the youngest one being ignorant, foolish-headed. He knew but little. Every day the brothers made arrows. The people wondered, "Why the arrows?" They would not tell!

When they had finished a big bundle of arrows, two great quivers filled with them, they said to the people, "Brother and I are going up on the mountain to look around."

The people said to them, "Do not go! The *Gy-u-boo'-kum* will kill you, will swallow you down."

The brothers laughed and made the boasting reply, "We are afraid of no *puch* [i.e., snake]!"

The brothers went up the mountain with their bows and arrows. They came to where the snake had been killing and devouring the Indians, eating everybody who passed. They could not see any snake. The oldest brother had a leaf from a tree. He put the leaf between his lips and blew a loud, shrill noise. He did this twice, when they heard the snake answer with the same kind of noise, bleating like a fawn. The oldest brother made the call three times, and three times he got an answer. He said, "There! See the snake is coming to catch up with us."

Yes, it was coming all right. The brothers sat on the mountain, watching the snake coming fast. The older man said, "Yes, he sees us! He is coming fast to meet us."

The brothers jumped up and ran down the mountain. But they could not escape. The younger brother said, "Look for a tree. We will run up the tree. We cannot outrun the snake."

They saw a small tree and both of them ran up it. They saw the snake come under the tree, saw him open his wide mouth to swallow them. The men shot arrows into his mouth. But the arrows did not hurt him. The arrows dropped to the ground, glancing from his hard-cased mouth. The arrows did not hurt him at all! The oldest brother said, "What shall we do? Let us run down the hill."

The ignorant boy replied, "No! We will run up the hill. He will catch up running down the mountain ."

They stayed in the tree all day. The big snake would not leave. Under the tree he watched the men, ready to swallow them should they come down. They had one large quiver of arrows, and the ignorant one said, "We will throw this far down the hill. He will go after it, and we can escape."

So they cast the quiver off down the hill, and the snake ran after it. The men jumped from the tree and hurried up the mountainside. The snake saw them and began turning to come after them. He had a long body, and his turning was slow. The men saw him as he turned and started after them with mouth open. He came up the mountain fast, and the oldest brother said, "There he is coming after us! Brother, we are sure to die. He is coming fast, and we cannot get away."

The ignorant brother grabbed a rock as large as a man's head. He threw it with strength into the open mouth of the snake. The rock choked the snake. The ignorant one called to his brother, who was still running, "Wait for me! We will throw rocks and choke him. Now look out! We will roll this big rock into his mouth as he comes up the hill."

The older brother stopped. Sure enough, the snake came straight up the steep slope, getting close to them. The brothers shoved the big rock, which rolled straight into his open mouth. The rock choked him from his breath, choked him bad. The men stood watching him as he was dying, squirming and twisting all over. He closed his eyes. He was dead.

The brothers skinned the top of the snake's head with the horns and made a bonnet of it. Then they went home. They slept several days without eating anything. The people asked them, "Why sleep so many days?"

The brothers answered them, "We killed the big snake that has been eating so many of our people."

Nobody believed them in their boasting. The brothers showed them the cap with the horns. Still they did not believe them. The brothers then said to them, "You go see the snake! He is decaying now."

The people went and found the snake already stinking. The Wishoms could now cross the mountain in safety.

V. "Wishham Girls on Horses." Special Collections
Division, Univ. of Washington Libraries.
Edward S. Curtis, c. 1909, NAI173

III. TALES OF MAGIC AND THE MARVELOUS

22. STAR HUSBAND[125]

Some young girls were sleeping out in the open in the summer. They saw the stars, one big one and a little one. The younger girl said, "I will have the smallest for a lover."

And the elder, "I will have the larger." They slept. Toward morning something lay close to the younger. It was bright, like gold. This happened north of Spedis. She said, "Oh, something is lying by my side."

The older sister said, "That is the star you were wishing for." So they jumped up and went home.

Everybody came to see him shining there. Now it is gone. I guess someone threw it in the river. Sometimes it shines there.[126, 127]

23. THE STAR-ROCK OF RICHES[128]

That star was only seen by certain persons chosen to see it shining on the rocks. A poor boy might see it glowing, and that boy would become a wealthy man. That boy would find things easily. The same was true with the girl. She would become a rich woman. Now the secret of the star was not told to everyone. It was told only to a few. My father whispered it to me. He said, "Be sure to look for the star. When you see it, act quickly. If you have no handkerchief, tear off a piece of shirt, drop it over the rock quickly. Wrap it [i.e., the sparkle] up! Hold it fast and tight. Keep it, that piece of shirt or handkerchief. It will make you rich. Do not tell anyone, not even myself or your mother, should you find that star."

I believe it, the story given me by my father. It was not immediately after he told me that this I am telling you occurred. It was at *Wishom*, when I was with father fishing. It was nighttime. I saw it, a light as if from a star come down. It boiled like cooking water. It came in front of me, on the rocks. I tore a piece of my shirt and dropped it over that sparkling light as quickly as I could. As soon as I did this, it was all gone. Nothing was to be seen. I kept it secret, never told anyone.

I believe it to be a true story, told me by my father about that rock. After I reached fifteen or twenty snows of age, I became lucky. I got two or three horses, found them somewhere. I traveled and soon had race horses. I beat the Indians at the races, got rich. If I had children living, I would tell them about this rock, this star. It comes on wood as well as on rocks. I have no children, and I told nobody. But I have now told you [i.e., L.V. McWhorter] and this woman [i.e., inter- preter]. It might come to grown people, but it is best for children.

My first wife and I had children, but all are now dead. She did something with that piece of shirt. She did not know. Father told me to keep it secretly till I was an old man. I was doing this, but my wife lost it.

But it is not everyone who can find the lucky star- rock.[129] I think it is a gift from the Great Spirit. It is not for everybody.

24. COYOTE'S PEOPLE SING[130]

And again the people sang in winter. Everybody sang; also Coyote sang and Coyote's daughter, whose name was Salmon-Head-Fat, a maiden, sang. Nothing but grease was flowing out of her mouth. And then Coyote was told: "Your daughter is singing."

Then he said: "What is flowing from her?"

And then they told him: "Grease is flowing from her."

Then Coyote said: "My daughter will be a medicine-woman." And then he smoked--his pipe was made out of a stomach, a salmon's stomach. Dried salmon-flesh he filled into the pipe and Coyote, the medicine-man, smoked.

And then yet another one sang. Coyote was told: "Your son, Coyote, is singing."

Then he said: "What is flowing out of him?"

They said: "Blood is flowing from him."

Coyote said: "He is merely lying."

Now then everybody was singing. Now that *Itq!wo'l*[131] was singing and that *Ak!u'stxuia*[132] was singing: "On my back I carry my daughter; we two are dug up."

And then she was told: "Give us your daughter; you will let her fall."

But then she said: "No! Just in that way am I accustomed to carry her on my back; we two are dug up." Truly *Ak!u'stxulal* (sic) was her name, *Ak!a'lakia*.

Now that *A'dwoq*[133] was singing. Thus she said: "Only by my tail, only by my tail am I dug up." And just in that way would one dig her up today; one would not dig up all, but only half of the "wild carrot." Now that *Amu'lal* sang, that *Aq!o'lawa-itk*, and also that Buttercup sang.

Now that Grizzly Bear sang. Thus he sang: "*Ho ho ho'! ho ho ho ho'*!"[134]

Then said Grizzly Bear: "*Ha'4!*" Whoever shall have challenged me, his head shall I eat up." And Grizzly Bear struck the people.

And then they said: "Who will challenge Grizzly Bear?"

So then a man, small of size, said: "I will challenge him." And then he arose and the man said: "Somewhere it is sung all day long, 'Eat up heads.'"

Then he said to Grizzly Bear, "I have challenged you. Be quick and do something to me! Be quick and eat up my head! Quickly shall I run up into your belly and you, Grizzly Bear, will quickly die."

Grizzly Bear looked at him, then said to him: "O younger brother, we should not kill each other. Perhaps the people will laugh at us."

Also Rattlesnake sang. Thus he said: "Where I shoot my arrows, there is the sunflower's shade."

And then Rattlesnake said: "Whoever has challenged me, him shall I put cheat-grass into."

So then a man stood up and then he, Raccoon, said to him: "Somewhere it is sung all day long, 'The shade of the sunflowers, there I shall destroy the people.'"

And then the man said to him: "I have challenged you. Be quick and put the cheat-grass into me! Be quick and bite me! Quickly shall I warm my hands, and your eyeballs will become all white. You, Rattlesnake, will die."

Now also Crow sang. In truth they were all singing, and truly they were thinking: "Now it will become warm." Truly they were calling the West Wind and trying to make warm weather, for indeed, they were feeling cold. Everybody was singing and now she, Crow, sang. Now then the wind was blowing; it rained and the West Wind blew. And then Crow went out and took her fish-bag and then found fish. The wind was blowing hard and the fish were forced clear up to shore. And then Crow caught a big salmon, and then Crow ate it.

Then Bald Eagle caught sight of Crow as she was eating the salmon. And then Bald Eagle took it away from her and flew up away with it.

Then Crow said: "Let me have a fish-gill!" Bald Eagle took one and struck Crow with it, and she became all covered with black blood. To this day she is black and her name is Crow. But that Bald Eagle became white about her head. To this day her name is Bald Eagle; she is all white in her head.

25. COYOTE AND ANTELOPE[135]

Coyote went on. Now then Coyote heard that way yonder people were gathered together. In truth they came to get a shinny-ball. So then Coyote's children and Antelope's two sons went. The seven went for the shinny-ball,[136] went to where the people were assembled. They arrived there.

The name of one of Coyote's sons was Big-Gristle; another one's name was Big-Backbone; another one of Coyote's sons was named Big-Fin; another one's name was Big-Adipose-Fin; there was one other, a daughter of Coyote and the youngest whose name was Head-Fat--she was a good runner.

And there were Antelope's two sons--those two were clumsy ones.

Now they went where the shinny-ball was; they had come in order to run away with it. They arrived and saw many people. There were Rabbit and Fox, both of them fast runners.

And then the shinny-ball was given to Big-Gristle, the oldest. He took it in his hand and ran away with the shinny-ball. Then Rabbit and Fox pursued him and gained on him. And then they seized him; they had overtaken him. They killed him and took the shinny-ball away from him.

Now they brought the shinny-ball back again. Again they put it in the next one's hands. Big-Backbone got hold of it. He ran away with the shinny-ball. And again Fox and Rabbit pursued him. They ran after him and he ran away from them. They overtook him and killed him, cutting off his head.

Now this time the shinny-ball was given to Big-Fin. He also ran away with the shinny-ball and again the two ran after him, overtook him, and seized him. They killed him, cutting his neck.

Next they gave the ball to Big-Adipose-Fin. Now he also ran away with it, and again Rabbit and Fox ran after him. They seized him and killed him, cutting his neck.

Now the ball was put into the hand of Head-Fat, Coyote's daughter, a maiden. And then she ran away with the shinny-ball. Then the two ran after her and she ran away from them. They pursued her and caught her. They killed her, cutting off her neck.

All the five children of Coyote had died. They had all been killed and had not held on to the shinny-ball. Now then those two sons of Antelope were given the shinny-ball. It was put into the hands of those two. Then they dropped it. They did not succeed in holding on to the ball.

And then the people said: "Now they will be killed here." Then they said: "Now they will be brought right there; they will be killed a little farther on." And then they were brought a little farther on. Then the fog became dark, all misty dark. And then they all said: "Now here I've caught him, hit him!"

Now in fact Antelope's two sons ran away with it; they ran away with the shinny-ball. Truly that ball was worth a chieftain's realm. Now then the two sons of Antelope took it along with them, but Rabbit and Fox did not pursue them. They looked at them and saw them now far off taking the shinny-ball along with them. Now they climbed up to two summits of the mountains and keep throwing the shinny-ball between them. Rabbit and Fox gave up following. The sons of Antelope had now gone far off and had the ball with them.

Those two people--Coyote and Antelope--were sitting quietly in the house. Now then the two sons of Antelope sang out: "Far away we two have left the children of Coyote; killed were they all."

And then they sang out again: "Far away have we left the two sons of Antelope; slain were the two."

And then they sang out again: "All were they killed, the children of Coyote; far away we two have left them."

And then again they sang out: "Slain were the two sons of Antelope; far away have we left them."

And then again they sang out: "Far away we two have left the children of Coyote; killed were they all."[137]

Straight on the two went. Now meanwhile Coyote had laid down a big stone in the doorway. And then he stuck in spits about the stone, stuck them circlewise near it. There Coyote stood. And then he listened while he, Antelope, lay down. Antelope knew about his two sons. Then one of Antelope's sons sang out five times. Coyote fell down senseless and died straightway; he fell over on the stone and all the spits pierced him. And then suddenly the shinny-ball was thrown into the house. Then Antelope arose and seated himself.

And then they chipped up the shinny-ball into little pieces and rubbed it all over their bodies. Then they wiped themselves on Coyote where he lay dead. They wiped themselves against his nose and against his ears and against his legs. Now Coyote is lying dead. And then Antelope and his two sons said: "What shall we do?"

Then they went out of the house and said: "Where shall we go?"

And then they said: "Let us go to the sky."

But on second thought they said: "We should not go to the sky." So then one of them said: "Let us go on the tops of the grass so that Coyote may not find us." So then Antelope and his two sons went on the tops of the grass. On they went and passed three nights. And then they went to sleep.

Coyote came to and awoke. And then he said: "I've slept altogether too long." Then he started to pursue them and looked all around to follow them by their tracks. Then he thought: "How, where have they gone?"

He could not find their tracks, so he went and pursued them in any direction at random. And then on Coyote went. He went and went until he became thirsty. So he went to the water and drank of the water. Then he looked closely and caught sight of a person in the water. He was scared off and was afraid.

Then he thought: "The person is going to kill me." So he loosened his arrows and got hold of them; he pulled them out of his quiver. Now he thought: "I shall slay the person."

And then he looked closely. The person was still in the water. Then he shot every single one of his arrows at him and thought: "Perhaps he has died now." He went and looked at the person; the person was there just as before.

And then again he took a stone. He thought: "Now I shall throw the stone at his head. He will die." Coyote went and got a stone and then threw it at him. He struck him with several stones.

He went to look at the person. He was by no means dead. And then he thought: "How is this?"

Then he defecated his two feces and asked them: "How is this?" He said to them: "Now tell me."

And then they said to him: "We two shall tell you. Your children, Coyote, did go, the five went for the shinny-ball. Also Antelope's two sons did go, those two. There your children, Coyote, were killed. The two sons of Antelope alone took the shinny-ball with them. And then they cried out, 'Coyote, your children have been killed.' Thus said the two sons of Antelope.

"Now they arrived home at the house, but you died; all the spits remained stuck in your body. Now then the shinny-ball came, and Antelope and his two sons put it all over themselves. They broke the shinny-ball up into small pieces and then rubbed it over themselves.

"And then they went; they stretched you. They said, 'Where shall we go?' And then they went on the very tops of the grass. Now that is your own reflection, Coyote, that you have been looking at all along."

Coyote said: "Why certainly! Just so, of course. Where did Antelope and his two sons go?"

"Yonder they went."

And then he went on and took his arrows. He went and went, also overnight; all night he went. Again all day he went; again all night Coyote pursued Antelope and his two sons. Again all night he went. He went and went and crossed the river.

Now then they were sleeping. And he caught sight of them sleeping in the mountains. He saw them in early morning. He got some dust, threw it at them, and said to them: "You shall be no chief. You are an animal and your name shall be Antelope."

And then they started to run away, all gray now. They were no longer of golden hue in their bodies.

Now then he said to them: "You should be no chiefs. I am Coyote. And thus shall people say, 'Now these--Antelope and his two sons--Coyote did magically transform.'

"The Indians shall be chiefs some of them, but you are Antelope.

"They will say; 'This Antelope did Coyote change by magic.'"

Coyote said: "Salmon is a chief, Eagle is a chief, and some people also shall be chiefs. I am Coyote, I am no chief." Across the river did they do thus--on the other side of the river did thus do Coyote, Antelope, and his two sons, in the valley of *Xat!Ena'uwa*.[138]

26. COYOTE AND DEER[139]

Coyote went on and on; straightway he arrived at Deer's house.[140] And then the two of them sat and sat. And then Coyote said: "Now I shall go home."

"Yes," said Deer to him. And then he took a knife and just cut off a piece of meat from his body. And then it was given to Coyote.

And he also stuck in a piece of wood into his nose. And then his blood flowed out; the bucket was full. And then it was given to Coyote. Now then he went home to the house.

Now once more Coyote went, and again came straight to Deer. And again he cut off a piece of meat from his body; again the meat was given to Coyote. And again he stuck a piece of wood into his nose. His blood flowed out; the bucket was full. And again it was given to Coyote.

And then Deer said to Coyote: "If ever you should be hungry, you should come to me." Coyote assented.

And then Coyote, on his part, said: "It is well that you, on your part, should come to me."

Deer said "Yes" to him. "I, on my part, shall go to your, Coyote's, house." Thus he spoke to him.

And then Deer, in turn, went to Coyote's house. Straightway he arrived. Now there Deer sat quietly.

And then Coyote thought to himself: "Now I, in turn, shall give a little meat to Deer." So then he seized his wife and laid her down on the ground. And then he cut her, whereat the woman burst into tears.

Then Deer jumped up and said to him: "Let the woman alone. I shall give you meat." So then he just cut off a piece of meat from his body; then the meat was given to Coyote and his wife. And he caused blood to come out of his nose and gave the blood to Coyote and his wife.

And then Deer started off to his house. And then he said to the two: "If ever you two should be hungry, you should go to me."

Then the woman said to Coyote: "You are wicked, Coyote. I am not Deer. Look at that Deer! Everyone will swallow his meat. My meat is not good. Likewise you, Coyote, are different; you, Coyote, are a person. No one would ever eat your meat. Thus people will say, 'Coyote is an eater of dead things.'"

VI. "Wishham Child." Special Collections
Division, Univ. of Washington Libraries.
Edward S. Curtis, c. 1909, photo NAI176.

IV. COYOTE AS TRICKSTER

27A. COYOTE AND *AT!AT!A'LIA*[141]

And then Coyote heard that *At!at!a'lia*[142] and Owl were stealing people. So then Coyote went; Coyote cut up some rushes. And then he dried them. He tied the rushes on all over himself: on his head and on his hands-- on every possible part. And then Coyote went along. *At!at!a'lia* was coming. And then Coyote caught sight of *At!at!a'lia*. He tried to turn aside, but without success. Now At!at!a'lia headed him off.

And then Coyote stood still; Coyote's body was rattling in all its parts. Then *At!at!a'lia* said to him: "What did you do to yourself?"

Then he said to her: "I would not tell you. I would first have to do that same thing to you yourself before I should tell you."

And then she said to him: "What did you do to yourself to make your body rattle?"

Then he told her: "I put pitch all over my body, then burnt myself in the fire."

At!at!a'lia said: "It is good that you do that same thing to me. You shall put pitch on my body."

Coyote said to her: "Well, I'll put it on you."

And then both of them went on. Very soon both Coyote and *At!at!a'lia* arrived at the furnace.[143] Coyote saw many people mourning. There in the furnace their children were sitting two by two.

And then Coyote said to the people: "All of you stand up." And then the people stood up.

Then he said to them: "All of you get some pitch." The people went, and then they got some pitch. And then they came bringing pitch.

Then Coyote said: "All of you rub it on over her body." He rubbed it over the eyes of *At!at!a'lia*.

And then he said to her: "If I shall do thus to you also, O *At!at!a'lia*, if I put the pitch over you, you will burn all over your body. And then you will become strong, and the people will all be afraid of you."

And then *At!at!a'lia* said: "Now it is well that you put the pitch on my body also."

And then they two went to the furnace, and he put the pitch on her. He said to her: "I, Coyote, must let you know just when you, *At!at!a'lia*, will be burnt sufficiently." And then he pushed her in, and she burned.

Then said Coyote: "You people cut four pieces of wood so that they be forked." And then they fastened the pieces of wood onto her--to the front part of her neck and to both her arms and to her legs. Then they turned her over, and *At!at!a'lia* burned.

And then *At!at!a'lia* said: "Now I am burning."

Then said Coyote to her: "I, Coyote, must tell you when you're done, not you. He turned her over and said: "I must tell you."

And then said *At!at!a'lia*: "I am burning!"

Coyote said to her: "Soon I shall let you know." She burned all up; *At!at!a'lia* died.

And then Coyote said to the people: "Now all of you can go home!"

Now he caught sight also of Owl, of whom, in truth, *At!at!a'lia* was the wife. And Owl was bringing along some more people. And then Coyote took hold of some ashes.

Then Coyote said to him: "By what right, per-chance, would you, Owl, do thus to people? No! This day your name has become Owl." And then he threw the ashes at him. Owl became all ashy gray.

And then Coyote said: "Very soon will come here the Indian people. Whenever an owl is heard, the people shall say, 'Now an owl is hooting; now surely some person will die.'"

And then said Coyote: "Now you people can go home. I have now killed *At!at!a'lia*."

And then Coyote said: "No longer would you, *At!at!a'lia*, do thus to the people. Now I am Coyote; you have this day died, *At!at!a'lia*." Thus he did at Wishram.[144]

27B. COYOTE AND *TAH-TAH KLE-AH*[145]

Coyote (*Paht-Paht*) was traveling along when he saw ahead of him, coming towards him, a *Tah-tah kle-ah*.[146] He was scared, bad scared! He said to himself, "I am gone! I cannot help myself! The old woman will catch me! She will carry me in her big basket to her roasting place and cook me and eat me. What can I do to save myself?"

Then Coyote called on his sisters for help. He had to scare them with rain before they would tell him what to do. They said, "Go to the wet place, the swamp, and get the jointed weed. Cut the joints; string them on your leggings so they will rattle when you dance. Make them dry. Fix them all over your leggings and do the dance when *Tah-tah kle-ah* comes up to you."

"She will like the music of the rattling and will say to you, '*Eh!* You look fine. How do you do that?' Do not stop dancing; do not answer the old woman. Only laugh, and she will again ask you. Then you laugh and answer, 'You are cowardly! You would not do what you would have to do, what I did.' Five times she will ask you, and the fifth time you tell her. 'It is hard work; but if you are not cowardly, you can do it. It is dangerous, very severe. You must have pitch all over yourself; burn it off, and you will be as you now see me.'"

Tah-tah kle-ah agreed to do as Coyote said, and Coyote helped her cover herself with pitch. Then Coyote set fire to the pitch and burned her to death. Coyote laughed at *Tah-tah kle-ah*, laughed to see her die. He said to her, "You cannot be so great. A new people are coming, a people different from us. You cannot be devouring these new people, the Indians, when they come. You are now a nobody, a nothing."

28. COYOTE AND HIS DAUGHTER[147]

Now Coyote, his wife, and his children were living together. And then Coyote said: "Now I shall soon die. When I shall have died, straightway my 'trading friend,'[148, 149] looking exactly like me, will come and marry my daughter--thus will my 'trading friend' look, like me." And then Coyote died, so then they buried Coyote in the earth.

And then Coyote arrived, and straightway the people thought: "He who has come is the man that Coyote spoke of." So then the maiden, Coyote's daughter, was given to the stranger,[150] Coyote's "trading friend." And then the people said: "Coyote himself said, 'I shall die. A man will come and you shall give him my daughter.'" So the woman was given to him. The two lived together, slept together about five nights.

And then the people said: "How is this! But he is

just like Coyote!" And they said: "Where you people
have buried him, there do you go and look for him." And
then they went and looked for him where he had been
buried.

Coyote thought: "Now they have recognized me,
since they have gone to look for me where I have been
buried." Coyote ran off and laid himself down where he
had crawled out, and slept. And then Coyote said: "I give
you people the death omen."[151]

And then Coyote said: "Always shall you people
do thus to your younger sisters. Now I here have done
thus; I have married my daughter, have stolen her this
day. Now always shall people do thus."[152]

29. COYOTE AND THE SUN[153]

Now Coyote is going towards the sun.[154] Then he
arrived there. "Well," he said to the Sun, "It is good that
I shall be your slave and that I shall follow you about. I
shall work for nothing. You are chieftainess."

So she said "Yes" to him. Early next morning the
Sun arose. Wherever she went, there also Coyote followed her. Oh, dear! He looked on and saw everything.

Early next morning they two went again. Again,
as before, he saw various things--in what various ways
people were acting, how women were eloped with, or
what was stolen, what bad things were done, who was
killed--everything Coyote saw.

At last he became uneasy. Then he cried out: "I
see what you people are doing."

Again he saw them. As before, he cried out
again: "I see you."

Then she did not want him. She said to him:
"Now I shall have taken you with me long enough. You

are too mean. It would not be good that you should always tell on people. There would soon be trouble." It is because of this that we do not find everything out.

But if Coyote had become the sun, everybody would today be betrayed in his secrets. In this way did Coyote in vain try to become the sun. And then he gave it up. There he stopped; he had arrived at the end.

This is the story of Coyote. Thus did the men of old in ancient days relate the tale. Today there are no longer such men of old.

30. COYOTE AND SKUNK[155]

There were Coyote and his younger brother Skunk.[156] Now then Skunk got sick. And then Coyote said to him: "Brother, now you will be doctored. Surely, I shall get a medicine-man. I shall get Raven. I shall tell him and he will doctor you."

And then Coyote told the people who were to act as drummers to beat time: "Now Raven is going to doctor."

And then Coyote got some pitch and stuck it up into Skunk's rectum.

Then indeed Raven doctored. And then Raven said: "He is not sick in his body; it is all in his belly alone." In truth, Skunk had only excrement and discharges of wind in his belly.

Then Coyote said: "Now let us take my younger brother outside. He will go to urinate." And then he said to them: "All of you will go and slowly lift him up. You will take hold of him by his anus." So then he was carried out.

And then Coyote took hold of the pitch; he pulled out the pitch from him. And then Skunk discharged wind.

And then the small deer all died. Now then Coyote went
out. And then he closely examined the little deer. Coyote
took all the fat ones, Skunk took all the lean ones.

And then Coyote said to him: "Just so, indeed.
Your ancestors, O skunk, were not fond of fat. My
ancestors were eaters of fat."

And then the two of them lived together again;
the pieces of meat they ate in quiet. Now they lived
together for a long time. And again Skunk got sick. And
again Coyote went to tell the people, the big deer. Again
the two of them did as before. And again Skunk got sick.
And again Coyote went to tell the people, the antelopes.
Again the two of them did as before. And again Skunk
got sick. And again Coyote went to tell the people, the
wild mountain sheep. And again the two of them did as
before.

For the fifth time Skunk got sick. So then Coyote
said to the elks: "You people shall go [i.e., to Skunk]; the
medicine man will doctor; you shall drum." And then the
elks went to Coyote's house. Then, indeed, he put some
pitch up into his younger brother's rectum. And then the
elks sat down. Now then Raven doctored. And then the
elks drummed.

Thus Raven sang: "Only grass is filled into his
belly, *L!ak wagwa'li*;[157] only grass is filled into his belly,
cu' cu'."[158]

And then Coyote said: "Now let us carry out my
younger brother, and he will go and urinate." And then
the elks took hold of Skunk and he was carried outside.
Now then Coyote was first on top,[159] outside of the house.
And then he took hold of his younger brother by his
head-hair. Then he was taken hold of by all; Skunk was
lifted up. Then Coyote removed the pitch from him. And
then he defecated and discharged wind. The elks all
jumped off, cleared the underground lodge, and all went

out. None of them died.

Again Coyote went to tell the people, the large deer.[160] But he was told: "We will not go." Truly, Coyote and Skunk are not good. If Coyote comes again, then we shall not go," said the big deer.

Then Coyote said: "Now you people shall go. Again you shall go and drum. My younger brother has become sick."

Then they said to Coyote: "We shall not go now."

Then he went off again to the antelopes. He said to them: "Now you people shall go; again you shall go and drum. My younger brother has become sick."

They said to him: "We shall not go now."

Then he went off again to the bighorn sheep. Again his experience was as before. Then he went off again to the elks. Again his experience was as before. The people had become afraid; none of them went.

31. EAGLE'S SON AND
COYOTE'S SON-IN-LAW[161]

Eagle married Coyote's daughter. And then they two dwelt for some time. And then a child was seated in her womb and she gave birth to a male child, Eagle's son. Now then Eagle went out hunting. Eagle's wife was sitting in the house. And then she thought to herself: "Now I will return homewards and leave Eagle behind."

So then the woman ran away. She ran and ran. Then she hung the child, Eagle's child, up along the trail. Straightway she ran on, ran until she arrived at Coyote's house, she being his daughter.

And then Eagle, arrived at his and his wife's house. The woman had disappeared. And then Eagle ran along the trail. He followed the woman, his wife. He ran along the trail. And then he saw the child. Eagle's son was hanging up along the trail--Coyote's daughter had hung up her son. Now then he slowly took hold of him and released him. And then he took the boy, his son, with him to the house. And then he kept him to himself. Now then the boy grew up and became strong, a big man he became.

Now Coyote's daughter had gone on. Soon she became a married woman [again]. Eagle's wife took a [second] husband. The man who married her was named Fish Hawk. Now then Coyote said to his daughter: "How is it, daughter, that you are somewhat sucked? Did you not leave your child behind there?"

And then she said to her father: "You are very wicked, Coyote. Why do you speak thus? If I had had a child, I should not have abandoned him."

Now then Coyote's son-in-law, his daughter's husband, became a racer. And at running he always left all the people behind. A racer, a fast runner he became.

Now Eagle's son became a full-grown man. And then the same, Eagle's son, said: "Now let us go. Let us go and look at Coyote's son-in-law." So then the people who Eagle's son took along went with him in great numbers. Now they arrived where Coyote was dwelling. They marched around the village, passed the houses. Jack Rabbit, a racer, had been taken along. The people looked about slowly.

And then Coyote said to his daughter: "How is it, daughter, that yon man looking like a chief resembles you?"

Then his daughter said to him: "Enough now, be quiet! How can you say thus, that yon chief is my son?"

And then the people stopped marching and camped for the night. Next morning Coyote's son-in-law and Jack Rabbit were to run, were to race against each other.

And then daylight came. The people said: "Now the two of them, Coyote's son-in-law and Jack Rabbit, are to run, are to race against each other."

And Coyote said: "Sir Jack Rabbit, Jack Rabbit! Sir Jack Rabbit, Jack Rabbit!"[162, 163] Now then the two ran, Coyote's son-in-law and Jack Rabbit. And then it rained and Fish Hawk became wetted through. He tried to run, but in vain. He fell right down, for Eagle exercised his supernatural power upon him. Jack Rabbit left him far behind. So then Eagle's people won out.

Many were the people that Eagle had brought with him. And then Eagle's people camped overnight. It was morning. And then they all started to go home, and Eagle said to his people: "You shall cut to pieces all their arrows and bows tonight.

"You, Mouse, will cut them to pieces.

"You too likewise, Rat, will cut the arrows and bows to pieces." Thus Eagle spoke to the two of them.

And then it became dark. Now then he said to Mouse: "Now go and look for Coyote's son-in-law and his daughter, where they are accustomed to sleep."

And then Mouse ran off. He went to look for them, then caught sight of them. Straightway he ran and came back again: straightway he came running to Eagle.

Mouse said: "Now I have seen the two. They are sleeping yonder."

Eagle, said: "I am going to kill them now." And then he went off. Straight on he went until he got to the two.

And then he caught hold of Fish Hawk and turned his head about. And then he cut his neck, cut it right through. Then he caught hold of his mother too, and turned her head about. And then he cut her neck, cut it right through.

Now then Eagle said to her: "You acted badly towards me, that is why I have killed you. You carried me when I was a child, and then hung me up on the trail. You did not take pity on me, but there on the trail you threw me away. You are very wicked."

Now he had killed the two. And then he stuck their heads onto their bodies. He laid them down and covered them over. Now the two were dead.

And then in the morning Eagle's people got ready, and were all about to go home. And then Coyote said to his daughter: "Now wake up, daughter! Eagle's son, the chief, is about to go home." And then Eagle's people got ready to go, and passed around him.

Now then Coyote said to his daughter: "Now arise! You too look at Eagle's son!" Again they passed around him. And then the people went off.

Now then Coyote tried to wake up his daughter and his son-in-law. They kept shaking and shaking. And then he saw that their necks were cut through, and that they were dead.

And then Coyote said: "Before now I was thinking that Eagle's son had not come for nothing. Perhaps she had somehow done something wrong to her son, so that her son killed her. Now today I have found out."

And Coyote said to his people: "Well! Now get your arrows and your bows and we shall fight." The arrows and the bows were gotten, but to no purpose. None of the bows had its bowstring, none of the arrows had its feathers, none of them had their arrow points. Mouse and Rat had eaten them all up at night. Thus the myth.

32. COYOTE AND THE
PREGNANT WOMAN[164]

Coyote again went on and traveled up the river. He met a man whose feet were tied together, and whose legs were full of pieces of wood. He was turning somersaults and standing on his head,[165] and he kept crying: "Alas!"

Coyote met this same man and said: "What are you doing?"

"Not of my accord am I doing thus. My wife is soon to beget a child; therefore have I thus come for wood."

Coyote took hold of him and disentangled him. He put the pieces of wood in order, and tied them together with a hazel-bush rope. And then he asked him: "Where do you live?"

"Yonder I dwell," said the man.

"Let us go," said Coyote. "Go first while I carry these pieces of wood on my shoulders." And then he said to him: "You should handle the wood thus--look at me-- whenever you go for wood."

And then he packed it on his head; Coyote put it on himself. Then the two went towards the man's house, and arrived at the house. He had packed the wood good and strong. "Moving along in this way, man, should you handle the wood. You should pack it good and strong, moving along thus."

They entered the house. He saw the woman. Her body was sound, only she had one of her hands covered up.

He examined her hand carefully. It turned out that a small thorn was sticking in her little finger, and that it had white pus in it. He turned it over, made the swelling burst, and pulled the thorn out from it.

"No!" he said to him. "Not in this way is she to become pregnant. This which has been sticking in her is what people call a thorn.

"Thus should you treat her from now on, and you will cause her to be pregnant. See me copulate with her!" And then she became pregnant with a child in her womb. Then she gave birth to it.

"In this way should you deal with a woman. Now this infant has become your own child. Thus should you people do in this one village."

33. COYOTE AS MEDICINE MAN[166]

A certain old man was sitting in the trail with his penis wrapped about him just like a rope.[167] And then Coyote passed by him and went on a little beyond. He saw some women jumping up and down in the water. And then he thought: "I shall borrow from the old man his penis."

He went over to him and said to him: "Friend, would you not lend me your penis?"

And then the man said to him: "All right, I shall lend it to you." So then Coyote took it and carried it along with him. Then he put it onto his own penis.

Then he shoved it under water right where the women were jumping up and down. One of the women jumped up, the penis got between her legs, and it remained stuck a little ways. And then she became ill (?).

Then the other women took hold of her and brought her yonder to shore. They saw that something was sticking to her, but they could do nothing with her. They could not cut it out of her with anything. And then they took hold of her and carried her a little farther away from the water.

Coyote was far off across the river, and they dragged him into the water. Coyote shouted: "Split a stone as a knife; with it you will cut it off."

They said: "What did some person tell us? He said, 'Cut it off with a stone knife.'" And then they looked for it and found a stone. They split it, and with the same they cut off the penis from her. It had run up right into her. That Coyote over yonder cut it all off. Then he turned his penis all back to himself. Immediately Coyote went on again. He arrived somewhere, and laid himself down there.

Now this woman was sick. The other women took her with them and carried her straightway home.

They looked for a medicine man and found the Raven.[168] They said to him: "Now you will treat her;" then he assented. He went to treat her; he had consented to do so.

And then he doctored and doctored until he said: "There is nothing in her body, there is no sickness in her body." Thus did speak the Raven.

And then the people said: "Yonder is a certain Coyote, who is a medicine man." Then they went and said to him: "What do you think, will you treat her? We have come for you."

And then he said: "Well, I could not go so far on foot. There must be five women without husbands. No! Five women will have to come for me. They will just carry me on their backs."

And then they went and said to five women who had no husbands: "Now you will go and bring the old medicine man."

Coyote yonder split some alder bark and chewed it. Then the women came to meet him, and he said to them: "I am sick in my breast." Then he spat. He showed them that what he had spit out was red and pretended that it was blood.

"You will just carry me on your backs so that my head is downward, in order that the blood may slowly go down to the ground. If my head is turned upwards, my mouth will perhaps become filled with blood, so that I shall die. It is good that my head be down so I shall not die."

One of the women straightway took him on her back. The youngest one carried him first; she carried him with his head turned down. She went along with him. And then straightway he put his hands between her legs. Immediately he stuck his hands into her private parts and fingered them. She thought: "Oh! The old man is bad. The old man did not do good to me." So then she threw him down on the ground. Then he spat blood when she had thrown him down.

One of the older sisters spoke and said to her: "It is not good that you have hurt the old man."

And then one of the women again took him on her back. She went along with him. Again, as before, he mistreated her. Again he put his hands into her private parts. She did not carry him long; she also threw him down.

Again one of the sisters said to her: "It is not good that you have thrown him down. You have hurt the old man. Look at him. Blood is flowing out of his mouth again, he is coughing."

And then she also put him on her back. Now she was the third to carry him. To her also he did as before; he fingered her private parts. She did not carry him long, but threw him down also.

And again one of the women said to her: "Oh! You have not treated the old man well. Now he is continually spitting out much blood. The blood is flowing out of his mouth. You have hurt him badly."

And then the fourth woman took him on her back. That woman also went along with him. He treated her also as before, fingering her private parts. She also threw him down. Behold, now they were approaching to where the girl was lying sick in the house.

Now another one of the women, the oldest of all-- she was their oldest sister--said to them: "How you have treated the old medicine man! Look, blood is flowing out of his mouth. Now he is close to dying. Why have you done thus to the old man?"

The four women said among themselves: "Thus has the old man done to me." One said in like manner: "He fingered my private parts." They said to one another: "Now she too will find out. She will think that the old man is bad, after all."

Now also the other one, the fifth woman, took him on her back and went along with him. He treated her as the others. Now the house was nearby, and there she threw him down.

And then people were gotten to where the woman lay sick who should sing for him,[169] while he was to treat her. They obtained animals of such kind from the land, large deer who could make much noise. They were to sing out loud.

Coyote the medicine man[170] said: "Now lay her down carefully." And then they laid her down. The people who were to sing for him seated themselves. The medicine man said: "I alone would not treat her. Put something around her here to hide her from view, so that I may treat her well." And then they took rushes and put them over her to hide her from view. Now there he sat by her, and said to them: "If I turn my hand up, then you shall sing."

Then he took up the song, and they started in singing. And then he treated her. He spread apart her legs. He stuck his penis into her and copulated with her. She called out: "The old one is copulating with me."

He put up his hand and said to them: "Now go ahead, sing hard." And then hard they sang and sang. The two parts of the penis stuck together. Truly, that was the same penis which they had cut off with the stone knife; that that Coyote had penetrated her with halfway. Thus he copulated with her. The two parts of the penis recognized each other. They stuck together.

And then he pulled it out of her. Straightway she became well. Her mother asked her: "How are you feeling now? Have you now become well?"

"Now I have become well, but the old one has copulated with me."

"Well, never mind, just keep quiet. Now the old one has done well to you."

And then the old man was told: "Now she has become your wife."

He said: "I do not want a woman. I am walking about without particular purpose. I desire no woman." Then he went out of the house. He left them.

34. THE STORY CONCERNING COYOTE[171]

And then Coyote went on. He went and went until he seated himself. And then Coyote looked all around. Then Coyote sucked himself. Thus he did: he turned up his penis, and bent down his head so that he stooped down. Coyote said: "You[172] have not done me good." And then Coyote locked up the story of his obscene act. He did not wish that people should find out about it. So he headed the story off. But then the story loosened itself. They[173] caused it to break out from its prison.

And then everybody found out what Coyote had done to himself. Now Coyote became hungry. Then he thought: "Now I shall eat." And then he went among the people.

But they said: "Coyote has acted badly. He has sucked his own penis." And then Coyote went on again.

He thought: "Yonder I am not known. Truly now they shall not find out about me."

He went on until he came to another house. But again the people were laughing among themselves. "Now Coyote has sucked his own penis," again the people were saying to one another.

And then he thought: "Truly now I am found out." So then he went on. Then again he entered a house where an old person was dwelling. He went into this one and saw that the person had sores all over.

And then he said: "I am hungry."

Then the person said to him: "I have no food. I have this flesh of mine which you see, my ugly flesh." And then she gave him to eat of this flesh of hers; she gave it to him on a plate.

She said to him: "I have no food. This bad flesh of mine I shall give you to eat." So then she gave him it to eat. Then he ate, but did not eat in real truth. He did not swallow it. He let it fall down until there was a little left of it. And then he put it into his quiver and tied and took it with him. He took a little of the sores with him. He went out of the house and went on.

He went and went until he came to some people. He got scent of something to eat. And then he said: "You are eating alone, but you will save a little for me also. I too will swallow and eat some."

And then he went for some stones. Coyote bored them through with holes. He said: "You are eating alone."

And then he sat down. He was tired out. Then he turned and got hold of his quiver. He untied it and pulled out what was inside. Behold, there in his quiver was one entire salmon. There was another entire salmon inside, and he put that down. He started in eating, and ate it all. He ate up his whole quiver; ate his bow.

And then he sat down. He had eaten them [i.e, his bow and quiver] all up, including his quiver. Then he thought: "I shall go back. Truly it was a salmon which she had given me to eat." So then he went. Straightway he arrived there. And then he entered where she had given him to eat; there he went again.

But she said to him: "I shall give you no food whatever. Just now Coyote has been here. I gave him to eat, but he threw away all my flesh. He did not like it, so he threw away all my flesh. Now I shall give you nothing to eat." And then Coyote scolded the old woman because she did not give him anything to eat. Then Coyote became angry. And then Coyote went on again. He arrived at another place.

VII. "Wishham Female Profile. Special Collections
Division, Univ. of Washington Libraries.
Edward S. Curtis, c. 1910 NAI165

V. TALES OF CONFLICTS AND ADVENTURES

35. A CASCADE INDIAN LEGEND[174]

A Cascade Chief had many wives and a big, round lodge. Every morning he would go into the water, bathing. He could walk on it as on the ground. He would only sink in it just a little.

When a child was born he would ask the mother, his wife, "What is it, boy or girl?" If it was a boy, he killed it. If it was a girl, he let it grow. This was a law he always followed.

He had one woman [i.e., a wife] from *Nom-i-neet*.[175] Her baby came a boy. The Chief asked her, "What is it?"

The mother wanted to keep her child, and she answered, "It is a girl." She had to lie to save its life.

She kept the baby for several suns, and then told the Chief, "I would like to go to *Nom-i-neet*. I want to show my girl-baby to the people there, my own people." In this she lied to the Chief again, telling him when she would return in one moon's time.

So he let her go, and she went for good. She went and stayed, for she was afraid he would kill her baby. The boy grew to be ten snows old. He practiced to become strong. He grew rapidly to manhood. The Chief had long feet, longer than any of the warrior's feet. He kept loose dirt all around his lodge so he could see tracks even of the chipmunk.

When the boy had reached twenty-five snows, his mother told him all about his father, what he had done, and how he got up mornings and looked to see if anything came to his lodge. That night the boy went to the Chief's home and walked over the soft ground and entered his father's lodge. The next morning the Chief went out and saw tracks a little longer than his own. He thought, "Who can that be? Longer tracks than my own! My wife lied to me! The baby was a boy! It was he who made these tracks."

The Chief then picked two of the strongest men to go bring the boy to the Cascades. He said to them, "If he will not come himself, bring him."

The two strong men went to bring the boy. They found him in his mother's lodge, sitting on a bearskin robe. They told him, "We come to take you to your father." The boy made no reply. They spoke again, "You understand what we say! You better do it! We will take you anyhow!"

They grabbed him, both of them. They could not move him! He cracked the bones in the arms of both men. They went home, arms broken. When they got there they told the Chief, "We could not bring the boy. He is powerful! We have no arms now!"

The Chief sent more men, lots of canoes. They had no horses. When they got there, the mother had on a ceremonial cap of all colors. If you looked at her cap, you dropped dead. She was a powerful woman. The men were all killed.

The boy then carried a rock that many men together could not carry. He carried it a short distance and sat it down. It can be seen to this day on the bank of the *Neche Wana*[176] between the Cascades and Hood River. It is known as Castle Rock.

36. HOW YOUNG EAGLE KILLED
PAH-HE-NUXT-TWY[177]

Pah-he-nuxt-twy, a Chief, was cutting off the heads of the people. A bad man, he killed people when playing the bone game. He was not satisfied without killing some people.

Eagle heard about this. Eagle had two wives. One was Cricket; the other was Dove. These wives had two children, two boys. Eagle said to his wives, "I am going over there to find out who is killing all the people. I am putting up this feather. Watch it! If blood appears on it, then I am dead. You will know that I have been killed."

Eagle hung the feather and said again to his wives, "Watch the feather all the time." Eagle had fine hair, long hair. He wore lots of shell wampum, and buckskin leggings and shirt. He looked fine, all dressed in the best of everything!

Eagle went! He traveled one sun and camped. The next sun, he did the same thing, traveled and camped. The third sun, he traveled and camped. The fourth sun, he traveled and camped. The fifth sun, Eagle traveled all the time that it was light. It was about sundown when he came to where Indians were camping. He sat down on the ground close to the camp. Eagle found two old women there. One of them said, "Oh, my sister! A man comes into our lodge. I think he is a chief."

Eagle was a tall man, good-looking and clean. One old woman said to him, "I never saw you anywhere before. This is the first time that I have seen you."

Eagle made no reply, did not talk. The old woman told him, "There is the Chief at the bone game. He destroys men! Young man," the two old women said, "you have come only to get killed. He has destroyed many chiefs."

The bad Chief was on his knees at the bone

game. He said, "*Eh*! Somebody has come." This bad Chief knew! He said to Blue Jay, "Go over to the old women's lodge and see who is there."

Blue Jay came to the doorway of the lodge and said to Eagle, "The Chief wants you to come and gamble the bone game with him." Blue Jay looked at Eagle and was nearly blinded! He went back to the Chief and said, "You sent me! I am nearly blind. My eyes are put out."

The Chief told Whitefish to go see who was over at this outside lodge of the old women. Whitefish went and said to Eagle, "The Chief wants you to come and gamble." Eagle looked at Whitefish. Whitefish's mouth was cut way back. Whitefish ran home, his mouth big.

The next Fish, a fish with a small mouth said, "I will go! I will put my finger in my mouth." Small-mouthed Fish went and told Eagle to come and gamble with the Chief. He then put his finger in his mouth. Eagle looked at him, and burned his mouth red.

The Chief told Crab to go see who was at the women's lodge. Crab went and said to Eagle, "The Chief wants you to gamble with him." Eagle looked at Crab, burning him red. Crab ran home, scared! He said to the bad Chief, "You asked me to tell the Chief to come and gamble with you. I am all burned up!"

Then the bad Chief sent Cottontail. The Chief said, "Go tell him who is Chief, that I want to gamble with him."

When Cottontail delivered this message, Eagle went to gamble with the bad Chief. He took all the people who were in the old women's lodge to go gamble with him. That was the way, the rule. They got to the bad Chief's lodge. They went in and all sat down. The Chief said to Eagle, "If I beat you, I will cut your throat. If you beat me, you will cut my throat."

They commenced to gamble. The best were *Cas-*

te lah and Cottontail. They were against Eagle, and Eagle
lost. The bad Chief said, "I will have to cut your throat."
    Eagle was not afraid. He answered the bad Chief,
"All right!"
    Then the bad Chief cut Eagle's throat. He cut off
his head and hung it up like a flag; he left the body lying
on the ground. Eagle had told his wives, "Watch the
feather! Watch it all the time! If blood appears on it, then
I am dead. You will know that I have been killed."
    When Eagle was killed, blood dropped from the
feather. The wives said, "Eagle is dead!"
    When the blood came, the two wives with the
children moved camp. Coyote [*Paht-paht*] was not far
away. He knew that Eagle was dead, and he took the two
children. He was a Chief! He played Eagle [i.e., disguised himself] to get the two women and children.
    Now Cricket thought that it was Eagle, her
husband, but Dove knew better. Dove cried all the time.
They went traveling for one sun, then camped. Next
morning they traveled, then camped at night. Dove
followed behind, crying. The third sun they traveled till
it was growing night; then they camped. Fourth sun they
traveled, then camped. The fifth sun they traveled, then
camped and traveled no farther. They would stay in this
camp a long time.
    The two boys went out and did the same as
Indians. They grew up like Indians. The youngest boy
was strong, powerful strong! He practiced every day how
to make his strength grow. He pulled up small trees,
twisted them like ropes. He cast heavy rocks from him,
practicing all the time. Then he pulled up big trees,
throwing them like spears. Big rocks were hurled out into
the river. Bigger rocks, still bigger, were pitched across
the *n-Che-wana*.
    Finally Young Eagle was a grown man, and he

set out, going on the trail of his father. He followed his
father's tracks, resting where his father had rested, where
his father had sat down, camping where his father had
camped. Four times, four suns he traveled and camped.
Then the fifth sun he came to the lodge of the two old
women. Young Eagle sat down and looked. The lodge
was far from the village. That was why his father had
gone there. For a long time Young Eagle sat and looked
at the old women, looked and looked at them! He was
better-looking than his father, with buckskin moccasins,
leggings and shirt, with many shell-wampum strings. His
hair was long and fine-looking. One old woman said to
him, "Oh, young man, you have come to the wrong
place! There is a bad man, a bad Chief near here. I do
not want to see you killed!"

Then the two old women told him all about how
his father was killed. A fine big man, all fixed up nice,
Young Eagle went to gamble with the bad Chief. He won
the points, won the sticks fast. Only one more stick, one
more point was left to win. The bad Chief was scared! He
said, "We better quit right now."

Young Eagle would not quit. He made reply,
"No! When you gambled with my father, he did not say
'quit'."

Young Eagle won the game. When the last stick
went across to his side, the bad Chief said, "Let me go
safe! Do not kill me! Save me!"

Young Eagle would not let him live. He answered
the bad Chief, "No! I will not do that. I must cut your
throat!"

Three times the bad Chief asked to be let go
alive. Three times Young Eagle refused. Four times the
bad Chief wanted not to be killed. Four times Young
Eagle would not let him remain alive. He said, "No!
When you won the game from my father, you killed

him."

The fifth time the bad Chief asked to live, he offered Young Eagle everything he had for his life. But Young Eagle refused. He cut the throat of the bad Chief and told him, "After this, there will be no more killing at the bone game, only play in gambling. That will be all the bone game will be used for."

The bad Chief had lots of people on his side. They wanted to get away, wanted to escape when their Chief was killed. Young Eagle had five *e-Quo-quy mah*[178] on his side. Two fires were burning not far apart. Young Eagle had his *Quo-quys* on either side from these fires. The people who escaped the flames were killed by the fierce *Quo-quys*. That was the end of *Pah-he-nuxt-twy*, the bad Chief. Since that time there has been only betting in the bone game, and no killing.

Young Eagle took his father's head down from the pole. He took it to where the body still lay on the ground and put it back in place again. He had some paint, and he rubbed it all over his father's dead body. He did this a second time. Three times, four times he painted the body.

The fifth time he rubbed the paint, Eagle came back to life. He got up and went home to his two wives. Coyote was there, and when he saw Eagle, he cried, "Oh, my grandchild! I took care of all while you were dead. All are here now!"

Eagle replied, "All right! I know what you have been doing. You go up on this tree. A nest of birds is there."

Coyote went up the tree. When he got the nest, no birds were there. Young Eagle commanded him, "You stay there forever!"

That tree and Coyote are a great cliff along the *n-Che-wana*.[179] It was Coyote's punishment for what he had done. He can be seen there to this day.

37A. THE SALMON STORY[180]

Now the five wolves and Coyote, they and Skunk killed Salmon.[181] They seized Salmon's wife and ate him [i.e., her?] all up. One of his [i.e., her?] eggs dropped down. And then it rained. Then it was loosened up and went on to the river. Now the salmon egg floated in the Great River.[182] And then it grew into a salmon and became strong. He became a well-grown Salmon.

And then he went, went to look for those who had killed his father. Then he met a woman in the trail. And then he opened her apron(?).

She cried: "It is not good that you have opened it." She wept.

And then he said to her: "I shall make your apron(?) beautiful by means of dentalium shells." And then he made beautiful her apron.

Then she said to him: "Yonder dwell Coyote and Skunk. And farther yonder are the wolves who have killed your father. Way yonder dwell the five wolves."

And then Salmon went. Straightway he arrived at where Coyote and Skunk were dwelling. They were living in an underground lodge. And then Salmon examined his hand.

Then they two said: "He [i.e., Salmon] will not come as far as this. I think not." Then Salmon went into them, and they saw him. And then Skunk and Coyote started in crying; he went up to meet them.

They spoke to him. Coyote said: "When your father died, ever since then, I, Coyote, have always been weeping, also Skunk."

"Now you will give back to me the bow, the bow

of my father whom you have slain." Coyote took hold of a bow; then gave it to Salmon's son. It was given to him, and he turned it about. It broke to pieces.

And then Salmon beat him and said to him: "Give me another bow, my father's bow. What have you done with the bow?" Coyote gave Salmon's son another one. The bow was given to him, but again it broke to pieces. And then again he beat him.

A third bow was given to Young Salmon. He turned it about, and the bow broke to pieces. And then again he beat him. Then Coyote gave him another bow, the fourth. He turned it about. Again, as before, the bow broke to pieces. And then again he beat him.

Now Coyote gave him still another one. He took it and turned it around. He spanned the bow. Now he had gotten his father's bow; now he recognized it.

He said to the two: "You two have killed my father; now this day I have obtained his bow." He seized Coyote. And then Coyote was dragged down to the river, while Skunk was thrown up to the mountains. Thus he said to Coyote: "You, Coyote, shall prowl up and down along the river." And also to Skunk did he speak in similar manner. Thus did speak Salmon's son. Thus did he treat Skunk and Coyote, two of those who had killed Salmon's father. Now he had taken revenge for his father on them; thus he did with them.

Now Salmon's son went on again. Straight on he went. And then he heard a woman weeping. Then he thought: "Perhaps this is my father's wife who is weeping." And then he went on. Straight on he went into the house. She looked at him and recognized him.

She thought: "Perhaps it is the son of my husband Salmon who was slain. Perhaps it is his son."

And then she said to him: "Your father was slain by five wolves. In this very house they are to be found;

here they dwell. They will come presently." Then he sat down in the house and transformed himself into an old man.

And then one of the wolves arrived in the house. The wolf said: "*He'mm*, there is a smell of salmon." And then he violently pushed against him, and the old man staggered to and fro.

Then the woman said to the wolf: "That old man is your father-in-law and my father. Let him alone."

Another one came and also said: "*He'mm*, there is a smell of salmon." And then he violently pushed against him, and the old man staggered to and fro.

She said to him: "Let the old man alone, he is my father and your father-in-law."

Still one other wolf arrived. Also he treated him likewise. She said to him: "That is your father-in-law and my father. Let him alone."

The fourth wolf arrived. Also he treated him thus. He pushed the old man about.

Then she said: "Let him alone. That is your father-in-law and my father." Now also the eldest wolf arrived; now they had all arrived. Then the old man took a good look at them.

And then the five wolves said to the woman, her whose men they were--all the five wolves were her husbands--"Now you will tell the old man, your father. Now let our father-in-law make arrows for us."

Then she said to the old man: "Now you will make arrows for these five."

"Yes," he said, "I shall make them." They slept overnight. It was morning and then the old man made the arrows. Their supposed father-in-law made them.

He took out one arrow; yet another arrow he took out; yet a third one he took out; yet a fourth one he took out; and one arrow besides, the fifth, he took out. He took with him the five arrows in order that he might kill them. And then they slept overnight. Daylight came, and he finished the arrows. And then he gave the arrows to the wolves. Then he transformed himself back entirely to his original form. Now the wolves came back home in the morning, and he went out of the house.

And then Salmon looked all over the land. [He said] thus he thought: "Now this day I shall kill the wolves who have slain my father."

And then he exercised his magic power upon the water. The sun rose and it became warm; the sun shone strong. Then all the water dried up. There was no water to be found. And the Salmon made just one spring of water among the mountains; at *Wa'xcam*,[183] indeed, he made the water. Just one spring of water Salmon made, plainly seen by all. Now, then one of the wolves became thirsty. So he went to a certain small river to quench his thirst, but in vain. He did not get any water; the river was dried up. And then the wolf caught sight of the water that Salmon had made. Now he was thirsty, so he went to the water.

And then Salmon made some small trees, a few bushes; near to the water he made them. Then Salmon sat down well prepared in the bushes near to the water. Now the wolf went on and saw the water. Straight on to the spring he went. The wolf went to drink the water; then started in drinking it. Salmon exercised his magic power upon the water. So then the water sank down a little, and the wolf's eyes just disappeared from view. Then he shot at the wolf, and the wolf fell down; he was dead. And then Salmon took hold of the wolf. He had killed him, and so threw him away.

He went back to his place. Salmon seated himself. He had killed [i.e., a wolf] completely and thrown him away. Again one other wolf went to the water. Now

he also started in to drink it, and again Salmon shot at
him. Again one other wolf died. Again he took hold of
him and threw him away. Again one other wolf, the
third, went towards the water. He also started in to drink
it. Again Salmon shot at him and killed him. He took
hold of him and threw him away. Again one other wolf,
the fourth, went towards the water. He started in to drink
it, and again Salmon shot at him. He killed him, took
hold of him, and threw him away.

    The smallest and youngest wolf also went towards
the water. He arrived at the water, but did not drink of it.
Salmon thought: "He will drink of it," but in vain. The
youngest wolf did not drink at all. And then he cried:
"*U6*;" thus did the youngest do. And then Salmon
thought: "It is not well." The wolf escaped to the woods.
Now Salmon's son had killed four wolves; they had slain
his father, Salmon. If he had slain all five, there would be
no wolves today; but he killed only four, for one had
been scared away, their youngest brother.

    And then Salmon went to the house where his
stepmother was living. Then he arrived at the house, and
said to her: "Now I have slain four of the wolves; only
one, the youngest wolf, was scared away." And then he
said to the woman: "Now let us two go home." Then the
two went on; he took her along with him. I do not know
how many times they camped overnight when he laid her
down. Salmon laid the woman down, belly up. There was
a child inside of her. As it turned out, there were wolves
in her womb.

    And then he stepped on her; one tiny little wolf
came out of her. Again he stepped on her belly; a tiny
wolf came out from her belly. In this way five little
wolves came out of her. Then he killed the little wolves.
There he built a fire; there in the fire he put them. Thus
did Salmon. And then they two went on; he took with

him the woman, his father's wife. This woman was the Dove. Truly it was her husband, Salmon, who had been killed. The Dove is always wailing: "*U*', *u*'." Whenever the salmon comes, they kill him at Wishram, and then the Dove cries.

Straight on he went with her, straightway he came with her to some water. And then they got hold of a canoe and seated themselves in it. Then he said to her: "Now I'll sleep, while you alone will paddle." Salmon said: "Now I'll lie down to sleep, while you, woman, will paddle alone." And then he lay down to sleep.

The two drifted long about on the water. And then she began to feel ticklish in her feet. Then she looked and found a maggot on her feet. And then she looked carefully at him, and saw maggots crawling about all over his body. The woman cried, and he awoke.

And then he said: "It is not good that you have awakened me. You have disturbed me in my sleep."

Then he got hold of the paddle, took it away from her. He transformed the rocks and hollowed out the rocks; the rocks had a hole bored into them. He wedged the paddle under her and took hold of the woman. He moved it and threw her off with the paddle into the rocks. Then he abandoned the woman. He had been disgraced because she disturbed him in his sleep. So then Salmon went on all alone. Long he went, and far away he went.

Now, there he remained quietly. I know not how many years, how long he remained. Now, then he heard two old people talking to each other: "You are a bad distributer, and not good. Let us two put a cheek on each side. I myself think there should be also an eye to each side. And let us put half a vulva on each side.

"Thus did the one say to the other: "Oh, well! I shall take both eyes for myself."

The other one said to him: "You should not take

both to yourself. We two must divide them--one to each." Four times did he hear the two thus argue and talk to each other. As it turned out, those two were ravens.

And then he said to them: "What are you talking about? What are you speaking of to each other?" They said nothing at all to him. Now they still kept talking to each other, and he listened to them. Now they spoke again as before.

And once more he said to them: "Well, what are you talking to each other about? Tell me too!" Again they said nothing at all. They were arguing excitedly.

Again he said to them: "What are you telling each other?" Again they said nothing at all. And then again they kept talking to each other as before.

Again he said to them: "What are you telling each other?"

And then they said to him: "We two have found a person."

Then he said to them: "Where did you find the person?"

They answered him: "Far away from here we found him."

And then he said to them: "In what way did you come to get him?"

They replied to him: "No! We found him among some rocks."

Then he said to them: "What is that same person, a woman or a man?"

They said to him: "A woman."

"How long is it since you have seen her?"

And then they said to him: "Let this present moon have become exhausted and add yet one moon and a half --(so long is it since) we have found her."

And then he thought: "Perhaps they have really found a person."

Then he said to them: "Tomorrow you two will go; you'll go and look for her."

And he asked them: "Well, how have you been going all along?" Then in his heart he wished for a wind, and it arose.

And he asked them: "How have you been managing to go all along?" And then he heard them as they showed him how they managed. They flew up to the sky, but then the wind struck against them; and then almost immediately they came near striking down against the ground. But he, Salmon, endowed the two ravens with magic power.

And then they looked for her. They went to look for her where they had seen her. Now they went on. Straight on they went, and I know not how many times they slept overnight. And then they arrived there again. Then they turned back home towards the house. They said to him: "There is a person who is near to dying and is thinned out."

He said to them: "What could you do with her?"

Then one of them said: "We might carry her on our backs."

And then he said to them: "I shall lay down a stone on you."

They said 'Yes' to him.

And then they interlocked their wings, and he put down on them a rather small stone. They flew off with it and came back with it; and he loosened it off from them. Then he put a somewhat larger stone on them. And again they carried it with them, and the stone rested quietly on them. Again they came back with it, swaying their bodies from side to side. Again he loosened off the stone from them. Again they did as before, four times in all. The fifth time also he put a stone on them. Again they flew up with it, carried it about with them, and brought it back to him.

Then he said to them: "Now for my sake you will go and get me the woman."

And then they answered him: "No!"

Then he said to them: "You will go to get her for me." Thus did Salmon speak to the two ravens. In truth it was Salmon who had laid down [i.e., abandoned] that woman; now he wanted her.

Then they consented. "Now we shall go and get you the woman," they said to him. And then they went, went to get her. Straight on they went and straightway they came to her.

She was afraid of them and thought: "Now they have killed me."

But then they said to her: "Do not be afraid. We have come for you."

She consented to their proposal. "Whither will you take me?" she asked of them.

And then they said to her: "We shall carry you to our chief."

Then she said to them: "What will you do with me so as to carry me?"

They answered her: "You will lay yourself down on our backs." And then they neatly interlocked their wings; there on their wings she lay down. So then they took hold of her.

And then they went on, the two bearing her along. Straight on they went and brought her home into the house. Straightway they put her down. She had no hair left at all and they brought her home lean. And then Salmon took some oil. Then he poured the oil out over her. Five times he poured it out over her and she came to completely.

Now she was beautiful all over. Her hair grew out from her and her body was beautiful in every way.

The name of that same woman was Dove, Salmon's wife. "As for you two," he said to the two ravens, "your name shall be for all time: Raven. Thus shall you be. Whenever you shall cry *"ka'k, ka'k,"*[184] people will say: 'The two ravens have seen something, no doubt.'" Thus the tale.

37B. SALMON MYTH[185]

Five wolves had a house. They stole Spring Chinook Salmon's wife. They all went hunting. Spring Salmon made the springs dry up, so the wolves thirsted. They went around and around. They said, "Hmmm, that is a salmon smell." They could not keep still; they were wild because they smelled salmon. The springs all dried up so that they all died except the youngest. That is why there are wolves now; the youngest was saved. Then Spring Salmon took his wife again.

They went down the river in a canoe. He told his wife he was going to sleep. "Do not wake me. You will be captain in this canoe. We will go straight down[stream?]. If you see anything do not be afraid." He lay down where he sat and slept. As they went along she saw a worm crawl out of his head; salmon got wormy. So she pushed him away. "*Haaa,*" he cried.

They reached a big rock a little below Lyle [i.e., in the vicinity of this small Washington town]. He said, "Oh, Wolves' wife, you hurt me." He made a hollow in the side of the rock with his paddle just big enough to sit in. Then he placed his wife on the blade of the paddle and put her up there. She had nothing to eat. This was punishment because she hurt him.

He paddled a long time until he came to his house. He had two big crows or ravens. They used to fly about and on their return he would listen to what they said. Finally one said, "I am going to have the eyes."

The other said, "I am going to have the cheeks. You can have the eyes."

He heard them and said, "What do you see, that you talk that way? Do you see something?"

The crows said, "Yes, we saw a woman. She is in a rocky place: no one can get there. She is very poor, a nice looking woman." It was his wife.

So he said, "You fellows can go this morning and bring her on your backs. Do not kill her. Bring her here."

The crows said, "Yes, we will try." So they put their wings together and put something on this.

Then they flew up, and because it did not fall off, he said, "I guess it is all right. You can go fetch her."

So they went. That woman could not move. She cried. She said, "I cannot go; I might fall."

But they said, "No, we will take you. Our brother sent us." So they sat down where she was and crossed their wings. They told her to sit on that and place one hand on the shoulder of each. So she sat there and they took her. "*Kaw, kaw*," they called as they took her.

Anything Spring Salmon wished, he did. It was all right. So he took her for his wife again. She no longer starved. She was all right now. They lived together again.

38. THE ADVENTURES OF EAGLE
AND HIS FOUR BROTHERS[186, 187]

Now Eagle and Blue Jay and Beaver--they three and Sparrow Hawk and Chicken Hawk speared a seal. And then it dragged them along over the water, dragged them on and on with it. Then Eagle said to Beaver: "Now my hands are sick, so cut off the rope."

So then Beaver went and bit at the rope. Beaver's teeth all came loose, and his teeth fell over into the water.

Another one, Sparrow Hawk took hold of the rope with his claws. This time also his claws fell overboard into the water.

Next, Eagle took hold of it with his claws. Also his claws sank under water.

Next Sparrow Hawk [Chicken Hawk?] took hold of it with his claws. Now by that time they had been thrown onto land and came ashore. Truly Eagle and his younger brothers had been on board a canoe. They had speared a seal, and it had dragged them along with it, as in truth they were in a canoe.

And then they saw a woman. Those claws of theirs and their teeth were all gathered here where the woman dwelt. So they gathered there. As it turned out, that woman was the seal that had dragged them along with her.

And then they said to Blue Jay: "Now go and get our claws."

Eagle said to him: "Now you will go and get my claws and Beaver's teeth."

So Blue Jay went and said to the woman: "I have now come for the claws and teeth, O niece."

And then she said to him: "I am not your niece. Thus shall you speak to me: 'O wife;' and in that case I shall return them to you."

And then she took them with her and they went towards the house. All five of them she took with her straight on into her house. And then she put food before them. In truth it was all persons' eyeballs. She said to them: "They are huckleberries." In fact they were eyeballs, not huckleberries. And then they sank tubes down in themselves through their mouths reaching down straight to the ground. So then they pretended to eat the eyeballs.

Then she put food before them again. In truth it was brains. And again they ate it, and it went straight through them--truly a person's brains.

The woman said to them: "This is an *id'i'-nExt'* stew,"[188] but in fact she was deceiving them. Truly thus she thought: "I shall kill these men, Eagle and his younger brothers." She thought: "Indeed I shall kill them."

And again she took them along with her to a certain other house. And then she gave them a comb--in fact a hand, a dead person's hand. And they combed themselves with the hand.

And then she said to them: "Again to that one house yonder you shall go." In truth dead men's bones were being burned up as fuel where she brought them. And then they went inside the house. The smoke went up all murky. Truly dead men's bones were smoldering. And then Eagle took his younger brothers and completely sheltered his younger brothers under his wings. Then he turned to look at his wings. Eagle's younger brothers were all covered up out of sight.

In truth the woman thought: "I shall kill them. Eagle and his younger brothers will die." So then they stayed in the house while the smoke went up all murky. Dead men's bones were being burned as fuel.

And then a man was told: "Now they have died, so you will remove this smoke." So then he moved forward while sitting down in this manner[189]--in truth he was *Ixut!i'lili*.[190] He swallowed the smoke, and it slid down into his mouth. Now *Ixut!i'lili* had swallowed all the smoke. Eagle and his younger brothers were sitting perfectly unharmed. They were all brave heroes.

So then they sat unharmed; they had not died. And then again people came to tell them and they went to a certain other house. A woman gave them nuts and huckleberries to eat, and she gave them "*id'i'nxt*" (sic) stew to eat. In truth she who gave them to eat was the Squirrel, and she gave them good food. And then Eagle and his younger brothers ate well.

And then people came to tell them: "You will gamble at bones. We have come to tell you."

Then Eagle said: "Well, yes, we shall gamble. Although we do not know how to play bones, still we shall go."

So then they went and arrived there. And then Eagle and his younger brothers gambled at bones. Sparrow Hawk and Chicken Hawk, both of them were brave heroes; also Beaver, who eats sticks. Sparrow Hawk is an eater of birds; he strikes fear into everything, kills everything and eats it. Eagle is also thus, and Eagle is strong above everybody. He could easily seize a grizzly bear's son. And in fact nowadays Eagle makes even a grizzly bear afraid. Also that Blue Jay, their younger brother, if they should win in bones, then that one was to kill the people with his battle-ax. He was to strike the people with it and to chase them around. Truly they were all strong, they all alone, the brothers.

So then they gambled at bones. In truth, Rabbit was a player, a gambler at bones. Also Crab was a gambler at bones. In truth they all gambled at bones. Now then Crab took hold of gambling bones, and Rabbit took hold of gambling bones and they were forced up into his nostrils; the gambling bones were really in his nostrils. And then Eagle guessed Rabbit. Straightway did Rabbit's nostrils tear open and the bones flew out of his nostrils. And then that Crab took hold of the gambling bones and started in to avenge Rabbit. And then Crab sang. Also Crab was guessed and his hands were all cracked; the gambling bones flew out and his hands suffered big tears. Crab was burned all over, and you can see that he is red. Then Crab went to the water, went to stay there for all time. Nowadays Crab is always in the water. In this manner did Eagle guess him.

And so they won at gambling bones, and Blue Jay killed the people. Whenever they won he struck the people with his battle-ax, which is here on his head. Now people again came to tell them: "You strangers will go to the sweat house."

And then they went towards the sweat house and came to put themselves into it. The sweat house had been built for them, in truth, entirely out of stones. So then they went inside of the sweat house. It was heated down below and it was made entirely out of stones. They stayed down below and then the sweat house was covered with five stones.

And then Eagle spoke and said to his younger brothers: "What do you think? Now we have died."

Then Beaver said: "I am a man; soon you shall see water." And then he turned a somersault; and again he turned a somersault; and again he turned a somersault; and again he turned a somersault. Now then some water had come to be on the ground. And then again he turned a somersault, five times in all; a lake had come to be. So there they stayed and bathed themselves in the water.

And then they took five small stones. Then they threw a stone into the water and the stone fell in with a splash: "*lpu2*". And then the people said: "Poor, poor Blue Jay! Now Blue Jay's heart has burst." Thus said the people outside.

And again the brothers inside threw another stone into the water, and again it was heard splashing: "*lpu2*."

Then again they threw one other stone in; outside it was heard splashing:"*lpu2*." Now three stones had been thrown in.

And again they threw another stone into the

water, and again outside it was heard splashing: "*lpu2.*"
The fifth stone they threw down into the water with a
splash: "*lpu2.*"

And those outside said: "Now Eagle has died."
The people said: "Now they, Eagle and his younger
brothers, have all died. Now all their hearts have burst."
And then they took off the stones which were covering
the sweat house. Again they took off a stone; again they
took one off; again they took off the fourth; again they
took off the fifth.

Now a Blue Jay had seated himself in the doorway and had taken his battle-ax in hand. With the fifth
stone the door was entirely uncovered, and still was Blue
Jay sitting in the doorway. And then Blue Jay rushed out
and again killed the people. Then they all went out of the
sweat house. They were not dead at all.

And then again people came to tell them: "We
have come to tell you that we should all gamble at
'*waqi'lukck.*'"[191]

"Yes, we shall go," said Eagle.

So then they went and Eagle said to his younger
brothers: "Who of you will do it?"

Beaver said: "I shall do it."

"Yes," said Eagle.

And then Beaver went to the woods; and Beaver
stuck sticks onto himself all over his belly. Now then the
Black Bear lay down, lay with belly up. And that Beaver
lay down with belly up; both Beaver and Black Bear lay
down with their bellies up. And then a cedar tree was
taken with pebbles all clinging to its butt end. Then the
cedar, the pebbles clinging to its roots, was slung up into
the air. The cedar came falling down on Beaver's belly.
Far off bounded the cedar; the cedar fell down broken to
splinters.

Beaver was lying quite unharmed. He was not

dead at all, and arose.

Now that Black Bear lay down, lay with belly up.
And then a cottonwood tree with pebbles clinging to its
roots was slung up into the air and the cottonwood tree
fell down on Black Bear.

Eagle had exercised his magic influence upon it.
Eagle had put strength into the cottonwood tree, and the
cottonwood became heavy. Black Bear's belly burst into
pieces and the body of Black Bear bounded off in fragments. Black Bear was dead.

Eagle and his younger brothers won, and then
Blue Jay again killed the people.

And again people came to tell them: "We have
come to tell you that you should go and get a maiden's
tiny little dogs." So then they went, straight on they went.
They saw what proved indeed to be five Grizzly Bears.

And then Eagle exercised his magic power upon
the Grizzly Bears, so that they became quite small. Blue
Jay quietly took hold of a small grizzly bear. Eagle
quietly took hold of that other one. All five of them took
hold of the Grizzly Bears, each taking one Grizzly Bear.
And then they took them with them towards the house
and came home with them. Straightway they put them
down in the house, and then the Grizzly Bears started in
fighting in the house among themselves.

And then the people said: "For what reason have
you brought them?"

The brothers were told: "Go and put them back
again in that place in which you got them."

And then Eagle said: "You people were saying,
'Bring them.'" And then they took hold of the Grizzly
Bears, took them back again, and went to put them down
again. Then they arrived back again and Blue Jay again
killed the people. So they had won once more.

And then again people came to tell them: "Let us

gamble again. We shall wrestle on a rope stretched out across the water."

And then Eagle said to his younger brothers: "Who of you will wrestle on the rope?"

And then Blue Jay said: "I shall do it, I am a man." Truly that was Squirrel who was going backwards and forwards on the rope. So then both that Blue Jay and Squirrel wrestled there on the rope. Blue Jay struck Squirrel with his battle-ax. Squirrel died and drifted downstream. The people were seated while the two had them look on; the people looked. And then Squirrel was seen drifting down dead. Truly Blue Jay had struck her and truly he had killed her. And then Blue Jay returned to land and killed the people again.

And again people came to tell Eagle and his younger brothers, all brave heroes. And then they said: "Yes, we shall go." They went and then they were told: "We shall wrestle."

Then Eagle said: "I, Eagle and another, shall wrestle." Truly that was Buzzard who was wrestling with Eagle. And then the two took hold of each other, interlocked their wings and caught hold of each other by clinching each other's claws. And then up they went to the sky.

Now then Eagle said to his younger brothers: "If my body should fall down, straightway shall you dip it there in cold water. If Buzzard's body should fall down, straightway shall you put it into warm water."

Eagle's body fell, and straightway they dipped Eagle's body in cold water. Also Buzzard's body fell, and straightway they dipped it in warm water.

That Blue Jay is carrying water now and his eyes have become blinded; now he has been made a slave. And that Chicken Hawk is sitting in the house and one of his eyes has burst. And that Sparrow Hawk, the hero, is now sitting in the house; now he sits with his eyes bedimmed. And that Beaver is now eating sticks. But Eagle, their elder brother, and Buzzard had now mounted up to the sky. Now Buzzard and Eagle are holding on to each other by interlocking their bodies. They have reached up to the sky and their bodies are nothing but bones. Thus did the two wrestle.

And then Eagle cried out: "Where now is my brother, Sparrow Hawk, my brother? Now I have been overcome by Buzzard."

And again Eagle cried out and called upon him; again as before he cried out to him. And then Sparrow Hawk was heard in the house; now one of his eyes was burst.

Then again Eagle cried out to *Gayaxila'da*,[192] the hero. Eagle said to him: "Where now is my brother, *Gayaxila'da*, my brother? Now I have been overcome by Buzzard." In this way did Eagle call out.

And Chicken Hawk was heard saying, "*gle'l, gle'l*"[193] in his heart.

Then again Chicken Hawk was called out to: "Where now is my brother, Chicken Hawk, my brother? Now I have been overcome by buzzard."

And then he awoke and came to himself. Also Chicken Hawk did as before; he was heard saying: "*gle'l, gle'l.*"[194]

And then Sparrow Hawk and Chicken Hawk became frenzied and tore thus right through the house. Then the two rose up to the sky and went to look for their elder brother. They went on and straightway caught sight of him as a tiny dark speck in the sky. Then they came up close to the two combatants and they seized Buzzard. Sparrow Hawk and Chicken Hawk, the two younger brothers of Eagle, cut off the neck of Buzzard and threw down her head. It fell down there below where the people were dwelling. Straightway her head was dipped in warm water.

Then slowly the two unloosened her claws from him, for she had pierced through and caught hold of his heart. Straightway they threw the claws down, and they fell into the water. And then they carried Eagle back with them to the ground. They took hold of him by his arms and arrived with him on the ground. And then he brought himself to. Eagle took some grease and then poured it over himself. Five times he poured the grease over himself and he recovered entirely. But she, Buzzard, died straightway, while Eagle did not die at all. Thus did Eagle and Buzzard wrestle.

And then Beaver said: "For my part I shall go to stay always in the water, and there I shall eat wood."

Blue Jay said: "Now I for my part shall be here in this place, and the people will say, 'This is that Blue Jay and he did his deeds hereabouts.'"

And Sparrow Hawk said: "Now I for my part will be in this place in the woods; and they will say, 'That Sparrow Hawk is looking on.'"

Chicken Hawk said: "I for my part will be anywhere at all, all over shall I be. As to me the people will say, 'Chicken Hawk, the hero, kills birds every-where; everything he swallows.'"

And Eagle said: "Now I for my part shall be in the mountains forever and ever. I shall not be seen at all. Only once in a great, great while will anyone see me.

"The people will say, 'Eagle has come; here is Eagle flying about, in order that Eagle may take from the Grizzly Bear his son--he fills him with dread. Strong is Eagle. So he fills a deer with dread also, and also him could Eagle seize. He could just chew at a deer hide and it would become buckskin. Thus could Eagle do with it.'"
In this way took place the tale.

39. THE FIVE EAST WIND BROTHERS
AND THE FIVE THUNDER BROTHERS[195]

The five East Wind brothers were dwelling far away in a certain land. And then the oldest one said: "Now, O younger brothers! Now I shall leave you. I shall seek to find where the people are assembled together. Mind you, if I am alive, I shall come back to you within five days. If not, truly you shall think to yourselves, 'Now something has happened to him.'"

"Yes," they said to him.

He started out on his journey. He goes and goes. He came to an old woman whose house was smoking. Therein he entered. She turned her head and looked at him. For a long time the two remained silent. And then she said to him: "O boy![196] What, pray, are you journeying for?"

"Well, I am seeking to find where the people are assembled together."

"Yes," she said to him, "yonder they are assembled together." She directed him towards the setting sun. "I shall just tell you that they are not assembled together for nothing. Now, the Thunder brothers have consumed all the people. They are singing their supernatural dance song. If indeed you think to yourself, 'Now I am going to die,' then go! You will just find out that you are no longer alive. Now, surely indeed[197] the people go in one way.[198] Such alone is the assemblage here."

"Yes," he said to her. "Indeed, for that indeed am I journeying."

He camped overnight five times. He did not come home to his brothers. The second brother said: "Now I shall go and look for our elder brother. How is it that he is absent? Perhaps many people have assembled together."

"Yes," said his younger brothers to him.

He said to his younger brothers: "I shall be away from home for about five days." He too came to the old woman. Just as before she told him about the assemblage. He is away from home five days.

"How is it!" said the third brother. "They are assembled in great numbers. Now I for my part shall go and look for the two [i.e., the brothers]." He too, like the others, was absent. He also came to the old woman. Just as before she directed him.

The fourth brother said: "I for my part shall go now and look for them [i.e., our brothers]." Just like the others he said to his younger brother: "If I shall have camped overnight five times, then I shall not come home." Five nights passed; he did not appear.

And then the youngest brother got ready. He too went. He went and went until he met Coyote.

"O boy! Whither are you going?" said Coyote.

"Well, I am seeking to find where they are assembled together."

"Well, friend! We two might very well go together. I also am seeking to find the assemblage."

"Just as you like! Let us then go together." And then they two went. They went and went on a certain trail far away. They came to people.

And then Coyote challenged the people to play at gambling bones. They agreed to gamble with the two. They gambled all night long. The two were beaten. His friend was deprived of everything. Coyote now had no clothes at all.

Next morning the two went on again. Again they arrived in a certain land. Behold! Truly indeed people were assembled at this place. Coyote was spoken to: "With what shall we two join in in this assemblage?"

Coyote said, "Oh, well! I am somewhat of a fast

runner, friend, so that you will bet everything."

The two challenged the people: "Who will run with me?"[199]

For a long time the people were silent. A certain person was taken [i.e., selected], rather small and tall; in truth, Magpie. He and Coyote ran there and back. Both started out to run fast; Coyote alone was seen. They two ran down into a hollow; they ran up from out of it. Coyote alone was seen; Magpie was not seen, only a cloud of dust was seen. There truly he was following upon him. The people said: "It seems that we have been beaten."

The two ran down into a second hollow; they ran up out of it. Again, as before, Coyote alone was seen. The third time again he was alone. The fourth time again as before. The fifth time the two ran down into a hollow; they ran up out of it--now both of them were seen. And then the people got to disputing. Some of them said "Coyote." Some said "No! Magpie." Now the two are coming in a cloud of dust. They ran into the people. There Coyote was passed by. He and his friend lost.

Having absolutely nothing, the two now went on to a certain other village. "Well," said Coyote, "I shall try again. I shall gamble bones."

And then the East Wind said: "But what, pray, are we going to bet with?"

"No, friend," he said to him, "I shall be given blankets." As it turned out, that Coyote made the blankets out of the leaves of cottonwood trees, some greenish, some yellowish, some reddish he made. He patched together blankets with colored decorations. He deceived them in regard to the blankets. Since it was dark, they did not see them clearly. Many blankets did the two stake; they won.

Next morning they started off and left the people

behind. They went on; they went and went, up to a certain village. And then Coyote said: "Well, now I for my part shall depart. Yonder I shall go towards the rising sun."

"Yes," he said to him. "And I for my part, indeed, am going yonder towards the setting sun." There they parted from each other.

The East Wind went and went. He saw a small house smoking. Therein he entered. An old woman was sitting there.

She said to him: "Boy, what, pray, are you journeying for?"

"Well, I am going about without purpose. I am seeking to find the assemblage."

She said to him: "All by itself in that place, there is an underground lodge. There the Thunder brothers are singing."

"To them I am journeying," he said. He started off and went in that direction.

East Wind entered the underground lodge; it was evening now. He sat down close to the wall. He looked at the strange-looking people with bodies all reddish.[200] They were talking to one another in whispers. One of them asked him: "What, pray, are you journeying for?"

"Indeed, I hear that they are singing here, that they are assembled together."

"Yes," said one. "This one here sings;" a certain one was pointed to.

"Well, he is lying to you; this one here sings."

That one too said: "No! This one here sings." And thus they kept putting it off on one another.

East Wind said to them: "Hurry up and sing!" Now for a long time they sit silent. One of them stood up slowly,[201] saying: "Yes, boy, now indeed I shall sing." The eldest sang; five songs he sang. When he sang the fifth song, straightway the underground lodge became nice and warm. He sat down.

The second one stood up. He said: "Now, indeed, I also shall sing." He sang. Straightway their underground lodge warmed up. He sang the fifth song; immediately steam streamed up. He ceased.

The third one stood up. He sang. It got to be rather hot. He sang the fifth song. Immediately it got to be burning here and there, smoke streaming up in different places. He became silent. After a little while the smoke disappeared. They looked; East Wind was still sitting there.

They talked to one another, somewhat like whispering: "It seems, indeed, that this person is different from those that came before. Where he has come from I don't know."

East Wind said to them: "Why, hurry up! Start in singing! One feels rather comfortable when you keep singing. We were all sitting around nice and warm."

Quickly[202] the fourth one arose. He sang. Straightway now it began to burn here and there. He sang the fifth song. Their underground lodge was all fire. He became silent. They sat for a long time; the fire died away. They looked; the boy was still sitting. Again they talked to one another in whispers.

East Wind said to them: "Hurry up! Now, indeed, I have become cold. It was comfortably warm when you were singing."

The fifth and youngest arose. He just took a breath, and fire darted out of his mouth. He sang, he sang, he sang. He sang the fifth song; everything became fire. He became silent. It burned continually. They sat by the fire for a long time; it died out. They looked at East Wind; he was still sitting there.

They said: "This person is something different."

They were talking to one another in whispers.

East Wind said to them: "Hurry up! Start in singing now!"

They said: "We have sung enough."

"Yes," he said to them, "I too shall sing." They consented to what he said. He arose. Straightway an east wind blew nice and cool.

They said: "We shall each of us go out for a short while."

"No!" he said to them. "Sit quiet." He stood at the door. He sang the second song. An east wind blew strongly in the underground lodge. He sang the third song. It blew stronger. He sang the fourth song. Now they did not remain quietly seated. Now they started to shift in their seats; straightway ice formed and icicles projected. He sang his fifth song. Everything became congealed into ice. There the Thunder brothers froze.

Somehow or other the youngest [i.e., Thunder brother] broke through the underground lodge. He escaped. Truly thus they used to kill people. Whenever onlookers arrived, they used to seat them in that place. There visitors always burned. There his elder [i.e., Thunder] brothers had died. He took their bones and heaped them together. He stepped over them five times. They all came back to life in their proper likenesses. If East Wind had killed all five of the Thunder brothers, there would be no thunder today. Story story. May the weather tomorrow be as it was when the Thunder brothers and the East Wind came together.

40A. THE DESERTED BOY (I)[203]

Some time long ago the people said to a boy: "Now let us go for reeds." The boy was considered bad.

So then they said: "Now you people shall take him along when you go for reeds." And then they said to them: "You shall abandon him there." So then the people all went across the river.

They went on and arrived where the reeds were. And then they cut off the reeds and said to them: "If the boy says, 'Are you people still there?' you shall answer him, '*U*'."[204]

And then they all ran off. Straight home they ran, went right across the river. No person at all was left on this side; they were all on the other side.

And then that boy said: "Now let us all go home!"

"*U*," said the reeds to him.

He looked about long, but in vain. There was nobody. And then he too started to go home. He went following behind them. He ran until he arrived at the river, but there were no people to be seen. So then the boy cried.

And then he heard something sound: "*L! L! L!*"

And then he turned his eyes and looked; he dried his tears. Now then he caught sight of a wee bit of fire in a shell. And then that same boy took the fire and built up a fire.

And further he caught sight of some string, a small piece. Straightway he took it. And he went to the cache and found five 'Indian potatoes.'[205] And then he thought: "My poor paternal grandmother has saved for me the 'Indian potatoes," and my paternal grandmother has saved for me the fire, and my maternal grandmother has saved for me the string."

And then the boy made a fishline, and he made a trap out of the string. He set his trap for magpies and then trapped them. Then he made a magpie-skin blanket out of magpie's skin. He put it nicely about himself.

Also, when he went to sleep, he wrapped himself nicely in it.

And then he fished with hook and line and caught one sucker. Half of it he consumed; half he saved for himself. Next morning he consumed also the other half. Then he went to fish again and caught two suckers; one he consumed, and one he saved for himself. Next morning again he consumed the other one. Now next morning he went to fish again and caught three suckers. One and a half he consumed. Next morning again he consumed the other one and a half. Then again he went to fish and caught four suckers. Two he consumed, two he saved for himself. Next morning he consumed both of them. Now again he went to fish for the fifth time. The boy had now fished five times. He had now become a full-grown man.

And then he turned to look at his fishline. Behold! Ground roasted fish[206] was contained brimful in a hollow vessel. He stood it up on the ground. And then the boy sang.

Now then all the people were looking on at him, and then they said: "What has happened to him?" Truly, he became glad because he had caught ground fish.

Thus he sang:[207] "*Atse'*, *atse'*! My feathered cloak waves freely over me." In truth, it was *Itc!E'xyan's*[208] virgin daughter that had given him to eat.

Now then the boy had slept four nights. He slept through the fifth night. And then he awoke. A woman was sleeping with him. Very beautiful was the woman. Her hair was long, and she had bracelets reaching right up to here on her arms.[209] And rings were on her fingers in great number. And he saw a house all covered with painted designs inside. And he saw a mountain sheep blanket covering over both of them, him and his wife. Truly, that woman was *Itc!E'xyan's* daughter, and she had given him to eat. Plenty of "Chinook" salmon and sturgeon and blue-back salmon and eels, plenty of everything, she had brought. Now he married her.

Now the woman made food, and it became daylight that morning. Then the two remained together quietly all day. And they remained together for a long time. And then spring came. And then the people found out that he lived with her. So then his paternal grandmother and his maternal grandmother went across the river straight to his house.

And then he thought to himself: "The two old women are poor. Thus also on me did my paternal grandmother and my maternal grandmother take pity." So then he gave the two of them to eat. He gave the old women salmon, and he gave them sturgeon. And then the two old women started home. They went across the river.

For a long time they were there. And then the story got about, and the people said: "Oh! There is much salmon and plenty of sturgeon and eels and blue-back salmon at the boy's." Now snow had begun to fall gently, gently. There was no food among the people. The people were hungry.

And then the people said: "Let us too go to the boy." Now then his paternal grandmother and his maternal grandmother again went across the river first. And then they got close to the house. And then a great many people went across the river to the boy.

Now then the boy turned his head and looked. He saw the people crossing in a canoe in great numbers. And then he thought to himself: "It is not well thus when they abandoned me." Then, indeed, he caused an east wind to arise. A strong east wind arose and there was snow. All died in the water; the people were drowned.

Badly[210] the boy thought to himself: "Thus they did to me. They abandoned me." And again others went across the river. And them also he treated as before: a strong wind blew, and snow arose. And again they died; twice the people died. And only the two old women remained. Thus the myth.

40B. THE DESERTED BOY (II)[211]

There was a very mean boy at Spedis. He fought with the other children all the time. The boy's grandmother[s] had an underground house. An old man said, "We are going to take him into the hills across the river and leave him."

Those two old women said, "No!" They cried.

He said, "Yes, he is too mean." At last he took the boy across the river. The two old women never stopped crying. The men went over there to cut sticks for the hoop of the hoop and pole game. They left him there.

One young man said, "We will defecate." They made a face in the feces with a stick and told it, "If you hear a cry, you call out." They put another far inside the clump of bushes where they cut the sticks.

The mean boy said, "It is a long time now. I have lots of sticks." So he shouted, "Ho!"

Somebody shouted, "Ho!"

He called again and then went over there. Again he called and heard the reply. He went there, but there was no one. He saw the feces with mouths.

He said, "I guess they deserted me." So he took the sticks.

When he reached home nobody was there except the magpies. Everyone else was across the river playing the hoop and pole game. He went into the house and cried. He heard something going *k'e, k'e*, like a fire. He looked around until he found it; it was something to make string of.

He said, "I am going to make a trap to catch magpies." He made it and caught many of them. He dried the skins. He used the string to sew them together to make a blanket for sleeping. He measured: "It is long enough for me to sleep."

Then he went fishing and caught a chub. He roasted it at the fire and ate one side. He kept the other for the morning. He said, "Oh, I am all right."

So he slept under his magpie blanket. Next morning he put it on, tying it around his neck, and went fishing again. He got two fish. He cooked one and kept one for evening. "I am getting on all right."

Next morning he fished again. Pretty soon he got something; it was heavy and nearly pulled him in. It was put there by a woman of the river people, the daughter of *Itc!E'kian*, a river man. They had tied a big basket of salmon, camas, and berries to his line.

He pulled it in. "Oh, I have something." He opened it. "Oh, my!" He danced. As he danced his blanket flapped straight out behind.

The people who had left him now saw him. "Something happened to that mean boy. He is dancing close to the river." He took the basket to his house. Soon he ate and slept again. He was glad.

That woman got ready at night. She was a young girl. She had long hair. She made a nice house. She put nice blankets in it. The boy had nothing but his magpie skins. She wished him to be a man now. She put him in her bed.

In the morning he looked all around. He saw the blankets. He saw himself: "My, I am big." He turned and saw the woman. He was afraid and astonished by her nice clothes. He said nothing. She knew what he thought.

She said, "That food I sent you because you were poor and deserted. Now I have come to stay with you."

He said, "All right."

That morning the people saw it and said, "Look, that mean boy now has a good house. Smoke is coming out of it." They thought about him.

Those two stayed there until they had a little boy and a girl. They grew quickly. He told his wife. "I guess we will go to see my grandmother. Perhaps she is still alive." She agreed. He made a bow and arrow for the little boy. She made a little basket and digging stick for the girl. The boy tried to shoot. Those people across the river saw it and talked about him. But they never came across, because they were ashamed.

So the family crossed to see the man's grandmother. They traveled; the boy tried to shoot birds.

"Oh, a different man is coming," the people said. He knew because his wife had given him power. His grandmother, blind and poor, was sitting in the underground house, crying continually.

He went in and said, "Oh, you two are alive yet?"

One said, "*Eh.*" He told them who he was. They cried, "No, you are a man. That was a little boy."

He said, "Yes, that is me." But they did not believe him. He made them believe. So they returned across the river with him.

That is all I know of this story.

VIII. "Petroglyphs—Wishham." Special Collections Division, Univ. of Washington Libraries. Edward S. Curtis, c. 1910, NAI166

VI. TALES OF MONSTERS AND OGRES

41. EAGLE AND WEASEL[212]

Weasel and Eagle went along. They saw two women. Then Eagle told Weasel (to no purpose as it turned out): "Don't go to them."

Weasel assented to him.

They went on a little farther, and then Weasel ran off, ran after the two women. Then Weasel seized one of the women and knocked the woman over. And then the two heard the earth tremble. In truth, Eagle [sic] had seized the wife of a certain *Gayaba'xem*.[213]

And then the monster pursued them and made a terrible noise with his rattles, something like *Lali* it sounded. The earth shook, so angered was *Gayaba'xem*.

Now then the two saw that he was pursuing them. And then Weasel became afraid. They went back toward the rocks, where there was a cave. They entered into it.

And then *Gayaba'xem* came and bit at the rocks. The rocks kept shaking. And then Weasel went out and looked at him. He saw how his eyes were shining, and how he was biting the rocks.

And then Weasel thought: "When standing at his side, one could strike him on his nose." So then Weasel took hold of a stick this long.[214] And then he slowly went up to him, stood close to him.

Slowly he struck him; again he struck him; again he struck him; again he struck him; again he struck him.

And then *Gayaba'xem* died.

Now then he said to Eagle: "I have killed him now. You for your part are still afraid. Now come! Come here and look at him. He is dead now."

So then Eagle went; he looked at him. And indeed, *Gayaba'xem* was dead. Weasel had slain him. And then they cut him up. Everything they cut off: his skin, his head, his rattle; everything Weasel and Eagle cut loose.

And then the two started off and went on. Now then Eagle put the skin of *Gayaba'xem* over his head. So then he made a noise with his rattle something like *La'i*.

And then Weasel said: "Well! You are a chief and again do you now put it [i.e., the skin] over your head? Now I, Weasel, shall put it over my head." Thus Weasel said to him.

And then Weasel said to him: "If you do not give it to me, I shall kill you, Eagle."

So then Eagle said to him: "Now I shall give it to you."Eagle thought: "Truly Weasel says that he is bad."

To Weasel he said: "Now you, Weasel, put it [i.e., the skin of the monster] over your head!" And then he gave it to him, and Weasel put it over his head.

Now then the two went on. Weasel went behind, Eagle went on alone. Now, Weasel had the skin of *Gayaba'xem* over his head. And then Weasel made a noise:"La'2i2." Truly Eagle listened, there yonder Weasel was making a noise. And then he listened and Weasel was making a noise above. And again Eagle listened, listened to his younger brother.

And then Eagle thought: "It is not well that my poor brother be a person(?)." So then Eagle exercised his supernatural power upon his younger brother. Straightway Weasel fell down to the ground. Then Eagle loosened the skin from him.

And then Weasel was spoken to: "You are not fit for this, Weasel. This strong *Gayaba'xem* is something different from what is fit for you." Then Eagle loosened it from him. And then Eagle carried that same skin on his back.

Now then he and his younger brother went on. Then indeed Weasel thought: "It is not well that Eagle took it back again from me. Now I shall kill him." And then Weasel went on. He sat down far away. And then Weasel took his arrows and sat down across from the trail. And then they were shot at Eagle. In vain he tried to wound him, but he did not wound him. Eagle went on unharmed. Then again Weasel went to fetch his arrows and again went and sat down close to him. Now again he shot at his elder brother; again he did not wound him. Thus did Eagle and Weasel. Thus the myth.[215]

42. *TUH-TAN-NAH*[216]

Tuh-tan-nah [Tah-tah kle-ah] was carrying two little boys in her basket, taking them to her cave-lodge to eat. She came to a stream, not large, but about as wide as the length of a tepee pole. She went to cross this stream and began jumping back and forth in the water. Soon she stopped and listened. She said, "*Eh*! I thought I heard a voice say, '*Tuh-tan-nah's* children are burning up!'"

The two boys in the basket heard her say this, and they thought, "We will try that. Maybe we can get away!"

Then the boys five times made the call: "*Tuh-tan-nah's* children are burning up! *Tuh-tan-nah's* children are burning up!"

Tuh-tan-nah ran. She fell down! She jumped up, left her basket on the ground. She left the two boys and ran away fast. The boys took sharp rocks and pounded a hole in the bottom of the basket, and crawled through to liberty. They put rocks in the basket to fool *Tuh-tan-nah*. Then they ran away from that place, traveling as fast as they could.

An old man lived by the river. He was making sticks to play the ballgame. The two boys came to this old man and said, "We wish you would put us across the river."

Qash-qash knew! He answered, "All right! I will put you across the river."

Then *Qash-qash*, the kind old man, stretched out his long leg across the river, and the two boys walked over it to the other side.

When they had passed safely on the old man's leg and were resting on the other side of the river, *Tuh-tan-nah* came up and asked the old man, "Did you put somebody across the river? Two boys came this way."

Qash-qash made answer, "Yes, they went across."

"How did you put them across?"

Qash-qash was honest. He would not lie, and he told her, "I stretched out my leg and made a bridge to walk over."

Tuh-tan-nah was hard to convince. She said, "Let me see how you do this."

The old man put his leg far out over the water, made it to reach the other shore of the river. *Tuh-tan-nah* asked, "Can you put me across? They are my boys I am after."

"Yes, if you are not afraid, I will put you across."

"How do you do it?"

"You must step where I tell you, and I will put you across. If you don't, I will not put you across."

Tuh-tan-nah walked out on the leg-bridge. She came close to the knee. She stopped, was afraid to step on the knee. *Qash-qash* spoke, "Step on my knee right here!"

"No, I am afraid."

Three times, four times, *Qash-qash* told *Tuh-tan-nah* to step on his knee, but she refused. The fifth time the old man told her to step on his knee, *Tuh-tan-nah* did so. *Qash-qash* moved his knee, and *Tuh-tan-nah* fell into the river. *Qash-qash* saved the two boys.

One old man was fishing below in the river. *Tuh-tan-nah* came floating on the water. She grabbed hold of the rocks, but she would not stop, could not save herself. She came to the old man fishing. She caught him around his neck and then came ashore, not drowned. The old man took the rocks from her basket. When *Tuh-tan-nah* saw the rocks, she understood. She knew how the boys had fooled her, how they had escaped from her.

Tuh-tan-nah now traveled on down the river. Coyote [*Paht-paht*], wisest and greatest of all men, was coming up the river. He was nearly meeting *Tuh-tan-nah*. He did not know how he could pass her and not get killed.

43. THE BOY THAT WAS STOLEN
BY *AT!AT!A'LIYA*[217]

The chief's wife was cleaning up the house. And then they went to get grass and she cut it. Then she laid her child down and went off far away from him, while she was cutting the grass. Now she finished her work and went to her child. She arrived there. Her child was not to be seen. The only thing she saw, a single track, striped like a basket, where her child had lain.

They sought to find him, but in vain. He was not to be seen. And then they all went home. Now then the men went to search more carefully, took their arrows along. Again as before they found only a track; again as before it was striped like a basket.

So then they turned back and arrived home. They said: "There is no boy." And then all the people mourned.[218]

Now in truth it was that *At!at!a'liya*[219] who had stolen him. She took him straight to her children for eating. But then again she liked him and just raised him for herself. Now she used to go to dig up black snakes and frogs, or toads, and took them home with her. She used to roast them, and when tender, they were done. And then he used to eat them. Now he grew up quickly and became big.

She used to say to her children: "He is your younger brother." Now he saw they looked different from himself. Their flesh looked different from his own. His flesh was like a human being's. As for them, their flesh was marked in stripes.

Then he thought to himself: "Why, perchance, is it thus?" He was puzzled. But ever she spoke of him as her son, and he, for his part, thought much of her.

Whatever her children would do to him, she would take his part. She would say to them: "He is your younger brother."

Now he killed various animals, various birds with his arrows. Always she would say to him: "Do not go off in that direction." Now he was always hunting, and even killed a deer.

And then he thought: "Why, perchance, has she always been telling me, 'You shall not go off in that direction'?"

Then he thought to himself: "Now I shall go just

yonder."

And off he went in just that direction. He came to a narrow trail. There lay this stick. He was about to step across over it; then it arose. He was about to pass by it; again there was this stick. Then he stepped on it; it broke right in two.

"*A'nnanana*," groaned the person in pain. "Was it I, perchance, that stole him? And yet he broke my leg, and indeed I was about to let him know something.[220] My leg is valuable, my thighbone is of jingles,[221] of beads is my knee, of *alxa'plxap*[222] my ankle, of dentalium my shinbone."

Then he said to her: "Oh! But you did not tell me before." And then he made her leg well again, as it was before.

Then she said to him: "Wait, I shall go and tell your great-grandfather."[223] Then she ran off and a sprinkle of rain arose. Now in truth Thunder was her husband, and she went to tell him.

"Now I shall tell you. That one is not your mother. That woman is different from you. Your cradleboard is in the back part of the underground lodge, at the rear end. When you get there, then you shall split up pitchwood. Then you shall stick some of it into every part of the underground lodge. Then, when she goes off somewhere, you will set fire to the pitch, and her children will burn. When her children will have all burned, then go to yonder place, where an old man is dwelling." She pointed it out to him.

And then he went home. Then he did as directed. He stuck pitch about their underground lodge. Now then she went off again, went digging. Then he, for his part, pretended to go hunting. Then he turned back again and came to where they all were.

He said to them [i.e., the ogre's children]: "Let

me louse[224] you." So then he loused them. He laid them on his legs and they all slept on him. Then he tied their hair to one another's and set fire to them.

Now then he went off immediately. Again he turned back, again he went off. Five times he turned back, five tracks he made. And then he went to the old man; (first he got his cradleboard).

While *At!at!a'liya* was digging, her digging-stick broke right in two. "Oh, the stinker!" she cried, "Now he has done something to my children." Now then she went straight home. She arrived there; their house was all burning now. Then she tracked him at the first track he had made. Again she turned back. And then she became puzzled. Five times she tracked him before she followed him rightly.

As for him, he had reached the old man. He was fishing with a dipnet on the other side, across the river. Then he stretched out his leg across the river.

The Old Man said to him: "You shall not stand on my knee." So he went straight up to his knee and stepped over it. Now in truth this Old Man with the long leg was Crane.

And then he took him to his house. He made him vomit all those various bad things that he had been eating. Then he gave him all sorts of good things--bull trout, chubs, steelhead salmon, trout, Chinook salmon. He ate them, finished eating. Then he clothed him, gave him a leather cape and all sorts of clothing. And he gave him five quivers of arrows and a bow.

And then he pointed out his way: "You shall go to yonder mountains. There you will shoot upwards all these five quiverfuls of yours." Then he did just that.

The youth shot clear to the sky. He caused the arrows to stand one on top of another clear down to the ground. Then he climbed up there. As he climbed up, then also he took off his arrows.

The youth arrived up in the sky. Behold! He saw people. He met them and said to them: "Whither are you going?"

"No! We are going to ride on the heads of Indians." Now in truth those were the Lice, dressed all in black.[225]

Again he went farther ahead. Again he met still other people. He asked them: "Whither are you going?"

"No! We are going to hang on to the hair of Indians." Now in truth those were the Nits.

Again he went on farther ahead. Again he saw still others coming. "Whither are you going?"

"No! We are going to stay in the breech-clouts of Indians." Now in truth they were the Graybacks.

He went farther ahead and saw a person coming. He met him. He carried something on his back; it was tightly closed. Then he asked him: "What is this that you are taking along with you?"

"No! These are nights that I am taking along with me." Then he opened his box and it became entirely dark. Then he closed it again and it became all light again.[226] And then he passed him again.

He saw a person coming again. He met him. "*Ah, ah!*" he was groaning. He had been shot in the heart, an arrow stuck to him. A little farther ahead--there he fell down and died.[227] He went farther ahead; he saw a person coming in haste.[228, 229]

44. THE CANNIBAL WOMAN[230]

There was a girl and a little boy at Spedis. These two were very smart. They were looking for arrowheads, which they found. An ugly woman named *At!at!a'liya* came. She had a big basket in which she put them. She covered them and tied them in. Then she carried them to her house near Celilo. She had many children there, which she always roasted.

The girl hurt the boy. He cried, "Sister, you hurt me."

The woman said "[i.e., That is a sign that] my children got burned."

His sister whispered, "Say it again;" and he did.

The woman said, "Somebody hollered, 'my children got burned.' I will have to leave this basket."

When they reached there these two children were all right. The two cut a hole in the basket and got out. Then they stuffed the basket with grass and roots.

The two fled. The girl carried the boy some of the time. When they reached the river again, an old man told them, "I will take you over there."

The woman found that they were gone when she opened the basket. So she followed them. They went across in the old man's canoe, but she swam after them

She tried to catch them, but she was drowned. The old man took them across the river. She floated down until she stood upright as a big rock. She has breasts and her basket on her back. That is why there are no more cannibal women about. All the children are shown that rock.[231]

VII. TALES COMPARABLE WITH EUROPEAN *MÄRCHEN*

45. A WISHOM LEGEND[232, 233]

A boy made five quivers of arrows. He said to his parents, "I am going now." He went towards the sunrise. He traveled so far and stuck an arrow in the ground. He traveled on and placed another arrow. Thus he continued until all the arrows of one quiver were used. He did the same thing with his second quiver of arrows, and then the third quiver was used. Then the arrows from the fourth quiver were placed at distances apart, as had been the arrows from the other three quivers.[234]

Now he had reached where the sun comes up. He still had the fifth quiver of arrows, the last one. He started beyond the sunrise, placing arrows as he went. He came to a lodge where he found a young woman. She was the daughter, but her father was not there. He was a bad man, always traveling about, bringing people to his lodge to eat them.

The girl said to the boy, "My father is a bad man. He will kill you and eat you.[235] But I will hide you some way."

The boy answered, "All right! You can hide me somewhere."

The girl covered the boy with skins, placing them all over him. Soon they heard a great noise. It was a roaring like a big storm in the forest, a terrible thing to hear. The girl said, "My father is coming! He is bringing people with him to eat them."

The man entered the lodge. He said, "Daughter, somebody is here."

She answered him, "No! You smell the people you have killed and brought here."

He answered, "No, I smell somebody."

"No, you smell your own dead people," his daughter answered him.

"No, I smell somebody here," replied the bad father.

"No, you smell those you have brought here and killed," was the answer.

"No, it is a different person I smell," he continued.

"No, it is the same people you have killed," his daughter said.

"No, I smell one different from the others," he answered.

"No, it is not different. You smell those you have brought with you after killing them for food."

This was the fifth time that he had spoken thus, and five times his daughter had answered him, "No." This ended the talk. The bad father did not find the boy hidden under the skins.

The next day the bad father again went hunting for people to eat. The girl said to the boy, "You now see! This is the way my father does every day. I will help you if I can."

The girl knew that the boy was good. They talked five times about what to do, repeated five times what they thought was best. The boy said, "I will go bring all kinds of food. I will have everything cooked ready when he comes. He will kill people no more."

The girl listened and then answered, "He is coming! I hear his coming in the distance."

The boy had everything cooked, all kinds of birds

and animals.

The father entered the lodge. He spoke to the girl, "Daughter, I smell something nice!"

The girl made reply, "Yes, your son-in-law has brought all kinds of food."

Then the boy showed up. He said to the man, "When we eat, we will be through." They ate of what had been cooked. The boy said to his father-in-law, "Come outside."

They went outside the lodge. Deer, buffalo, elk, and every kind of animal good for food was seen like *moos-moos* (cattle) in the pasture. The man killed no more people for food. He said to the boy, "This is well, my son-in-law! I am glad you have come."

In time the young man became the father of a boy and girl. He now thought to go back to his own people, taking his wife and children. The old man gave his son-in-law a suit of buckskins, gave one each for himself, his wife and the two children. He gave his himself, his wife and the two children. He gave his son-in-law the entire country; so when he got back home, he would have the whole country to give to his people. When he arrived home, he told the people everything. The gifts and the land were given away among his people.[236]

IX. "Dip-netting in Pools-Wishham." Special
Collections Div., Univ. of Washington Libraries.
Edward S. Curtis, c, 1909 photo NAI208

III. TWO ORAL TRADITIONAL HISTORIES OF BRAVE DEEDS AND DARING

A. AUTOBIOGRAPHY OF *CHE-POS TO-COS* (OWL CHILD), ALSO KNOWN AS *SHAT-TAW-WEE* (LEADER IN BATTLE), WHOSE ENGLISH NAME WAS ALEC McCOY[237]

I. I was born at The Dalles, Oregon; we call the place Wasco.[238] I was born on the site of the old Wishom village which was burned by the soldiers during the Yakima War, 1855-56.[239] My father, *Pul-kus*, was of the Wishom tribe, while my mother, *An-nee-swolla*, was a Wasco woman.[240] I went to school about three years at Warm Springs. I got tired and went with a cattleman.[241] I could ride, was a chunk of a boy, and could ride well. I should have gone to school. Many say that William Charley[242] can read and write. I could have done the same had I not left school. I see all this now when an old man and too late.

II.   Entering in Portland, Oregon, [over the Southern Pacific railway along the Willamette River] when a boy I saw many lodges of Indians built of hewn lumber boards and bark.[243] No white men were here then; no part of the city of Portland was to be seen. Timber was here, and Indians with their canoes, bows and arrows. I came down from The Dalles with my people, sometimes in canoes and sometimes with horses. It was a bad trail traveling down the river in places.

Two Hudson Bay [sic] men disputed about which were the best canoe men, the Cascade Indians, or the Willamettes who lived where Portland now stands. A race was arranged between the two chiefs. The wager was guns, blankets, ammunition, and other goods. The two canoes, each with four or five men, started at the Cascades to race to [what is now] Portland. At the signal, the boats leaped ahead like racehorses. The Cascades pulled ahead, but the Willamettes drew up along with them. The Willamette chief stood up in his canoe. The Cascade chief told him to sit down or he would break his paddle. The Willamette did not mind him. He [i.e., the Cascade chief] repeated his order three times, and then with his power [*tahmahnawis*?] he broke the Willamette's paddle. He took up another one, which was also broken in the same manner. Then the Willamette sat down, and the race was continued, all rowing hard.

But the Cascades, used to rough water, were the stronger of the men, and they won over the Willamettes, who were not so strong with the paddle. They lived where the waters ran smooth and easy to canoe. It was a friendly race, done in one day's time. Camping, we usually spent two or three days making the trip, landing and hunting as we came.

III. It was while I was living at The Dalles, on

the Washington side of the *n-Che-wana* [Columbia River], when I was about twelve years old.[244] An old man used to tell me what to do. There is a deep hole down in the rocks, which is hid when the river is full. When the water is low, this hole is empty with only water in the bottom, but this water is very deep. It is way down and dark at night. The old man told me, "You take off your clothes; go down into this hole at night. Halloo first, then go head first into the water.[245] Do this five times. If you do this and do not lie to me, you will live a long time. Nothing will hurt you. It will make you strong; it will make you a good boy. If you do not do this, you will never be able to do the things of a man. You will not live long."

I went the first time. I was scared, but I did as he told me. I wanted to grow up strong. I left my clothes on the sandbar island. I went down the deep hole. I hallooed and went into the water headfirst. This I did five times, as the old man told me. This was in the fall. He never told me to do it except in the fall. In the summer, it must be something different [to do]. Sometimes he would send me twice, maybe three times each fall.[246] Yes, I would hear things, but I must not tell.[247]

He sent me up among rocks, by a burial ground. I saw fire streaks passing and crossing in the dark. Nobody saw it but me. I heard the dead talking. Once I lost sense, and I think that I was in the house. When I woke up, I was sitting in the graveyard. I was not scared. I saw and heard things in the dark, but I cannot tell them to you now. Only when I dance sometimes at night can I tell what I saw and heard.[248] Then it is all right to tell. Then I do not lose my power by telling.[249]

IV. When fourteen or fifteen years old, I went to Montana.[250, 251] I stayed with white men only. I worked for a rich man, a German named Koss, as I understood it. He had a big house, plenty of cattle and horses. I did right in everything, and the man liked me. He said, "You are the best boy I have working. You are better than any of the whites. I like you the same as my own boy. You stay here and go to school in winter and do chores. In the summer, I will pay you wages." He gave me good clothes. He had many hired hands, but I was the only Indian boy. He set a long table. It was made of iron and cost $250 at Deer Lodge. I thought, "I will be a big man, will grow up rich." He advised me how he took care of himself when young. He said, "I was a poor boy, but now I am the richest man in the valley. You do as I tell you. Take no whiskey. It will ruin you." He had sheep and cattle and mines. He had everything. I went to school there three winters.

But I did not like four walls about me.[252] Riding the open, I saw the wide desert plains, the high mountains, the streams, the woods. Something kept calling from out the wilds. I heard--I knew! It was the Spirit Power which I found when a little boy.[253] I have told you about it before. I knew what power had been given me. I knew what I must do. I left my best friend for the lands of the Piegans (Blackfeet) across the Canadian border. But after a short time I again thought to go back among whites. I needed money.

V. I found a job with an English army officer.[254] He had five hundred horses to break and gentle. We argued for a day and a half. I wanted five dollars for breaking and riding one horse. He offered me two dollars and a half. It was hard and dangerous work. A half-blood named Garry advised me to take the offer. He said, "They will not offer you any more. It is lots of money. You better take it."

I then told the officer I would take his offer. He asked me to stand up and raise my right hand. I stood up and with my hand up I agreed to break horses to riding for two dollars and fifty cents a head. It was too cheap. It was very dangerous--some awfully wild and mean horses. I was wild and a good rider, but I soon got tired.

I worked about three months. I did not like it. That spirit-voice still called me to a different life, a life for which it had fitted me. One white fellow was there and I said to him, "I do not like it here. Too hard. I will die before I get through. I am going to quit."

The man looked at me, sizing me up. He said, "Do not tell what I am saying to you. Do not repeat to anybody. Laws here are very strict. This is English country. Do not ask for pay. You will get nothing. If you ask pay and mention to quit, you will be sent to prison. You have a good horse. Better get on that horse and ride away. Do not ask for your wages."

I did as the half-blood told me. I said nothing; asked for no pay. I did not want to be locked up. Taking only my clothes, I rode away in the night. By break of day I crossed to the American side. I went to the Piegans in Montana, where I stayed eight snows. But I still held to the English I had learned. One white man asked me while I was there, "Where did you learn English? You speak plainer than schoolchildren." I explained how I learned to talk English. I never interpret if I do not think that I understand. At the end of eight years, I came back to my tribe here. My Piegan wife died within one snow when I did not return as I promised her. I have a daughter there. We exchange letters often.

VI. Owl Child served in the Modoc War of 1873 as a member of the famous Warm Springs Indian Scouts for the government.[255] He enlisted under the name of

"Jack Butler."[256] But he never received the well-earned pension to which he was entitled. He gave an account of the capture of Captain Jack.

"We were attacking the Modocs.[257] We lay down, bullets striking the rocks about us. One man said, 'Let's get out of here.'"

"All right," said *Topplesh*, who was brave, and he jumped first, going toward the Modocs. He jumped and lay down, jumped and lay down. Advancing, we finally got to the Modocs. One Warm Springs man, just before we made these advances, stood up and danced, defying the Modocs, making himself a brave man by making sport of the Modocs. He was shot through and through, from one side to the other, killed dead. His name was *Wah-sen-i-ke*.

We fought hard. When we first fought, we were cautious, did not like to show up [i.e., reveal themselves?]. We went ahead all the time. Different Indians got together at a nighttime council. "What you know?"

"Power," one would say. "When I sleep, I can tell you in the morning if I see blood on our side.[258] I can talk tomorrow." That man slept. "We are all right. Be careful. I saw nothing, and we will lose no man."[259]

Another fellow said, "If you see our enemies, do not get excited. Keep cool, keep going, make your hearts strong, make your heads clear. Do good work. Do not shoot till enemies show up. Go ahead all the time. That is my dream. When we get through with this, I will tell you more the next night."

When we fought away [?] ourselves [i.e., like?] snakes, we always had a song from our man, sending sleep to the enemy. (He held out his hand--waving to and fro). This gives us good strong minds and brings rest to us, while it makes the enemy sleepy.[260] The next morning he would say, "We will be all right. I saw no blood on

our side. But be careful. I think we will get them easy.
That is what we are here for. Go ahead and fight. Do not
be afraid a bullet will hit you."

This same thing he would do in the evening, not
morning, so he could dream and see. If he said, "I had
the dream. I saw blood on our side. Be careful yourselves." Then we may be killed. He worked on himself
this way every evening, all the same. He said, "We will
capture Captain Jack. I saw him, women and children.
We got him. What I say, always remember my words. I
am telling you that when we get him, it will be ended.
We will quit. This is the last time I will see him. I am
going to sing a song. Warriors, get your guns. Make a
dance like my song to win."

He made a song in the evening. The next morning, he said, "We got him, no difference how he fights.
Do not be afraid; we got him."

Captain Jack was captured that morning. When
we got there, Captain Jack dropped his arms, his guns.
He said, "When I heard you soldiers, I thought to give
up. But I fought. I thought, "If I give up, I do not care.
But why do I give up with the gun ready in my hand? I
do not know what makes me that way."²⁶¹

The song man said, "I said I was doing this to
you. My songs that I sing made it to you like that."

This is what the song man, *Tip-see*, said to
Captain Jack. This man was sort of a medicine man. He
had a long stick of hard wood [with gray bark and white
flowers] with notches cut in it.²⁶² He scraped another stick
over these notches making a strong noise.²⁶³, ²⁶⁴

VII. Owl Child has an ugly scar just above the
small of his back which he decorates with two circles of
red paint when doing the war dance, stripped as for battle

during the tribal wars.[265] Of this scar he gave L.V. McWhorter the following story.

"We were fighting, had been fighting for half the sun's travel through the sky. The Crows [Indians] came too thick, too many for us. My comrades ran way. I also went, but was the hindmost one. A Crow on a fast horse came after me. He had a big knife; and as I lay low on my horse, he reached out and struck me in the back. Not deep, for he could not reach far enough to drive in the knife. I was bad scared; the Crow was yelling loud and fierce. I had a good horse and I escaped with only a wounded back."

VIII.   In still another battle between Owl Child and the Sioux, he barely escaped with his life.[266] According to Owl Child, "There were eighteen of us in Chief Lone Man's band of the Blackfeet; and we were attacked by the Sioux who outnumbered us. We fought all day, all night, and the second day the Blackfeet escaped. I was on horseback when a Sioux struck me, hit me in the head with a gun, the lock sinking into my forehead. I must have fallen into the creek instead of being thrown in by the enemy. We were close by the stream, and I was knocked senseless and knew nothing. Three Blackfeet [had been] killed, and some of the enemy, but I do not know how many. I lost my gun and horse.

When I fell in the creek, I must have worked downstream. The water was deep, and when my life returned to me, I found myself against some drift, my neck against some brush, holding my head above water.

I was bad suffering for three days, thinking I should die. It was nighttime, nearly daylight, and I was sitting propped up, my head hurting me badly. I heard a voice just back of me, speaking over my shoulder. It said, "What did I tell you when you were a boy?[267] Have you forgotten? Did I not tell you that if you should ever get hurt or wounded, to go into the water and you would not die?"

I turned my head and I saw this fellow Otter [i.e., designating an otter skin] standing there behind me.[268] I said, "Yes, I remember now. My head hurting me, I could not think."

He spoke again, "Go do as I told you, and you will not die."

I crawled to the river and lay in the water. I dipped water over my head, putting it on my wound. I felt better and got well."

IX. On still another occasion, Owl Child escaped unscathed from seven Indians, and stole their best mount.[269] According to Owl Child, "I was living with the Piegans in Montana when it happened. It was in the evening, some time before sundown. I was hunting alone on the open prairie, in the buffalo country. I had a short, muzzle-loading musket and a big knife. I was dressed in breech clout and leggings only. I was riding slow. Soon my horse turned his head and looked off to the left. I did not look around. Soon my horse again looked to the left. I did not pay attention. I should have looked to see what was there, but did not do so. Then my horse stopped, half-turned, and watched in the same direction. Then I looked quickly. Seven Indians were riding towards me hard. They were about four hundred yards away. They were Flatheads and Nez Perce, who were at war with the Blackfeet. I did not run. I thought, "This is my last day, and I will die brave."

I was not scared. I got off my horse and stood on the side from the Indians. They came a little closer and then started to circle to the right. That is the way Indians always circle. They do not go to the left like you see in

the pictures sometimes. One Indian was in the lead, on a
fine black horse. I thought to kill that Indian. I shot
across my horse, aiming at the lower body of that Indian.
The ball did not rise in the sight, and I killed the black
horse. He fell and fastened the Indian's leg under him. I
first thought I killed them both, but the Indian was not
hurt. He got up, and then all the Indians came on me
before I got my gun loaded. They grabbed my gun and
knife. Four Indians caught my arms and held them out
straight and tight, two holding each arm. They did not
talk. I knew their minds. I was not of their tribes, and
they would kill me. I was a warrior and would die brave.

Then one Indian stood before me with a breech
loading carbine, only one breechloader in the bunch. He
raised his gun right in front of me only about five feet
away. He aimed at my forehead. I looked into that gun.
The gun snapped. The Indian worked the lever to throw
out the bad shell. He tried to throw in another shell, but
that shell stuck tight. He could not get it in place. He
worked at it and tried several times, but it would not
move. Then another Indian came behind me and struck
me on the left side of the head with his gun. You can see
this dent cut in my ear. That lick woke me up. I knew
what I would do. I was a strong young man, about
twenty-seven years old. I jerked down hard with my arms
and body. I went down on the ground free from those
Indians holding me. I did not try to get up. I quickly
placed my feet and hands on the ground and jumped
hard. I landed about across this *Pom-pom* house [about
twenty feet]. The Indians did not see me go. I looked
back and they were on the ground trying to find me.
They could not see me. They were grabbing hard. They
could not find me.

Their horses were feeding right close to us. I ran
and leaped on the back of a grey horse with an Indian pad

saddle. I leaped high and lit right astride of that horse. I hit with the bridle whip, and he jumped quick. I looked back, and the Indians saw me. They fired at me, but missed me. That grey horse was a good horse, a race horse, and I rode hard. The Indians got horses and rode after me and fired at me again. They did not hit me. They could not catch me. I had their best horse, and I was leaving them behind. I looked back and laughed at them. They loaded their guns as they rode, and fired at me again. I laughed, for they missed me. I crooked my finger at them and yelled bad words at them. I said, "You are only women. You cannot fight a warrior. You cannot ride fast horses like a warrior. Go home and break wood for the squaws. You are not men. I am a warrior and get away from seven of you. You are no good."

They whipped their horses, but after awhile they quit. I got away safe. That was one thing I did. I got away from seven Indians on the open plain. Not many ever do that. They got my horse, gun and knife; but I got their best horse. If I had had a breechloading gun, I could have shot several times as they came at me. I would have killed some of those Indians."[270]

X. Owl Child told of an adventure he had with a buffalo cow.[271] He said, "We were a party of Piegan Blackfeet hunting buffalo. I was riding bareback, stripped for the chase. I had a buffalo- hide-rope bridle, Indian style. It was looped to the horses's underjaw by a buckskin thong. Buckskin is soft and does not hurt the mouth, as does the hard rawhide-buffalo-rope.

I rode fast after a young cow, about three snows old. She was fat and almost black, and I could tell by the horns also as to her age. I threw my lasso rope made of buffalo hide and caught her horns and pulled on the rope. That cow stopped and came at me. My horse was smart.

He dodged her charge four times, and four times I
reached over and stabbed her with a big, heavy knife I
carried, made from a file.[272] Soon blood came from her
mouth and I knew that she was about to die. She fell and
soon breathed her last. My people came and found me
standing there by the dead cow, brave. No one had ever
done such work before.[273]

Another time Black Feather, a young man, was
charged by a great buffalo bull which killed his horse[274].
As the bull struck the horse, Black Feather leaped onto
his back and held tight to the shaggy mane. The bull ran
with the others of the herd and after going some distance,
Black Feather slid off from behind the bull and hid in
some bushes. The bull did not seem to know that he was
being ridden; did not try to throw Black Feather. Maybe
he only wanted to get away with the other buffalo; I do
not know. I saw it all but was not close enough to help
my friend. Usually when a hunter's horse was killed, he
jumped up behind another man and thus escaped. Sometimes the man was killed if he had no chance to mount
with a nearby friend.

XI.   Another time Owl Child was out hunting: we
were out after the buffalo.[275] It was in the Sweet Grass
Country, where these animals were plenty and fat. That
was a good grass land; and the name tells you that the
grass was nice to chew, the only place where the grass is
good to taste. There were several of us, a great many of
the Piegans, and the women were there to care for the
meat after the killing had been done. Always a hunting
party was made up of entire families, women and children with the men--different from the war party, where
only at times some brave women accompanied the
warriors.

As in war, in these hunting bands were always

some young men who showed their skill and daring by doing brave and dangerous acts. Maybe I was that way myself. It is what the white people call being "smart." I guess that is the way of all races of people. We were charging, riding fast in the dust of the buffaloes. I had a good pony, a fast-running horse, fine in sense. I knew what I could do when riding that fine-built horse. Above the rumbling beat of hundreds and hundreds of hooves, you could hear the challenge-call from some wild-riding warrior, dashing ahead where danger was thick should his horse go down from stepping in a hidden badger-hole. But I never saw any such accident in all my hunting and war trips.

One bull, a mighty bull, tall and long, I saw ahead of me and a little apart from the main pack of the herd. "*Eh-ou!*" I knew what I would do. I gave a loud call of my intentions, a call all who heard would understand. Then I rode faster, faster still, crowding that great bull closer against the flank of the herd. The bull was just like an out-riding guard to an Indian moving camp. He did not turn on me, but if he did I knew what my horse would do. Closer and closer I pressed that bull. I was close, but I did not try shooting. He was too big for good meat, and I wanted to do something else with him. I would show all the Indians what I could do. I crowded the bull hard against the close-packed herd, and once I thought he was going to charge me. But no. His face went straight fronting [to the front], and only a side-glance he gave me. He seemed not afraid.

Now my horse had drawn close enough to that bull. I had my gun and I must hold to it. I sprang from my bare-backed horse, lighting well on the back of that galloping bull. A leg on each side of him, my hand was buried in his shaggy mane. He did not buck, that bull! But he snorted, leaped away faster, never stopping. I held on, and the Indians were all yelling delight. They were witnesses to what I was doing--riding a big buffalo bull with his herd. I held my gun high and gave the whoop which told of victory. I rode some distance--not too far-- then jumped to the ground, bringing with me a wisp of the buffalo's mane. I would wear that tied to my hair. No, I did not stumble and fall. I struck the ground running. On my thumbs I gave a whistle-call, and my horse came swiftly to me. That was the way many war and hunting horses were trained. Yes, he was the same horse I rode when with the knife I killed the buffalo cow. Yes, he had a name. I called him *Ki-ets-ke*, "bald-face." A bay horse, he had a white face. Fine built, he was a good-looking horse.

That was one thing I did, rode a wild-buffalo bull and escaped with my life. I was then younger than I am now. I did not care, was not afraid. There was one other man, *Pox-i-pi*, (Weasel), a young Blackfoot warrior, strong and active. I saw him ride a buffalo bull when in the chase. He was not hurt in the riding. This added to his name as a big man. I was the second man to do this among the Piegans.

XII. Owl Child had another adventure with a sleeping buffalo.[276] It was when I was with the Blackfeet. It was winter with snow on the ground. We were hunting afoot, the hunters scattered about over the broken land, for the buffalo had sheltered among the canyons and washouts. I went up a canyon alone. I saw a buffalo bull lying down. He looked to me like he was dead. I watched him a good while. Then, I went up to him. Yes, he was dead. I kicked him, for he might have a little life. He did not move. I kicked him again. *Ech*! He had good life. He sprang up with a big snort. I jumped for a clump of bushes only a short distance away. That buffalo made after me. As I ran around the bushes, he charged me. His horn caught my blanket which I had wrapped around my waist, hanging down to keep my legs warm. He tore a piece from my blanket. He did not stop, did not turn after me. He galloped away, and I was saved with my life. If not for the bushes, I would have been killed.

XIII. While with the Piegans, I sometimes went with war parties to fight the Sioux.[277] I had joined the tribe and they gave me a name. It was *Che-pos tos-cos* (Owl Child). This name in Yakama is *Om-as-ish-tum*. The Piegans also called me *Shat-taw-wee* (a leader in battle).[278] *Shat-taw-wee* was a brave chief who had died. I was given his name. I was often in war. I will tell you a story.

While with the Piegan Blackfeet, many war parties went against the Sioux with whom we were at war. I often joined with such parties. We would form in the Sweet Grass Mountains, or at Buffalo Head where we lived, and travel to the enemy country. There we would scatter, scouting to locate the Sioux. We watched for small hunting parties and camps. Finding them, if favorable to success, we attacked, killing as many as we could. Or, capturing a band of horses, we skipped for home. Riding fast, we never stopped for long until out of pursuit danger. Seldom did we mix with a stronger party. A leader tried to avoid the loss of any of his warriors. That chief was greatest who returned to his village with scalps and horses, leaving none of his followers behind. No one liked the death wail in their own camp. Sometimes we were glad to return without spoils. I will tell you a story.

We were a party of about seventeen under Chief Lone Pine, a brave and cautious warrior.[279] We had gone into a country a little strange to me. It was a large Sioux camp. We lay hidden on a ridge across from the smaller of two rivers. We were watching for stragglers from the Sioux village. We might get a scalp or two, or some horses. At the joining of the two streams or nearly so we saw a great battle fought.[280]

The Sioux and Cheyennes were at war with the whites. They had scouts out watching for soldiers. We saw these scouts come running their horses. We saw the Sioux hurry to where they waited for the soldiers. *Eh*! There it was--a dust cloud rolling in the distance. Troops were coming, but not yet in sight. The Sioux were on horses all ready. The dust cloud was drawing nearer. Yes, now came the soldiers! They must not have known how many of their enemies were in hiding. They came at a trot, the commander in front. They reached the flat-like ground between the two rivers. Not very large this ground. *Eh*! *Eh*! The bugle sounded. The attack came. Indians rushed from hiding places, the shooting began-- loud yelling, loud whooping, guns going like bunched firecrackers. The bugle did not sound only twice, maybe three times. A bad mix-up! The guns were soon almost a solid roar. Dust and smoke; smoke and dust. Horse falling; men tumbling.

Soldiers were running, trying to escape. No use! Indians were all round, circling; warriors darted as hawks on flocked quail. No hiding anywhere. Blue coats; painted, naked Sioux, all mixing as waters of two rivers. Terrible fighting on both sides. Death everywhere. Not one soldier escaped. Horses were all killed. The com- mander was the last to go down.[281] We had no watch, but where the sun stood, the battle must be measured nearly two hours. When night came we left that place, returned home without scalps or horses.

XIV. Owl Child related how he fought to defend

his wife.[282] "I went from the Piegans with my wife. We traveled one day and one night. We got to Fort McCloud [i.e., Alberta] on the British line [i.e., the Canadian border]. We met three Indians, Canadian Indians. They were of the Blood tribe, but spoke the same language as the Piegans. They asked me, 'Where you from?'"

I answered, "Yes, from Piegan tribe."

They looked at me and talked to themselves. "He does not look like a Blackfoot. No! He cannot be a Blackfoot." Then they said again, "Where you from? You do not belong here. You look different. Your eyes are different."

My wife said to them, "He is all right. He belongs here."

They said, "No! He is different and not a Blackfoot."

Then I told them, "You are right. I do not belong here, but I come from the Blackfeet."

They said, "That is what we are asking you. No different how long you stay there, you do not belong there. You are from some other place."

Then I said, "I will tell you from where I come. I come from where the sun goes down. There is where I was born. There is where my people live."

They answered, "We are glad to hear you say that. You do not belong to this tribe." Then they asked the woman, "What tribe are you?"

She answered, "Piegan."

Then these Blood Indians said, "You are right. But he is different--different eyes, different head, all different."

It was about sundown and the Blood Indians said, "Sundown now. We better camp on the other side of the river. It is night now."

My wife said to me, "No! Tell them we will not

go."

So I said to them, "No! We do not want to go with you."

They answered, "No! You better come with us."

My wife again said, "No! They have nothing for us, nothing to give us. There is something wrong. They will harm us."

They now said, "You cannot go away. You must come with us."

I spoke to my wife, "We will have to go. They are the strongest and rule. We will go and see how it comes out."

So we went with them. We got to a camp place and stopped. We made a fire. It was almost dark. Quickly, as we built a fire, one man, tall and heavy--awfully tall and big--took my wife's hand and said, "You will be my wife."

I heard him say to his men, "Take that fellow." Then, quickly, I made a jump. They both shot at me but missed me. The horses were tied to bushes, and there was an open place in the bushes, like a stall or room. I went in there. The Indians did not follow me. They thought I was only one, and they could kill me easily if I did not run away.

I was not scared. I now knew what I would do. I took off all my clothes but the breechclout and leggings. I tied them on my horse. I left my gun tied on the saddle. I had a heavy knife as long as to my elbow. It was made from a file and sharp on both edges. A blacksmith made it, and an Indian gave it to me. It had a wooden handle and a hole for a buckskin string, a loop for the hand to go through.[283] I took this knife and put the loop about my wrist.

The Indians stayed at the fire. They thought, "Three against one. We will kill him if he comes back."

They were sitting about one hundred feet from me.

I held tightly to my knife and went around on the other side of the fire. I went on foot, stepped easily and kept back in the dark. The big man was sitting on that side of the fire, still holding my wife by the hand. I slipped in and got nearer to them. I would stop and wait. Then I went another step. I went without disturbance. I did not make any noise. The three Indians could not hear me as I came on them in the dark.

When I got close to the big man, he was talking to my wife. He was holding her by the right hand. I reached above with my knife and struck him hard on the top of his head. I split his head. He stooped [pitched] towards the fire. I grabbed him by the hair and pulled out the knife. A second time I hit him, and when I tried to pull away the knife, it broke by the handle. I pushed the Indian towards the fire.

When the two other Indians saw me kill their leader, they ran into the dark and I saw them no more. I did not scalp the dead man. I had killed him and that was enough. I took hold of my wife and said, "Stand up." She got up. She was glad to get away. We went to our horses and got on them and came away. We traveled all night till daylight. That day we got home safely. We saw no more of the two Indians.

Afterwards, I told my wife that I wanted to come and see my people. I planned to go back, but I never went. She died about one year after I left [before my visit was out]. I have a daughter back there, and I get letters from her and I often write her. I found out and wrote first.

In his later life, Owl Child was an allottee on the Yakama Indian Reservation. For many years he was an Indian policeman, and later a judge of the Tribal Court.[284]

B. A PERSONAL NARRATIVE
OF THE PAIUTE WAR[285, 286]

I, Louis Simpson, was soldier for two years when the people fought, [when] the Paiutes[287] were to be killed. The order was given to us; the chief gave it to us soldiers: "You shall slay the Paiutes. You shall rip open their bellies and cut their heads; you shall take hold of their scalps. And then you shall cut through their necks; you shall put the heads of the Paiutes ten paces off." The name of one [Paiute] chief was *Pala'i-ini*; the name of another was *Yawi'wa*;[288] they were both of them strong and wicked men, chiefs.

At 10 o'clock we started off. We did not see any [i.e., Paiutes] on the way. At 8 o'clock we camped. We started off one hundred and seventy of us; this many did we people start off towards the Paiutes.

And then we caught about five Paiutes on the trail. Immediately we bound them; they were not men, only children and women. We camped. And then we dreamt that we all became covered with blood.

And then in the morning our chief said: "Now do you make a fire and I shall tell you something."

So then we got up from bed, and then we took hold of *iqta't-sticks*.[289] And then we sang, now strongly we sang.

And then the hero said: "Now I shall tell you people what I dreamt. Now this day we shall die, I have seen the Paiutes. If we are to see them, it will rain." Thus said the hero. And again we sang, rubbed the *iqta't-sticks* together.

And again one man said: "Now I shall tell you

what I, for my part, dreamt. A grizzly bear ran away from us towards the setting sun. And then we caught only the grizzly bear's son.[290] Thus did I dream."

And then the people yelled their war whoop: "*wa+*"[291] and "*ma+*."[292] The Paiutes became afraid; they cried. And then daylight came. And then we got the horses and put the saddles on the horses.

Now then the chief said to us: "You shall go two by two; you shall not talk to one another today."

And then the chief said: "This flag[293] you shall well keep. Whenever you see this flag move three times from the ground, then you shall all look about. Thus you shall do." And then we started off.

Truly there were Paiutes not very far away; now the flag went on, went ahead. And then it moved, three times it moved from the ground. So then we went and looked about among ourselves. We saw houses of the Paiutes; they had seven fires.

Then indeed it started in to rain. And then the chief took out a spyglass. And then the chief said: "They are not Paiute soldiers." Then a box was taken and chopped open; it was full of bullets.[294] And then they were given out, fifty to each man. And then the guns and all the pistols were carefully cleaned; the guns and revolvers were loaded. Now then the people were all prepared.

One horse was carefully fixed up; here[295] feathers were tied on to a bobtailed horse, feathers. And then they said: "Now let us all charge on them." And then we rode the horses.

Now then we started out and all charged on the Paiutes; they had seven fires, seven houses. And then swiftly the horses went, we came up close to them. Now then thus we followed them -- with war whoops: "*wa+*;"[296] the guns were shot off.

And then the Paiutes came to a stand and seized

their bullets. Now then they shot; the smoke just darkened everything up about their houses.

We looked about and fought all day. [When] the sun [was] over there,[297] we stopped. [We] ripped open their bellies, cut through their necks, cut off the scalps, [put down] their heads ten paces off. We caught two children, one girl and one boy. We killed many of them, a great number.

Then it became night. Then we kept watch, looked after the horses all night. Now then the horses[298] were heard to neigh; in truth the [Paiutes] had under cover of darkness seized one girl and run off with her from us.

I whistled, and then a man said to me: "Go tell them! Let some more of us keep watch."

So then I went, and then I told them: "You fellows wake up! Some Paiutes have come again." And then many of us kept watch over the horses.

Daylight appeared. Now again we started off, and again we caught some Paiutes. And again they fought there; one of the women was killed first. And then they fought; bang, bang! went the guns. We caught some women.

I killed a Paiute, we shot at him; he, the Paiute man, had no shirt on, he was naked. I ripped open his belly, cut through his neck, cut off his scalp. There lay the Paiute without his head.

I arrived where we had been fighting; there were very many women. There were very many scalps, perhaps forty. Those to whom the scalps belonged had been killed. Thus they fought in the Paiute country named *Gwopha'ni* and the Paiute country named *Malhe'wa*.[299] So then we killed them all and caught many Paiute women. At night we bound them.

Now then we were taken; we went to a large

lake [where] there were many Paiutes. Straightway we were brought to the bridge, and then we were shot at. And then we [were?] called out by name, twenty men; ten men were brave warriors, also strong. Now ten were put in the rear; the packhorses were put in the middle. And then the men went on in front two by two; we first went on in front. And then straightway the people followed us in back of us, and our packhorses for the bullets in the middle of the people. Now then we went up to the bridge.

The captain said to us: "You shall not go back; you shall go ahead to the other side. If the guns will be shot at us, just go ahead. You shall not be afraid. Now that is how we are traveling; the command has been given to us. Now we can only die," he said to us.

"What do you think? Now will you do thus? Are you willing to die? [If so], lift up your hands!" And then we showed our hands.

Again he turned round and said to the [others]: "Now this day we shall die. What do you think? Now will you do thus? Are you willing to die?"

They said: "Yes! We all think it well that we should die this day."

Now thus we agreed: "Now this day we shall die." Whenever those who were in front advanced first, those in the middle would advance fast. So then we went on. So then the people went on; we went across. The Paiutes did not go across; we were first. Now then the people had gone across. There were only their tracks and their houses, nothing but logs.

And then we encamped there. Now then we kept watch at night in the mountains. Two of us went off that way; two went off that way; two again went off that way. Now we were to keep watch all night for their fire. Now we two caught sight of the fire.

And then he[300] said to me: "How about it, will you go or shall I?"

Then I said: "I shall go." Way off yonder I went to tell them; now I went. And then I arrived and told them: "We two have seen a fire over yonder."

The captain said: "Yes, let us go."

So on we went; straightway we came up to the man. Then we proceeded towards the fire. Then we all got at the fire, the [Paiute] people all standing around. It became light. And then they shot.

We killed all the Paiutes, about fifteen. And then we caught two of their horses; one horse had a sick leg and one was sore-backed, his skin all coming off. The Paiutes quietly sat on their sore-backed horse with his skin coming off.

Again next day, just as before, again we kept watch for a fire. All night long we moved and saw all the fires; in the morning we again caught many of them. Again we fought; we killed them all.

Again we saw their tracks in the snow. And then we followed them [until] it became quite dark. And then one man said: "I shall go in the man's footprints." So then he went on; we went [after him].

He said: "I give up; let somebody else try."

"I shall go in the Paiute's footprints, I first," said one man. He followed him in his footprints. Now then it had become very dark.

And then the man said: "Now let us camp here overnight." So then we camped there in the snow. In the morning we awoke and again followed the Paiute in his footprints. We came in view; now [i.e., we saw] the fire burning. Now in the morning we saw it. And then we looked about and got together in a bunch without saying anything. And then we loosened our guns, carefully cleaned them, and loaded them; we put bullets into them.

And then we went on.

We made a charge, we all yelled, "$wa+$"[301] at them. The Paiutes all jumped straight into the water; some of them we caught and killed. We caught one little boy here.

One Paiute man ran away; he dashed off. And then they headed him off. And then a man fired at him and wounded the Paiute in his hand, pierced it right through. And then the Paiute was surrounded; he also had a gun. Now then that Paiute shot it off. And then he was again shot at, and then he fell down dead. And then his neck was cut through, and he was cut in his head, and his belly was ripped open. In truth, that Paiute had been wounded in his arm.

So there they killed him; the Paiute's gun we took, his head they threw way off.

At daybreak there was an old Paiute woman there, without eyes, blind; her head they mauled with a gun. And then we ceased. There were no Paiutes to be seen.

Now then way off we caught sight of many of them, high up among the cliffs. And then we went on slowly; we went up a small river. And then farther on some Paiutes were talking excitedly among themselves.

Now then the one towards us spoke, a Paiute. Thus said the Paiute: "They are not whites, they are Wascos."[302]

And then another one said: "They are whites, not Wascos."[303]

And again as before the first one spoke: "They are not whites, they are Wascos."[304]

Now then our captain said: "Do not look around! Now they are uncertain as to who we are. Now those men are saying 'Wascos,' [but] do you just keep quiet."

And then this[305] Paiute man said: "Now I have

surely seen that they are soldiers."

And then [our people] became glad and yelled their war whoop: "*wa+*."[306]

And then yonder man across the river said: "I shall not go [i.e., to meet them]." So then he set fire to his house. Now then the Paiute's house burned, and then the Paiute ran off and escaped.

And then here two of our men went on, and four of their men went [to meet them]; very quickly they went ahead on horseback. Here they came together. And then the Paiutes shot at the two; they wounded one horse in his shoulder and one in his neck.

Now then [one man] looked about as he ran off, the horse ran away with him; in vain he tried to hold him back. We arrived there. And then the man said: "The Paiutes have wounded my horse, they have wounded the two of them." And then we quieted down.

Now then the man said: "The Paiutes are staying in a bad place. There is a fence [there] and we can't do anything to them."

Two men [went over and] stayed there at the cliffs. And then they came back to us, straightway they arrived. And then the two of them said: "The Paiutes are staying in a bad place." And then we all stopped.

Now then one man went off a ways. And then we heard yelling: "*wo+*;"[307] the [Paiutes] yelled the war whoop. As it turned out, the Paiutes had wounded the man in his leg. And then some [of us] jumped up and seized the man. And then they brought him hitherwards. And then we stopped there all day.

Now then the captain said: "Soon I shall give you all two hundred [bullets], and you shall jump upon the Paiutes."

And then the injured man's wound swelled, and he lay groaning thus: "*E,' E,' E,*"etc." Now the sun was nearly [down] way yonder.

And then the captain, his name was Billy Chinook, said: "Let us no longer stay here, but let us return home. If we stay here, the Paiutes will kill off all of our horses so that we had better return home now. That wounded man is sick, and perhaps he will die soon; now we shall take him with us."

[We said]: "Yes, indeed, let us return home now!" So then we got ready and were now about to return home. And then we bound the wounded man to his horse and put him astride him. And then we tied the man's legs.

Now then we went on straight to the river and waded in the water. And then the guns were shot [at us], but no one was wounded. Immediately when it was daylight, the guns were shot; they missed all of us.

And then the Paiutes yelled a war whoop to us; "wa+"[308] they yelled.

And then the captain said: "Now I want to speak to the Paiutes; who will interpret for me?"

And then a man said: "I will speak to the Paiutes. What do you think? What are you going to tell them?"

"I shall tell them that the Great Chief[309] has made up his mind that we fight for fifty years or one hundred years, so that you had better not be shooting.[310] You must first see us before you shoot at us; maybe you will run out of ammunition.[311] This one bullet I shall give you just for fun. Do you Paiutes listen, listen to me!" And then he shot off his gun.

In the evening he said to them: "That bullet I gave you just for fun. Now the great Chief has made up his mind that we fight perhaps a hundred years." And then we yelled thus: "Wa+."[312]

And then at night we went towards our camp.

We took the wounded man along with us, and he was
tied by his legs; the man had now become sick. And then
two horses went on, went on ahead of us towards our
camp. And then the two men [riding them] said to those
[in camp]: "The people are coming, and one man has
been wounded; now they are bringing him."

And then they made a fire here, another fire they
made here; four fires were made. Now there we arrived.
And then we passed around the fire. These men were in
our camp; and then they took us by our hands and shook
hands with us.

Now here we passed by the fire. And then they
said to us: "Who has been wounded?"

And then we named who had been wounded:
T!a'mlauwai. We told them that we had taken many
scalps, many Paiute [scalps]. And then straightway the
people sang the scalp song; all night long they danced
and went around with scalps in their hands.

Now then a certain Paiute boy was taken and
enclosed in a sack. We went right there up to the fire.
There he was taken out, there he ran about near the fire,
and the Paiute boy was captured [as though in war]. All
night long they sang, right up to early dawn, when the
sun just began to appear. And then the people stopped.

Now the man had become sick. So then a long
pole was set up, and then ceremonial feathers were tied
on top of the pole to a wolf's backbone, the man's guardian spirit.

The man said: "Now I shall die, and do you all
hear what I have to say what I learned when I was a boy.
Now then I saw[313] something as a boy, so that now I
shall tell you all what it was that spoke with me as a boy,
what I recognized. Now it is going to rain a little. Thus I
know, I found it out as a boy. I saw black [clouds] passing over the sky, and the sky turned white. And then it

rained. If it will not rain and if it will not hail, then truly
I shall die."

Then it started in to rain and to hail and the
wounded man said: "Now I shall bathe in the water, and
you will carry me." So then he was carried to the water
and put into it. And then the man recovered; surely
indeed the Paiutes had shot at his guardian spirit. He did
not die, he became well.

Everyone saw him, also I here saw him. Thus
the Indians have strong hearts; not thus are white people.
Indians could pass five days and eat nothing, nor would
they drink any water. So strong are the Wascos, they are
not cowards. So also they too, the Paiutes, are not cowards.

We passed three nights and there was no food.
And then we caught a very small jackrabbit; [we were]
thirty people. And then to each one a little bit [of meat]
was given; each one ate [his share]. Far away was our
camp; this small jackrabbit we thirty people ate. Then
we went each to his own home; straightway we arrived
at our houses.

Now again we set out; again we went to look for
the Paiutes. Then we caught them when the sun was
straight overhead. And then straightway we chased them
into the water, they escaped from us; the Paiutes all
swam off. And then way yonder in the water some
Paiutes would just appear. And then we would shoot at
the Paiutes. Then we camped overnight; in the morning
we again caught sight of them in the water.

And then we started home; we said to them:
"What do you Paiutes all keep hiding yourselves for?
Come, let us fight!" And then we shot off one volley.

We said to them: "This bullet we have given you
for nothing." Now then we started home.

We caught some Paiutes on the road. Now again

we fought there. One of the Paiute men had magpie-
feathers tied onto his gun. And then the Paiute was fired
at, he was shot; straightway he died.

Eight Paiutes were killed; their scalps were all
taken off, and their necks cut through, their bellies ripped open; to everyone of them it was thus done. We took
their guns, we killed them all. And then the people sang
with scalps; happy the Wasco people became.

Now the Paiutes ceased from the war. Now then
the Paiutes said: "Now we have stopped; we have fought
enough." We all stopped. We did not see *Pala'-ini*, Chief
of the Paiutes, nor did we see *Yawi'wa*, chief of the
Paiutes.

And then we took them all back with us. Straight
to Walla Walla we took them back; there we left the
Paiutes. Thus we and the Paiutes fought, fiercely we
fought. And the Paiutes are bad people, they are thieves.
Thus the government agreed, so that we fought. I,
Pa'pkEs,[314] fought.

Now I am alone, all the Wascos [i.e., who
fought] are dead. This day there are now only two at
Warm Spring[s] and I -- we three fought with the
Paiutes. Now today the Paiutes are good and speak English; they are peaceful. Today a Paiute's son and a
Wasco man's daughter marry. Thus Government helped
them."

PART THREE
APPENDICES

NOTES TO THE NARRATIVES

INTRODUCTION: LOCUS
AND CULTURE

1. The Wishram or Wishom Indian tribe (the term employed throughout this work) is probably the most studied, however desultory, of Southern Plateau Indian nations. In July and August of 1905 Anthropologist/Linguist Edward Sapir journeyed to the Yakama Reservation, probably to the Indian Agency headquarters at Fort Simcoe, the southwest corner of the reservation. With the aid of interpreters, Sapir collected numerous Wishom oral narratives which he set forth in his bilingual edition of Wishom tales in English, also his construction of a written version of the Wishom language. This opus was published, along with Wasco materials obtained earlier by Jeremiah Curtin, in *Wishram Texts, Together with Wasco Tales and Myths. . . PAES.* Leyden: E.J. Brill, 1909, 235 pp. + Introduction. Drawing on the rich ethnographic notes which Sapir also gathered, Anthropologist Leslie Spier with Sapir published *Wishram Ethnography*, UWPA 3/3. Seattle: UW Press, 1930, 299 pp. Still other works which relate of the Wishoms include: Spier, Leslie 1936. *Tribal Distribution in Washington*, GSA. Menasha, WI. G. Banta Publ. Co., p. 20; also Hodge,

Frederick Webb 1960. *Handbook of American Indians North of Mexico*, Part 2 [Repr.of BAE 30]. NY: Pageant Books, p. 965; also Swanton, John R. 1952. *The Indian Tribes of North America*, BAE 145. Washington DC: US Gov't Printing Office, p. 449.

The modern reader might well consult Sapir, Philip, Editor-in-Chief 1990. *The Collected Works of Edward Sapir*, especially Volume VII, *Wishram Texts and Ethnography*. William Bright, volume editor. Berlin: Walter de Gruyter & Co.. We stand aghast at this edition for, despite the importance of Edward Sapir's collected materials, neither critical updating nor further scholarship has been included for either *Wishram Texts*. . . or for *Wishram Ethnography*. Yet, over the 67 years from Edward Sapir's original labors to date, a remarkable body of theoretical and critical works plus many scholarly tools have been devised by which Sapir's original texts might have been related to other Southern Plateau tribes, or have been given the appropriate scholarly emendation possible at an earlier time, but not likely now. As a result, we know painfully little of the unique dimensions, the "characteristics" of Wishom narratives. DH

2. Throughout this work "Wishom" is used and for several reasons. First, "Wishom" is the term we have heard used presently on the Yakama Reservation. Second, according to LVM and the narrator of Tale 13A "The Wishom Tribe: A Story of Their Division and Separation," found hereafter, "Wishom" ". . . is descriptive of the deep, rumbling roar of the swirling, tumbling cataract of the Tumwater [or the Columbia River rapids] near which they lived. '*Wish-h-h-h-u-u-u-m-m-m*' is the manner in which this tribesman put it when explaining the significance of the name. *Tum-water* he interpreted as pertaining to the same element; thus, *T-u-u-u-m-m-m-water* is a 'tumming' roar of falling or rapid waters [the horrendous miles-long stretch of rapids on the Columbia River from approximately Celilo down to near Hood River]." The tribe's name, Wishom, seems an onomatopoeic rendition of the sound of the roar of falling water or the river rapids nearby their village sites--translating possibly as '**People From Where the Waters Roar**.' But see also Tale 14 "Why the Wishram are Called Ilaxluit," hereafter. DH

3. See Spier, *Tribal Distribution in Washington*, p. 20. And see also Spier and Sapir, *Wishram Ethnography*, p. 164-167, especially p. 165, the map showing locations of Wishom and other villages. DH

4. This writer recalls the great 1948 springtime flood of the Columbia River. In lieu of his June high school graduation, he was employed sandbagging river dikes against the river which had risen 30 ft or more, had quickly wiped out Vanport, a WWII commu-

nity of some 80,000 war workers.DH

5. With the advent of the hydroelectric dams on the Columbia River, and with the elimination of the roaring white water rapids, few Pacific Northwesterners recall the meaning of a "dalles" or how the city of The Dalles, OR, likely obtained its name. According to *Webster's Third New International Dictionary of the English Language, Unabridged,* a **dalles** is ". . .the rapids in a river confined between walls of a canyon or gorge [i.e. in this instance the Cascades Range]." DH

6. At least two brief mentions of a great flood over Central Washington occur in Yakama tales, *Ghost Voices. . .*: see 7A, also 45. DH

7. The severity possible in winters over the area was recorded by Jeremiah Curtin in our "Introduction" to *Celilo Tales,* pp-. 7-8. And in 1969 this writer and family witnessed the ravages of a fierce late December storm through the Columbia River Gorge in which ferocious easterly winds, remarkable low temperatures, and a powerful storm front brought freezing rain, but then changed quickly to heavy and blowing snow which quickly exceeded the capacities of giant rotary snowplows. And soon Freeway 84, connecting Portland, Oregon, to Boise, Idaho, was shut down. DH

8. For example, see hereafter Tale 5B "The Origin of Fish in the Columbia." DH

9. Wilke, Steve, et al., 1983. *Cultural Resource Overview and Survey of Select Parcels in The Dalles Reservoir, Oregon and Washington.* Seattle: Geo-Recon International. See Vol. I: "Fauna," pp. 21-23. DH

10. Hines, Donald M. 1994. *Tragedy of the Wahk-shum: The Death of Andrew J. Bolon, Yakima Indian Agent, As Told by Su-el-lil, Eyewitness; Also, The Suicide of General George A. Custer, As Told by Owl Child,* Eyewitness. Issaquah: Great Eagle Publishing, Inc., p. 25. DH

11. See Sapir and Spier, *Wishram Ethnography,* p. 159. And in *Wishram Texts. . .,* p. xi, Spier notes that his informant Pete McGuff recounted that about 150 Wishoms (c. 1909) were still able to speak their own language, including those on the Yakama Reservation, and also those who regularly lived at the "fishing village" of Wishram on the Columbia River. DH

12. See note 1 above. This work is included in the newly published *The Collected Works of Edward Sapir,* Vol. VII, previously cited. DH

13. *Wishram Ethnography*, pp. 159-161. DH

14. In the preparation of this volume we have made use of Ault, Nelson A.1959. *The Papers of Lucullus Virgil McWhorter*. Pullman: Friends of the Library, State College of Washington, 1959, 144 pages. Very recently, an updated calendar of the McWhorter Papers has been prepared. We have not had the opportunity to examine this work. DH

15. Bødker, Laurits 1965. *Folk Literature (Germanic)* Vol. II, *International Dictionary of Regional European Ethnology and Folklore*. Copenhagen: Rosenkilde and Bagger. DH

16. Thompson, Stith 1946. *The Folktale*. New York: Holt, Rinehart and Winston. DH

17. Thompson, Stith 1966. *Tales of the North American Indians*. Bloomington: Indiana University Press. DH

18. Oral Traditional History was discussed in some detail in *Tragedy of the Wahk-Shum: The Death of Andrew J. Bolon, Yakima Indian Agent,* already cited. See esp. p. 79f.: "Oral traditional history accounts like those of Owl Child and of *Su-el-lil* demonstrate extraordinary knowledge of and unique perspective on violent deeds over which darkness lingers in written history. First, a strong visual orientation focuses on observed particulars, on a spatial order of mayhem, of a murder, or of a fierce battle. And action marks both accounts. Second, the extraordinary recall of details attests to the power of memory of *Su-el-lil* and of Owl Child. Third, the medium for tribal annals is oral tradition. This is history which is narrated, performed rather, again and again before groups of listeners. And the oral traditional history episodes of both *Su-el-lil* and Owl Child assume a relatively fixed form within a narrative framework. . . .But the historical validity of these two accounts demands corroboration from historical records of the time, and, more importantly, corroboration from archaeological field investigations." Further intersections of "official history" with "Oral Traditional History " are examined in Hines, Donald M. 1990. "Native American Narratives of First Encounters with Whites," *The Folklore Historian, Journal of the Folklore and History Section of the American Folklore Society*, 7:31-44. DH

19. See *Wishram Texts*, pp. 204-227. And see note 286 below. DH

20. Our assembly of Owl Child's autobiographical elements told to McWhorter is described in note 238 below. DH

21. Some of Owl Child's exploits have been previously published. See Hines, Donald M. 1987. "Accounts of Heroes and of Great Deeds from the Yakima Indian Nation," *Fabula* 28:293-306. DH

22. Thompson, Stith 1955. *Motif-Index of Folk-Literature: A Classification of Narrative Elements in Folktales, Ballads, Myths, Fables, Medieval Romances, Exempla, Fabliaux, Jest-Books and Local Legends*. Bloomington: Indiana University Press, 6 Vols.. And see Thompson, Stith 1966. *Tales of the North American Indians*. Bloomington: Indiana University Press. DH

PART TWO
THE TALES OF THE WISHOMS

I. TALES OF THE ORIGIN OF MAN, OF ANIMALS, PLANTS, PHENOMENA

23. Sapir, pp. 42-47. Told by Louis Simpson with Pete McGuff. DH

24. Lapwai is located in the western part of the Nez Perce Indian Reservation. It lies just south of the Clearwater River, an eastern tributary of the Snake River. The town is the site of the Nez Perce Tribal headquarters, and is about 20 miles east of Lewiston, Idaho. DH

25. According to Sapir, *Itc!E'xyan* is here used to refer to a "mountain monster" and is used in text IB "Coyote and Itc!E'xyan" hereafter. Sapir continues that a "merman" is supposed to be half fish and half man, while the former "mountain monster" is described as resembling rather a sphinx. [Note: no sphinxes are located within Eastern Oregon, Eastern Washington, Northern Idaho]. DH

26. "The monster had been wont to devour all beings that passed by by drawing them to himself with his breath. "*Fu2*" represents the sound made by sucking in air." [To comprehend this sound and also others hereafter, see the phonetic symbols listed on pp. xiv, xv, of *Wishram Texts*.] ES

27. This is a motif borrowed by the Wishoms from the Nez Perce, borrowed by the Wishoms in recent times. See Herbert J. Spinden, "Myths of the Nez Perce," *Journal of American Folklore*, 21 (1908), p. 14. DH

28. Sapir, pp. 40-43. Told by Louis Simpson. DH

29. "The *Itc!E'xyan* or Merman of the Wishram, evidently as far at least as his name is concerned, is identical with the gambler's protector

itc!x.ia'n of the Lower Chinook, among whom also his dwelling is supposed to be in the waters." See Boas, Franz 1894. *Chinook Texts*, RBAE 20. Washington, D.C., pp. 220-222. [This work is cited hereafter as *Chinook Texts*.] See also Boas, Franz 1901. *Kathlamet Texts*, RBAE 26. Washington, D.C., p. 19. {This work is cited hereafter as *Kathlamet Texts*.} Even today, the imagination of the Wishram peoples certain bodies of water with mermen, as for example, a lake in the mountains south of Fort Simcoe [early in this century the agency town of the Yakima Reservation] is said to be *ayatc'E'xyanix* [peopled with mermen]." ES

30. "Coyote used the tree to climb up to the heart, which was dangling high up out of reach." ES

31. McWhorter: told by Chief Menineck, August 1922. DH

32. "*Is-tam-ma*: 'animal baby,' youngest of any 'animal family.'" LVM

33. "*Wish-pooch*: 'beaver.' It does not appear to belong to the Yakima language proper. Chief Menineck (originally *Menine-okt*) belonged to the *Skein-tla-ma* tribe, residing on the *n-Che-wana* opposite the mouth of the Des Chutes River (located 8-10 miles east of The Dalles, Oregon, on the Oregon side of the Columbia River.) The tribe became amalgamated with the Yakimas under the Treaty of Walla Walla, 1855, which was signed by the Chief's father, whose name he inherited. The narrator declared that *Wish-pooch* stands for beaver not only with the Yakimas, but with all the kindred *n-Che-wana* bands as well. The student of native languages and dialects on the Yakima Reservation is destined to be confronted with many confusing problems." LVM

34. "*Wahk-puch-pal*: 'Poison-snake people.' Doubtless here is found the true origin of 'snake' as applied to certain Shoshonean bands [of Indians], especially the Bannocks and Paiutes, who came in direct contact with *n-Che-wana* tribes of Chinookan and Sahaptan linguistic families. It has been generally supposed that the name 'snake' originated from the very expressive tribal identification signal used in the sign language of the plains Indians, a serpentine-like movement of the hand with index finger extended. Hoffman, however, was of the opinion that this sign applied to the weaving of the grass-lodges; this the Bureau of American Ethnology regards as reasonable, since the Shoshoni 'are known as 'grass-house people' or by some similar name among numerous tribes.' See Frederick Webb Hodge, ed. *Handbook of American Indians North of Mexico*, (New York: Pageant Books, Inc., 1907-1959), Part 2, p. 557.

"With all due deference to the eminent authorities cited, it does not appear logical that the haughty warrior-Shoshoni should adopt as his differentiation sign a symbolism as stringently expressive of woman's domesticity. Such supposition contradicts all known traditions of the race. 'Snake' is strongly suggestive of a subtle craftiness, an ability to insidiously creep up on the enemy, a truly proud attainment sought by every ambitious warrior. Recognizing this trait of superiority in the Bannock-Paiute, and expressing the dread and antipathy in which they were held, the enemy-tribe of the *n-Che-wana* dubbed them *'Wahk-puch pal,'* which became abbreviated 'Snake.' With this distinctive sobriquet fastened upon them, the sign of the crawling serpent as indicator of tribal affiliation was adapted.

"For several generations a ceaseless warfare was carried on by the Bannock-Paiute against the Umatillas, Wascos, and bands now comprising in general the Yakima tribe. The origin of this war is traditional. It is claimed that at one time the Bannocks and Paiutes occupied territory around what is now Pendleton, Oregon, and Walla Walla, Washington. An attempt to seize upon the coveted fisheries of Tumwater [the Columbia River] and vicinity, and *Top-tut* on the Yakima, proved their undoing. The various bands, joining forces, drove the aggressors into Eastern Oregon and Idaho, where they ever afterwards remained. From that time on, predatory forays between the hereditary enemies continued until the authority of the United States Government became established over the warring factions. The brunt of the retaliatory raids on the part of the allied tribes fell to the more warlike Wascos, Umatillas, Klickitat, and *Pish-wan-a-pums,* or Yakima proper. In these forays women and children were ofttimes carried away into captivity or slavery. Aside from a life of servitude, the captives were generally admitted to all the tribal privileges, often intermarrying and raising families. Children born of such parents were not subject to slavery." [See Wishom tale #16 below which makes mention of a 'Snake Indian slave boy.' A similar account is told by the Yakamas, also mentions a 'Snake Indian' slave boy.]

"During the forepart of the winter of 1894-95, fifty Bannocks came to the Umatillas with an exchange of gifts, when the tomahawk was formally buried. A feature of the occasion was the staging of a mutual war dance in the snow on the bank of the Umatilla River, above Thorn Hollow [Eastern Oregon]. The hardy Bannocks stripped as for battle, but the less demonstrative Umatillas were content to retain their full native costumes against the biting cold. To this friendly mingling can be traced the present modified war dance of the Umatillas and Yakimas. The step is more quick and vigorous than formerly. It also heralded the adoption of new-patterned regalia such as the 'feather bustle.' The gorgeous war bonnet of eagle feathers was never a feature of Yakima tribal life." LVM

35. "This is the low gap through which the Satus-Goldendale Road passes. *Pouen-kute* is the south fork of the main Satus River." LVM

36. Sapir, pp. 106-117. Told by Louis Simpson. DH

37. "We have just been told that Coyote and Eagle had each lost two sons. *Itsxa'n* 'my son' (instead of *ickxa'n* 'my two sons') is inconsistent with this statement, but it has been thought advisable to leave Louis Simpson's inconsistencies uncorrected." ES

38. "Perhaps this means: 'Probably you think that--.'*Qadac it!u'ktix*' = probably.'" ES

39. "*Nikciamtca'c* is now supposed to be the person represented by the markings in the moon. The name *Nikciamtca'c* occurs also in a Kathlamet myth. See *Kathlamet Texts*, pp. 20-23, though in an entirely different connection. But a change in gender is obvious." ES

40. "In other words, it was near daylight." ES

41. "That is, our wives and sons." ES

42. McWhorter: told by *Ye-mow-wit* (Jobe Charley), 18 September 1925. DH

43. "To an inquiry, the narrator described the trail ascended by Fox and Coyote as consisting of power within mortals to make the journey; there was no visible trail to be seen. The power of this bodily transportation was destroyed or closed by Coyote." LVM

44. McWhorter: Told by *An-nee-shiat*, May 1918. DH

45. "These Sisters are now the *Weet-weet yah*: the cliff swallow, 'smaller than the killdeer.' The Yakimas call them *Tic-teah*, or *Tea-tic*. These active little birds travel up the river shore ahead of the fish. Salmon and even eels will not appear until after these swallows have first heralded their coming in the manner prescribed by the wise Coyote. They especially travel with the blue-backs, but they come first with the chinook salmon. The *Weet-weet yah* no longer have any control over the fish, other than where to go. The laws of Coyote stand to this day." LVM

46. "*Ho-ho lah-me*: 'river of crows.' This is Wind River, Skamania County, Washington." LVM

47. "*Lou-le pol-me*: definition uncertain. It is Klickitat for White Salmon River. A band of the Klickitat tribe residing on this stream was known by the same name." LVM

48. "*Why-phot*: A Klickitat name pertaining to the mouth of the Klickitat River. The same appellation applies to the *n-Che-wana* where it enters the *At-tah cheech*: the ocean." LVM

49. "*Klah-ti-hut*: 'dropping over.' Falls of the Big Klickitat. This name does not appear to be of the Klickitat-Yakima proper. However, Indian place-names are often multiform." LVM

50. "*Y-yum*: 'above,' a designated, or known place. In the present instance it refers to a certain locality 'above' The Dalles, on the *n-Che-wana*. It was a noted tribal fishery, opposite *Skein*: 'cradle-board.' The resident Indians were known as *Y-yum pums*." LVM

51. "This drama was enacted on *Skein* Island; if not voluntary on the part of the devotee, the 'charm' proved ineffective. [Cf. motif D1782. Magic results obtained by imitating desired action. {Sympathetic Magic: rolling about on sand of beach / capturing slippery salmon brought up to beach.} *Al-o-tut*, whose aquatic achievements are noted elsewhere herein, was one who often volunteered to carry out the rules and laws laid down by Coyote governing the fishing on the island. *Al-o-tut* died about 1900. To the Indian, there are many mystical signs to be found on *Skein*. The imprint in solid rock of the track of the black bear, the grizzly bear, the wolf, coyote and other animals are some of the wonders encountered. The island has ever been a great resort of the Indians during the fishing season." LVM

52. McWhorter notes: "In May 1918, when I was camping with a band of Indians on the *n-Che-wana* near Timberman's Ferry above Pasco, the tribesmen called my attention to the cool, dry wind which set in from the north-northwest regularly each mid-day as depicted in the legend. Eels dressed and hung on an improvised scaffolding on the beach and protected from the direct rays of the sun were soon cured in the best of condition." LVM

53. "The exact location of this ancient failure of Coyote was not ascertained to a certainty. The interpreter pointed out to McWhorter the high first river bench on the Four Brothers Ranch near Timberman's Ferry, a saw-like notch in the hills, far up the *n-Che-wana*, as the scene of Coyote's unsuccessful experiment. He said, 'It is a considerable distance above White Bluffs. I have not been there in many years, but the channel bed is plainly traceable. The rocks placed by Coyote in building the fish traps are still in position. I do not know the location by the white man's name.'" LVM

54. "This was a romantic phase of Indian life. I was well acquainted with the daughter of *Te-yiash*, Peace Chief of the Yakimas, who was wooed and won while gathering berries on this wild bluff on the Wenatchee gorge. The aged woman was visibly perturbed when her daughter volunteered to tell me about her mother's courtship." LVM

55. "It will be noticed that the Yakima River is not included in the scenes of Coyote's exploits in this legend. The grandmother, *An-nee-shiat*, was raised on the *n-Che-wana* proper and was not conversant with Yakima folklore. She said, however, 'Coyote created a riffle fishery somewhere in the Yakima, above its mouth and below *Top-tut*.'" LVM

56. This narrative is made up of incidents which are told as separate tales elsewhere. For comparable accounts of Coyote or White Skunk being delayed on their return due to the marvelous reshaping of landscape into its present natural barrier see in *Tales of the Nez Perce*, 8 "Coyote Causes His Son to be Lost," p. 64; also 35 "White Skunk and Eagle." For the account of Coyote originating taking of salmon by spearing, see Wishom tale #13 "Coyote Spears Fish" below. And again, the episode of the stolen salmon is comparable to "Coyote and His Anus," *Tales of the Nez Perce*, pp. 57-60. And see also Wishom tales 9A "Coyote and the Mischievous Women;" also 9B, Tom Simpson's version, "Coyote and the Mischievous Woman" in which the sisters are transformed into birds, harbingers of salmon. DH

57. Sapir: pp. 3-7. Told by Louis Simpson. DH

58. Sapir was taken with the striking parallel of this narrative with Pliny Earle Goddard's *Hupa Texts*, U. Cal 1 (Berkeley, 1904), pp. 124,125. [This text is cited as *Hupa Texts* hereafter.] In this narrative, *Yimantiuwinyai*, the Hupa culture hero, is also fed with eels by a woman who guards all the salmon. DH

59. "That is, the Columbia River. The word *wi'mal* of the text is never used to refer to any other river. All other streams are denoted by *wi'qxat*." ES

60. "This explains why the coming of the swallows is synchronous with the first salmon run in the spring." ES

61. McWhorter: told by *Che-pos to-cos* (Owl Child), October 1916. DH

62. "Some Indians contend that the five head-coverings used by Coyote on this occasion were large bivalve shells of an unidentified variety, while others speak of them as five horn spoons." LVM

63. Appropriate here is motif D1782.1. Magic results obtained by imitating desired action: rain. [Sympathetic magic: spewing droplets of saliva / the imminent fall of rain.] DH

64. "*Y-yum*: 'fish-tail.' Now, Celilo, Oregon." LVM

65. "This is where the diversion dam of the Sunnyside Canal is built, the Yakima River. During the construction of this fish trap, Coyote's ear caught the sound of water pouring over *Top-tut*. He stopped work, listening! '*Oo-oo-m-m*!' came the distant rumble of the cataract. Coyote said, 'This is too close, too close to *Top-tut*.' "He then tore the trap out, leaving only a trace of it where a few fish may be caught. It was called *Koop*." LVM

66. "Another version of this legend has it that there were five brothers of Coyote, and that one of them continued directly up the *n-Che-wana*, while one went up each of the following tributaries, constructing the various fisheries to be found along these streams: the Snake, the Yakima, and the Wenatchee rivers. One of the brothers in some way reached the Clearwater River in Idaho, and Salmon Lake in Montana, in the region where Chief Joseph made his last stand, the Nez Perce War, 1877." LVM

67. Sapir, pp. 152-165. Told to Pete McGuff--narrator not specified. DH

68. "Species not certain." ES

69. "The exact rhythmical values of the syllables of the song sung here by the grandmother (also by Raccoon above) are undetermined. According to Sapir, the narrative was written down and forwarded by mail by his interpreter." [An attempt has been made here to reform Raccoon's and the Grandmother's language into stanzaic format of a song.] ES

70. "A sound supposed to be characteristic of the pheasant." ES

71. "No explanation could be obtained of the meaning of *Wala'lap* or wicked beings beyond the fact that it signifies some sort of mythical being. One of the old men of the tribe said that Coyote himself did not know what it was, but merely wished to excite Raccoon's curiosity so as to get a chance to waylay him, kill him, and eat him." [Compare *Kathlamet Texts*, pp. 152-154 where, according to Sapir, the *waLax lax* invented by Coyote evidently corresponds to the Wishom *wala'lap*. And Sapir, not distinguishing between 'versions' and 'variants', lists text 7B of "Raccoon and his Grandmother" as a second installment, with evidently a break in the narrative.] ES

72. "Perhaps a humorous contraction of the Wishram *it'i'laq*: 'grasshopper.'" ES

73. Molale, or Mollala is thought to be the western dialect of the Waiilatpuan stock. But it was also a tribal group dwelling perhaps 150 miles westward of the Wishoms, on the westerly slopes of Mount Hood, the Willamette Valley. DH

74. Sapir, pp. 152-153. Told by Louis Simpson. DH

75. "This short text is merely a fragmentary version of the preceding narrative. It supplements the former, however, by the somewhat more detailed explanation it gives of the markings of the raccoon. With both versions cf. *Kathlamet Texts*, pp. 142-154." ES

76. Sapir, pp. 98-103. Told by Louis Simpson. DH

77. "Said by Pete McGuff to mean 'shiner, a small freshwater fish of the minnow kind.' Both shiner and chub belong to the genus *Leuciscus*." ES

78. "It is not at all clear what is meant by this statement." ES

79. Sapir, pp. 103-105. Told by Louis Simpson. DH

80. "This tale errs in assigning the greater strength to West Wind. In fact, wintry East Winds are a formidable feature of the region. Indeed, East Wind would seem, initially at least, the stronger wind, until supplanted by the mild "chinook winds" from the south, etc., which mark the end of winter's cold." DH

81. Sapir, pp. 6-9. Told by Louis Simpson. DH

82. "That is, with which to catch them, so elusive were they." ES

83. "It does not appear what sort of water birds the mischievous women were transformed into, possibly divers." [But see McWhorter's text 9A "Coyote and the Two Sisters of the *n-Che-wana*," esp. note 13, wherein the two sisters were changed into the *Chi-collah*, a small bird of the swallow variety, the cliff-swallow, the *Tic-teah* of the Yakamas. This particular bird was the harbinger of the salmon runs.The tales or versions here also depict the transformation of the two women into birds.] ES

84. Sapir, p. 8-11. Told by Tom Simpson, brother of Louis Simpson. DH

85. "Tom Simpson took exception to the transformation incident in the first version (by his brother), when this was read to him, and denied

its correctness. The transformation to water birds (narrated by Tom Simpson) seems more appropriate than that into rocks, however." ES

86. Wishom tales or versions above depict the transformation of the two women into birds, but not rocks. Causation for such transformation is not apparent in Tom Simpson's version. See for example Wishom text 9A above; the bird transformation motif is included with the action of the tale text. But here such action seemingly exists separately. DH

87. Sapir, pp. 30-31. Told by Louis Simpson. DH

88. "'Dried Salmon: The Indian site called 'Dried Salmon' is now called 'White Salmon Landing,' and was formerly inhabited by both Chinookan [more particularly 'White Salmon' and Klickitat Indians.] Salmon was often dried, pounded, and preserved in baskets, for use in winter, and to be traded off to other tribes who came regularly to The Dalles for barter." ES

89. *Lmuyaqso'qu*, or *Lmie'qsoq*, was about half a mile up the river from *Itk!i'lak* [see the map, Vol. II], and on the same (Washington) side of it. Its site is now occupied by the Burket Ranch. It was also occupied by the 'White Salmon' Indians [who spoke, with probably only slight variations, the same dialect as the Wishram and Wasco.]" ES

90. Sapir, pp. 26-27. Told by Louis Simpson. DH

91. "From a rope held by two posts slanting toward each other is suspended a basket trap into which the white salmon, in attempting to jump past, fall back." ES

92. "This site was located on the northern shore of the Columbia River, above the Cascades at the spot now known as Cooks' Landing, about half a mile below Drano. The word means 'eating place,' while *Sq!E'ldalpl* denotes 'it keeps tearing out,' the reference being to a lake connected with the river by a narrow creek." ES

93. Sapir, pp. 28-29. Told by Louis Simpson. DH

94. Told by Jobe Colwash, also known as Jobe Charley, a Yakama, time unknown. DH

95. Sapir, pp. 200-205. Told by Louis Simpson [Indian name *Me-nait*], with Pete McGuff serving as interpreter, summer, 1905. DH

96. A similar version of the *Wandering of Tribes* legend, or so we believe it,

was recorded by Mooney, *Ghost-Dance Religion*, p. 740. DH

97. "A Wishram village which was a short distance up the river from the main village *Nixlu'idix* or *Wu'cxam.*" ES

98. "Made with a high pitch." ES

99. "Without doubt the Yakima River is meant." ES

100. "It was not found possible to definitely locate all of these Sahaptin place-names. *NuL!a'-ik* was somewhat east of Wasco. *NuL!a'nuL!a* was about 2 ½ miles east of *Nixlu'idix*. *Txa'iauna* was at Summit, within the limits of the Yakima Reservation and some distance south of Fort Simcoe. *Po'uwankiut* was at Canyon, near Summit. *SA;tAs* is represented by Satus Creek of today. *IL!u'mEni* was at the head of Canyon Creek. *Pala'xi* was said by Pete McGuff to be near Wenatchee, north of North Yakima. [If this is correct, the name is evidently misplaced in the narrative, as it should come after 'The Gap']. The course of the supposed migration was thus east for a short distance along the Columbia; then north across the divide between the Columbia River and the Yakima River; and then along the Yakima River to the Wenatchee." ES

101. "'The Gap' is the narrow pass through which the Yakima River flows in breaking through the low range of mountains south of the modern town of North Yakima [Union Gap], Washington." ES

102. "This is its Wishram name, and may be approximately translated as 'the place where two mountains nearly touch.' *Patixkwi'ut* is the Klickitat or Yakima term." ES

103. "In the country of the Salish *Piskwaus* or *Winatshi*, who dwelt along the Wenatchee River, a western tributary of the Columbia River. See Mooney, *The Ghost-Dance Religion*, p. 736." ES

104. "Given by Pete McGuff, ca. 1924: 'an old lady [not identified] tells why the Wishram are called *ilaxluit*. I never heard this explanation before.'" [See Spier, *Wishram Ethnography*, pp. 164-165.] LS

105. "'I am an *Ila'xluit*;' or, freely, 'I am a Wishram.'" ES

106. "*Nixlu'idix* is the chief Wishram village. Thus, how it got its name." ES

107. Sapir, pp. 38-41. Told by Louis Simpson. DH

108. "*Sk!in* was the country immediately north of the Columbia River and east of the Falls or "Tumwater" inhabited by the Sahaptian Tribes

[Walla Walla Indians?]." ES

109. "Coyote is supposed by the Wishrams to have urinated on their Sahaptian neighbors to show their inferiority to themselves. This inferiority consists, among other things, in the use by the Sahaptians of a smaller and more rudely constructed canoe, as contrasted with the long, elaborately built craft of the Chinookan tribes. The use of this dugout or rudely constructed canoe is anticipated by Coyote himself." [Numerous photos, even some examples of the dugout canoe, manufactured by burning out a fallen tree, can be found over the region. Members of the Lewis and Clark expedition were shown how to make dugout canoes.] ES

110. "The *Ilka'imamt* were the Sahaptian tribes living on the northern and southern banks of the Columbia River, east [upriver] of the Wascos and Wishrams. They included the people of *Sk!in* on the north bank, and the 'Des Chutes' Indians [Wayam and Tenino] on the south banks of the river." ES

111. Sapir, pp. 18-25. Told by Louis Simpson. DH

112. "That is, the mouthless man." ES

113. Again, the mouthless man. DH

114. "Again, the mouthless man." ES

115. "Meaning, he whispered." ES

116. "The village, *Nimi-cxa'ya*, was a village of the Cascade Indians, and was situated on the Washington side of the Columbia River about a half mile below a high rock (*Ik!lamat*) now known as 'Castle Rock.' To make amends for their former mouthlessness, the people of *Nimi-cxa'ya* are (or were) said to possess particularly large mouths." ES

117. "This account of a famine at the Cascades was taken down in Indian from an old woman by my interpreter, Peter McGuff, who supplied also an interlinear translation. [See Sapir's original text.] The events took place about 1835." ES

118. "This text, like the preceding ['A Famine at the Cascades'], was taken down in Indian and provided with an interlinear translation by my interpreter, Peter McGuff, the source being an old woman named Sophie Klickitat. The events are supposed to have taken place at the Cascades long before the coming of the whites." ES

119. "*Ca'wac* ('Indian'), from Chinook jargon *sa'iwac*." ES

120. Note the similarity of songs learned by means of a dream: by the old man in this legendary account, also by successful youth on a *Tah* quest. DH

121. McWhorter: told in 1909, narrator unknown. DH

122. "Lame Sam with his son was hunting rabbits on the mountain slope of Medicine Valley, Yakima Indian Reservation, one winter day more than a quarter century ago. Sam came upon a trail in the snow which he could not identify with any game-tracks he had ever seen. There were the prints of lizard-like feet, and the sinuous track of a serpent body of prodigious size. The old hunter, remembering the stories heard in his young tribal days on the *n-Che-wana*, saw in his imagination the terrible *Gy-u-boo'-kum*. He called his son and they mounted their horses and hurried away from the dangerous place. It is supposed that the monster still haunts the desert mountain of the Medicine Valley." LVM

123. McWhorter: told by *Salatsze*, 1911. DH

124. McWhorter: narrator and time of telling unknown. DH

125. Spier and Sapir, p. 276. Told by Mrs. Teio. DH

126. "Mrs. Teio did not know of the sky root digging incident which is included in some versions of this tale. The Wishrams have the spider rope incident, but Mrs. Teio did not know it." LS

127. Compare the closing detail of this narrative with Wasco tale 7 "The Star Rock of the Tumwater." DH

128. McWhorter: told by Chief *Meninock*, August 1922. DH

129. "The 'star-rock' is not to be regarded as a solid substance, as the name would imply. It is the 'glow,' the 'sparkle' descending out of ethereal space, which settles or concentrates on the surface of a stone or other possible substance. It is the winning power' *tah* obtained from the Pleiades. The luck-glitter, typical of wealth, was secured with a handkerchief by the *tahmahnawis* hunters on the Ahtanum ridge [the Yakima Reservation] in the same manner as described by the Chief, who found his on the rocky shore of the *n-Che-wana*." LVM

130. Sapir, pp. 94-99. Told by Louis Simpson. DH

131. "A root referred to as 'wild potato' and said to be similar to the *amu'mal,* though of a finer grade and grain." ES

132. "A root referred to as 'wild onion;' it is similar to the *ak!a'lakia*, but is smaller in size." ES

133. "Known as 'wild carrot.'" [Sapir sketches the song tune sung throughout on p. 94.] ES

134. "[Sung or said] in a loud whisper." ES

135. Sapir, pp. 66-75. Told by Louis Simpson. DH

136. At least one form of shinny is a variety of hockey played by schoolboys in a schoolyard, using a curved stick and a ball or a block of wood. DH

137. On page 68 of his *Wishram Texts.* . . , Sapir records the approximate tune to which all of the magical-songs are sung. DH

138. "[This place is] now called the Goldendale Valley, Klickitat County, Washington." ES

139. Sapir, pp. 144-148. Told by Louis Simpson. ES

140. "This myth is perhaps only an incident in a longer tale of Coyote as unsuccessful imitator of the host. Compare Livingston Farrand, *Traditions of the Quinault Indians*, Jesup Expedition 2 (New York, 1909), pp. 85-91, especially pp. 87, 88. [This work is cited hereafter as *Quinault Traditions*.]" ES

141. Sapir, pp. 34-39. Told by Louis Simpson. Sapir also spells "At!At!A'Lia" as "At! At! A'Liya"--we have retained both spellings. DH

142. "The child-stealing woman-fiend *At!at!a'lia* of this narrative corresponds to the *Aq!asy'nasyene* of Kathlamet mythology. See esp. *Kathlamet Texts*, pp. 9-19." ES

143. "*At!at!a'lia's* furnace, or perhaps, better, barbecuing place was located on a small island called *At!at!a'lia itcagi'tkxo q* near the falls or 'Tumwater' only a short distance upriver from the main village of Wishram. It was reckoned as the extreme eastern point on the river of the Wishram [hence also Chinookan]) country. [Today, we might mark this as the upriver beginnings of the Columbia River Rapids, now inundated by a raised Columbia River and numerous hydroelectric dams.]" ES

144. "*Nixlu'idix*, [across the Columbia River and about five miles up from the present town of The Dalles, Oregon,] was the chief village of the Wishram, and contains the same stem element (*-xluid*) seen in

the generic name *Ita'xluit*, by which the Wishrams call themselves. The first person singular of this, *itcxlu'it* ('I am a Wishram') is probably the 'Echeloot' met by the Lewis and Clark
expedition. . . . ." ES

145. McWhorter: told by *Che-pos to-cos* (Owl Child), June 1923. DH

146. Under note 4, #18 "*Tah-tah kle-ah*," in *Ghost Voices*. . ., McWhorter
describes at least one instance of *Tah-tah kle-ah* used as a bug-
bear. The note also appears in this narrative under "Comparative
Notes" hereafter. DH

147. Sapir, pp. 104-107. Told by Louis Simpson. DH

148." [Sapir's interpreter] Peter McGuff explained the term 'trading friend'
thus: When one has a friend in another country [i.e. among
another tribe], he comes to see you or you go and see him. Both
are glad to meet each other; one gives the other a horse or anything valuable, the other gives something in return. Such are each
other's *ie'lpEt*." ES

149. In an extensive note to McWhorter, c. 1921, Chief Waters defines *Yah-
lipt*, or *Yah-y-lipt*.
"I do not know what the white people have to denote the form of
custom, the friendship among our tribes. *Yah-lipt*, is this way:

"I come to see you. I bring blankets, furs, beads, clothing and
many things with me. These, I give to you. I do not say anything.
I leave them without words. You are glad to see me. You take
me in and feed me; we are *Yah-lipt*. I am your *Yah-lipt;* and you
are my *Yah-lipt*. Maybe I have come from another tribe, come
with pack horses loaded for my *Yah-lipt*. I stay several days.
Then I say: 'Now I go back home.'

"You say: 'All right!' Then you order your boys, the young
Indians, to round up your horses. You select maybe ten, maybe
twenty of the best horses and give them to me. We have had a
good time, and I go home feeling fine.

"*Yah-lipt* is not loaning things, is not the way the white people do
business. White man goes to another white friend and wants
money. The white friend says: 'How long? When you pay back?'
The white man says: 'Thirty days, sixty days, I pay you back.'
That is not *Yah-lipt*. Indian never says anything about paying
back. Let it alone. Never speaks that he wants to be paid back.
That is good, the Indian way. The old Indian way of friends.

"Chief *Tommy Tash*, the Klickitat, would come from the White

Salmon to Chief Kamiaken of the Yakimas. Once he brought maybe forty Hudson Bay blankets; shawls and other goods, all packed on twenty horses. Twenty horses all loaded with goods for Kamiaken, his *Yah-lipt*. No words were said about the gifts. When Chief Tommy Tash was ready to return home, Chief Kamiaken had his horses rounded up and gave Chief Tommy Tash twenty of the best ones. This was *Yah-lipt*. The Chiefs were *Yah-lipt*.

"In my study of the Bible, I find the Bible a looking-glass. It reflects. It shows there was *Yah-lipt* among the Bible people. One man gets mad. He speaks bad of his neighbor. Maybe he strikes his neighbor. Then he thinks about what he has done. He finds that he has acted badly. He is sorry. He kills beef, divides it equally. He says to his neighbor: 'I was wrong. I was wrong in what I did. Take this meat. I have same amount; I give you half. Eat, and we will be friendly, forgetting the past. Let it all go, forgotten.' That is *Yah-lipt*; same as Indian have. By this I find that the Indian way is good; was good in the old tribe-days. It is not that way now. Young Indian goes to school and learns white man's business way. He is not *Yah-lipt* as was his father.

"The white man is not *Yah-lipt* to the Indian. He came here, took America from the Indians. He has not given in return. When the last day comes, the poor Indians will be on one side. The rich white people will be on the other side. God will know. He will know that the white man was not *Yah-lipt* when he took the poor Indians' land. It will not be good for the white man on that day. It will be better for the Indian who was always *Yah-lipt* until ruined by the white man."

150. *"Ciwa'nic*: 'stranger' in Yakima. Used regularly for the Nez Perce." ES

151. "This refers to the belief by Indians that the howl of the coyote foretells the approach of death." ES

152. "Coyote is thus the first to commit incest. The incestuous conduct of some people is traceable to him." ES

153. Sapir, pp. 46-49. Told to Pete McGuff - narrator not specified. DH

154. "This narrative fitly closes the Coyote cycle,[or so Sapir felt,] as in it Coyote reaches the farthest point to the east possible--the home of the Sun, who is conceived as a woman (*aga'lax*, 'sun,' is feminine in gender). A widespread [tale] of which this seems to be a kind of variation, or with which, at any rate, this is related represents the various animals in council as to whom is to be the sun. All are tried, but some objection is found in every case

except in that of the one who is now the sun. Coyote also is tried, but is derided for his tale-telling [gossip-mongering]; life would be impossible with him for the sun." See Tale 29 herein. ES

155. Sapir, pp. 148-153. Told by Louis Simpson. DH

156. "Compare *Kathlamet Texts*, pp. 79-89, where *ip!e'cxac* [Wishram *Ip!icxac*] is translated as 'Badger.' The Kathlamet story, however, would seem to apply better to the skunk than to the badger; and it is possible, as confidently affirmed by my interpreter, that there is here an error on the part of the Kathlamet informant. Skunk is *ap!e'sxas* in Kathlamet." ES

157. "These two words [expressions] seem to have no assignable significance. Raven means that Skunk has nothing the matter with him, except that his belly is all filled up with grass. *Cu' cu'* is whispered." [Sapir includes a tune line on p. 150 of *Wishram Texts* for these expressions.] ES

158. See the previous note. DH

159. "The exit to Coyote's house [*watcE'lx*, 'underground lodge, cellar'] is here implied to have been by way of the roof." ES

160. *'Itquctxi'lawa* properly means deer and other kinds of big game." ES

161. Sapir, pp. 132-139. Told by Louis Simpson. DH

162. "*Sapa-* or *Sipa-* is sometimes used as a 'high-sounding,' apparently titular, prefix to the names of mythological characters. Compare the names of Coyote's four sons in "Coyote and Antelope," herein [tale 25 above]. It is noteworthy that Jack Rabbit's name is here provided with the archaic *wi-*pronominal prefix, instead of the ordinary *i-*." ES

163. As perhaps a chanted portion of the text intended to further highlight the grandiose character for Jack Rabbit, Sapir gives us a melody line, *Wishram Texts*, p. 134. DH

164. Sapir, pp. 24-27. Told by Louis Simpson. DH

165. "A similar motif of men walking upside down occurs in *Quinault Traditions*, p. 85." ES

166. Sapir, pp. 10-19. Told by Louis Simpson. DH

167. "Compare this narrative with Franz Boas's 'Traditions of the Tillamook Indians,' *Journal of American Folklore*, 11 (1898), pp. 140, 141.

Also see James Teit's, *The Shuswap*, Publications of the Jesup
North Pacific Expedition 2 (New York, 1900-1909), p. 741."
[This work is cited hereafter as *The Shuswap*.] ES

168. "Raven plays the part of medicine man in Wishram mythology, [or so
 Sapir observed.]" {Cf. the story of "Coyote and Skunk," above.}
 ES

169. "*Idiaxi'lalit* [cf. *-gila-it*, 'to doctor'] denotes properly "medicine-man"
 in his capacity of 'doctor,' dispeller of disease; *idiage'wam* is
 used as equivalent to 'shaman' in its wider sense of one who can
 inflict harm on others by his control of spirits. Not every
 idiaxi'lalit or 'doctor' was such a 'shaman' or '*-tama-noas*,'
 though an *idiage'wam* could generally cure disease. In the text
 the two words are used interchangeably for 'dispeller of disease.'"
 ES

170. "Accompanied by a gesture in the recital." ES

171. Sapir, pp. 30-35. Told by Louis Simpson. DH

172. "That is, the 'story' of what he did, which would spread among the
 people; and make Coyote the butt of their jokes. A curious mate-
 rialization of the mere idea of a narrative or report into an entity
 independent of the narrator is here exemplified, similar to the
 common conception of a name as a thing existing independently
 of its bearer." ES

173. "The text is obscure. It is said that Coyote requested all things present
 not to carry off the 'story,' but forgot about the clouds (*itka'*),
 just then sailing above the spot. Not bound by the promise, they
 tore out 'the story' from its fastness and conveyed it to the
 people. Thus was explained how all had heard of Coyote's
 obscenity, though no one had witnessed it, and though he himself
 did not tell anyone of it. North of the Columbia River, and opposite the town of Mosier, Oregon, may still be seen a long, high
 mountain called *Idwo'tea* or 'Story,' in which Coyote attempted
 to lock up the 'story.' Its clefts are due to the sudden force with
 which the 'story' broke out." ES

174. McWhorter: told by *Che-pos to-cos* (Owl Child). DH

175. "The Wishom name for Hood River" [a stream as well as a town on the
 Oregon side of the Columbia River.] LVM

176. "'Big River,' applied in general to the Columbia River. Previously
 spelled '*n-Che-wana*.'" LVM

177. McWhorter: told by *Che-pos to-cos* (Owl Child), October 1923. DH

178. "Wishom plural for grizzly bear." LVM

179. "The scene of this legendary account is along the *n-Che-wana*, between Wishom and Hood River, Oregon, the closer proximity being in favor of the first-named place." [Along the Washington side of the river?] LVM

180. Sapir, pp. 48-67. Told by Louis Simpson. DH

181. "The Salmon [narrative] of the Wishram presents several striking analogies, [for Sapir,] with that of the Lower Chinook. See *Chinook Texts*, pp. 60-67. Salmon and Eagle are the two most heroic figures in Wishram mythology, and the deeds of the former form what is evidently one of the most popular tales of the Chinookan tribes." ES

182. "That is, the Columbia River." ES

183. "*Wa'xcam* is on the Yakima Reservation, four miles east of a point about midway between Fort Simcoe and Block House." [Perhaps Sapir is referring to the vicinity of *Wahk-shum*, or Simcoe Mountain {near Goldendale Washington}, and the murder of Andrew Bolon, Indian Agent, 1855, as related in McWhorter, Lucullus V. with Hines, Donald M. 1994. *Tragedy of the Wahk-Shum: The Death of Andrew J. Bolon, Yakima Indian Agent, As Told by Su-El-Lil, Eyewitness; Also, The Suicide of General George A. Custer, As Told by Owl Child, Eyewitness*. Issaquah WA: Great Eagle Publishing, Inc.] ES

184. "Done with a very high pitched voice." ES

185. Spier and Sapir, p. 273. Told by Mrs. Mabel Teio. DH

186. Sapir, pp. 74-93. Told by Louis Simpson. DH

187. "For a very similar narrative of a non-Chinookan tribe, [Sapir directs us to *Quinault Traditions*, pp. 102-105] the places of Eagle, Sparrow Hawk, and Chicken Hawk in the Quinault narrative are taken by 'Blue Jay's chief,' Landotter, and 'another man' respectively. Blue Jay and Beaver are characters in both narratives." ES

188. "This is an Indian stew made of two roots [*adwo'q* 'wild carrot' and *amu'mal* 'wild potato'] to which dried fish was sometimes added." ES

189. "This was indicated by an appropriate movement." ES

190. "This is some species of bird, but my interpreter was unable to identify it." ES

191. "This term refers to a contest designed to test physical power or endurance. The one who withstood the most pain won the game [or contest.]" ES

192. "This is another species of hawk, whose identification is uncertain. It is described as a small hawk with a sharp wing bone." ES

193. "[To be sung in a] high pitch." [The tune is provided by Sapir, *Wishram Texts*, p. 90.] ES

194. "[Uttered with a] high pitch." ES

195. Sapir, pp. 120-131. Told by Pete McGuff. DH

196. "[Said] in surprise." ES

197. "[Implied here is] the matter-of-courseness, as it were, of the destruction of the people: 'They just go right in, and are destroyed without further ado.'" ES

198. "That is, they do not return." ES

199. "Literally, "Who we two shall run?" ES

200. These are the fire-people with whom the Thunder brothers are associated." DH

201. *"Wa'x* has reference properly to the burning of fire, with which Thunder brothers are associated. He rises slowly to his song like a fire starting into burn. It is not probable that the literal meaning of *wa'x* is here lost sight of." ES

202. "Here the term *wa'x* denotes the opposite of 'slowly rising,' because of the short vowel.' ES

203. Sapir, pp. 138-145. Told by Louis Simpson. DH

204. "[Given in] rather a high pitch." ES

205. "Known generally [among Indians of many tribes] as 'wapato.'" ES

206. *"Ats!Epts!Ep* was a mixture of dried fish and pieces of flesh mashed up fine and kept in fish-oil." ES

207. "He sang while waving the blanket over his shoulders. The song is

repeated several times." [Sapir gives the melody line on p. 142.]
ES

208. "The Merman was the guardian of the fish supply. [See Wishom tale 2
"Coyote and *Itc!E'xyan*," above.] Also compare the Chinook
Its!xia'n (gambler's protector)." ES

209. "Indicated by a gesture." ES

210. "That is, without pity, with sinister thoughts." ES

211. Spier and Sapir, pp. 274-275. Told by Mrs. Mable Teio. DH

212. Sapir, pp. 116-121. Told by Louis Simpson. DH

213. "[According to Sapir, a fictional] monster said to look like an alligator."
ES

214. "Indicated by gesture." ES

215. "This is all that Louis Simpson knew of the [narrative,] but it is by no
means all of it. It was said, according to Sapir, to be more particularly a Clackamas myth, and to consist of a long chain of incidents located in the Willamette region.

"[According to Sapir,] it corresponds, doubtless, in a general
way, to the *Kathlamet* 'Myth of the Mink' in *Kathlamet Texts*, pp.
103-117. The mink and panther of that myth correspond to the
weasel and eagle respectively of the Wishram version. A fragmentary account of the myth, obtained in broken English from
another informant, contained the incident of a violent rain following upon the divulging by Weasel of the name of a certain place,
confided to him, after much coaxing on his part, by the unwilling
Eagle. The exact correspondent of this incident is to be found in
the *Kathlamet* myth referred to, on pp. 112-113." ES

216. McWhorter: told by *Che-pos to-cos* (Owl Child), October 1923. DH

217. Sapir, pp. 164-173. This myth was taken down in phonetic Wishram
and forwarded with interlinear translation by Pete McGuff, the
original source being an old Indian woman named *AnEwi'kus*.
Despite several attempts to get the whole myth in its complete
form, it had to be left unfinished as here given. It is evidently a
variant of the Kathlamet 'Myth of *Aq!asxe'nasxena'* [See Boas,
Kathlamet Texts, pp. 9-19]. ES

218. A similar track in the dust after an infant is found to be missing is
recounted in Wishom 19 "The *Gy-u-boo-kum* (I)" above. DH

219. [Compare Wishom tale 27A "Coyote and *At!at!a'lia*," esp. footnote 142 herein.] Pete McGuff [wrote that this mythical female being] "is supposed to be a kind of a person, but much larger than an ordinary person. No one today can give the exact description, nor has anyone seen one." ES

220. This being is likely Meadowlark. Often, in narratives over the plateau, as the result of an accident Meadowlark's leg is broken. But thanks to the kindness of the person who caused the injury, the leg is splinted, usually with "brushwood." Out of gratitude Meadowlark prophesies, provides solutions to dilemmas which will be met by the traveler. DH

221. "The '*ik!alamgwadid*" [or jingles] are described as a tin ornament of the shape of a funnel; several were tied close to one another to a belt or saddle, and produced a jingling effect. Pete adds that surely the '*ik!alamgwadid*' was made before Indians ever saw tin. 'To my knowledge, it was made of horn or bone in olden days. Perhaps dewclaw rattles are referred to.'" ES

222. "No explanation of this term was given. Probably some sort of beads or other ornament is referred to." ES

223. "All progenitors from the fourth generation back, i.e., beginning with one's great-grandparents, are included in the terms *ilxt!a'max* (masc.), *alxt!a'max* (fem.)." ES

224. "*L!E'k!!Ek* properly means 'to uncover or open' something by taking off a lid. The idea of 'lousing' is here derived from that of 'opening or parting the hair' when looking for." ES

225. The episode of fleas, et al., as people about to descend and to afflict Indians also appears in Wasco Tale 2 "Ascent to the Sky and Return to the Earth." DH

226. An episode of bundles containing the darkness, held by the Ground-Squirrel people, also appears in Wasco tale 2 "Ascent to the Sky and Return to the Earth." DH

227. The episode of a man, shot through with an arrow and who dies, also appears in Wasco tale 2 "Ascent to the Sky and Return to the Earth." DH

228. "[According to Sapir, this narrative doubtless] continues very much like its Kathlamet correspondent. See *Kathlamet Texts*, p. 13." ES

229. Despite several attempts to record the complete narrative text, it had to be left unfinished as here given. For Sapir it was evidently a

variant of the Kathlamet "Myth of *Aq!asxe'nasyena*." See also
Kathlamet Texts, pp. 9-19. DH

230. Spier and Sapir, p. 274. Told by Mrs. Mable Teio. DH

231. "The narration was interrupted at this point." LS

232. McWhorter: told by *Che-pos to-cos* (Owl Child), 7 June 1926. DH

233. Though incomplete, this narrative conforms essentially to A-T 328. *The
     Boy Steals the Giant's Treasure*, Jack and the Beanstalk, in Aarne
     Antti and Stith Thompson 1961. *The Types of the Folktale; A
     Classification and Bibliography*, FFC 3. Helsinki: Academic
     Scientiarum Fennica.. For other versions of "Jack and the Bean-
     stalk," related among the North American Indian nations, see
     Thompson, Stith 1966. *Tales of the North American Indians*.
     Bloomington: Indiana University Press, p. 357, note 287h: *Fie-fi-
     fo fum* (G532.1). DH

234. Of interest in this version is the absence of motifs by which the hero
     might climb to the sky: e.g., F54.2. Plant grows to sky (Jack and
     the Beanstalk); D983.1. Magic Bean; F815.7. Extraordinary
     vine. Likewise absent is F53. Ascent to upper world on arrow
     chain. No vertical image or concept appears at all. Instead, in a
     practical, matter-of-fact **horizontal** way, the hero blazes or marks
     his trail by means of arrows stuck into the ground that he might
     find his way back. DH

235. Also of interest, the girl's father may be a bad man and a cannibal, but
     he seems not a giant. And he possesses no marvelous device
     which the youth might steal, take below to earth. DH

236. "This story is incomplete. Owl Child said at this point, 'I do not re-
     member just right. This story ends nice, has a nice ending. I will
     ask Sallie [his wife] about it and will tell it to you some other
     time. It is a fine-ending story.' This was June 7, 1926." LVM

237. *Che-pos to-cos* or Owl Child was also known as *Shat-taw-wee* [Leader
     in Battle], a name given him by the Piegan Blackfeet Indians of
     Montana. His English name was Alec McCoy (See also note 256
     hereafter.) This autobiography was begun narrated to L.V.
     McWhorter on July 13, 1911. But Nelson Ault's *The Papers of
     Lucullus Virgil McWhorter* (Pullman: Friends of the Library,
     State College of Washington, 1959), in folder 1534, lists approxi-
     mately fifty pages of varied manuscript plus notes. My examina-
     tion indicated that these were not clear copies but drafts of auto-
     biographical episodes and legendary matter, including many
     corrections and duplications, taken at different dates over the

fifteen years following Owl Child's start at his autobiography
made with McWhorter. I have therefore taken up these later
additions, episodes of adventure and danger which Owl Child
recollected, and have assigned roman numerals and placed them
all in a chronological order. Spelling and names have been retained from the original drafts. Only slight emendations have
been made in the version here, to cope with matters of paragraph-
ing, complete sentences, etc., all for the sake of the reader's
ready understanding. McWhorter's notes are richly detailed, and
these are included. Begin 13-18/1534, pp. 13-18 in folder no.
1534, "The McWhorter Papers." DH

238. But Owl Child notes here and in Sec. III hereafter that he was living at
the dalles (not at the city on the Oregon side of the Columbia
River), but on the Washington side of the river.The Dalles--at the
rapids and white water --is simply a modern point of reference.
DH

239. To corroborate Owl Child's autobiography, we have related it to Sapir,
Edward and Spier, Leslie 1930. *Wishram Ethnography*, UWPA
III, No. 3. Seattle: Univ. of Washington Press, pp. 151-300. This
text will be cited hereafter as *Spier*. See especially the references
describing "Wishram Villages," pp. 164-167. DH

240. "He had the flattened head distinctive of chieftain lineage. His father
was half Umatilla, half Wishom [Wishram]. His mother was half
Wasco, half *Wy-um* or *Wy-yum* (Fishtail)." LVM

241. "He left the cattleman after becoming embroiled in an escapade resulting in tragedy." LVM

242. William Charley led Lucullus Virgil McWhorter to *Su-el-lil* (Yakima
George), and to the oral traditional history narrative of the murder of Andrew J. Bolon, Yakama Indian Agent. As a boy *Su-el-lil*
had been an eyewitness to the murder. William Charley not only
served as interpreter between his father-in-law and McWhorter,
but also provided McWhorter with a number of Indian folk narratives. See McWhorter, L.V. with Donald M. Hines, ed., 1994.
*Tragedy of the Wahk-Shum; The Death of Andrew J. Bolon, Yaki-
ma Indian Agent, As Told by Su-el-lil, Eyewitness; Also, The
Suicide of General George A. Custer, As Told by Owl Child,
Eyewitness.* Issaquah WA. DH

243. This segment, 59/1534, "A Canoe Race on the Columbia River," was
narrated by Owl Child on 7 June 1926. DH

244. Beginning 19/1534 the "Acquisition of Spirit Power, or *Tahmahnawis*
Power of *Che-pos to-cos* (Owl Child)", no date. DH

245. See *Spier*, p. 240. The youthful ordeal of a nighttime dive into the unknown, frightening depths of a riverside pool was demanded of other youths besides Owl Child. DH

246. See *Spier*, p. 239, concerning the training regimen for Wishom youth preparing to seek Spirit Power or their *Tah*. DH

247. The magical appearance of the Otter-spirit to Owl Child in later life, when he is desperately wounded and trapped and near death, recalls his youthful ordeals by water and possible acquisition of his *tah*. See Sec. VIII hereafter. DH

248. This account would seem to be Owl Child's search for his *tah*, or Spirit Power. Commonly among the Nez Perce and other Plateau tribes, boys and also girls at about age twelve would be led to a distant mountain where for several days and nights, sans food or sleep, they would await the visitation of an animal, bird, etc., whose magical spirit would remain with them all their lives. Not all youth found a *tah*, though they might return again and again to await its coming. In Sapir's *Wishram Texts*, in "Winter Bathing," pp. 189-191, Peter McGuff describes a portion of his youthful training, but admits that he did not succeed in obtaining Spirit Power. DH

249. See *Spier*, p. 240. DH

250. "Autobiography," resumes here from 13/1534: July 13, 19ll. DH

251. See note 241 above here. DH

252. Begin here 35/1534; no date. DH

253. See *Spier*, p. 240. DH

254. Continue here 35/1534: July 13, 1911. DH

255. Begin "Modoc War: Owl Child," 48-54/1534: no date. DH

256. "Owl Child related here also that his Wasco Indian name was *Snle-hi*, no known meaning. It was inherited from his maternal grandfather, and given him by his father. His mother was Wasco, his father Wishom." LVM

257. See "Warfare," *Spier*, pp. 228-232. DH

258. Cf. *Spier*, p. 229, concerning dreamlore prefiguring the group's fate in the combat to follow. DH

259. The Warm Springs warrior possessed shamanistic powers of foretelling the future through his dreams. A dream of blood would foretell disaster in the next day's fighting. He had this magical capacity thanks to his Spirit Power or *tah*, because he enjoyed the spirit power from a particular bird or animal. But his predictions gave courage to the Warm Springs warriors, and so they pressed ahead. DH

260. This is undoubtedly an observation by Owl Child of the words, the working of a magic spell, of Sympathetic Magic. Implications in the spellmaking include perhaps imitating the swaying of a snake, its reputed power to hypnotize its prey, etc. DH

261. No better attestation of a successful spell than from a victim of rather high repute. DH

262. See particularly 53-54/1534: no date. DH

263. See note 1, p. 206-207, of "A Personal Narrative of the Paiute War," in Edward Sapir's *Wishram Texts*. . . ., cited above. Known as the "*iqta't* stick, ". . . a piece of hard wood had a series of semi-circular notches cut into it. Another piece of wood was rubbed up and down over it, a 'thrilling' sound resulting. In the war dance, as practiced by the Wascos, singing and the simultaneous rubbing of the *iqta't* accompanied the dancing." ES

264. An interesting account by Louis Simpson, also a soldier "from the Warm Springs Reservation, Oregon," [p. 205] who fought in the Paiute Indian Wars in Southern Oregon, 1866-68, appears in Sapir, *Wishram Texts*, pp. 205-227. The narrative is included hereafter. DH

265. Begin "Owl Child's Adventure in Battle," 6/1534: no date. DH

266. Begin "Owl Child and the Sioux," 43-44/1534: no date [handwritten]. DH

267. See *Spier*, p. 240, concerning possession of multiple Spirit Powers. Here, Owl Child, according to his narrative, had at least two: Otter, and a Hawk. DH

268. Here Owl Child recalls the dazed state of mind he was in but also the magical presentiment of the Otterman, which directs him to remember his youthful training in past autumns whereby he was made to dive into deep, water-filled holes close by the Columbia River, both to find courage, but also to acquire a *tah*. See also note 247 above. DH

269. Begin here "An Adventure of *Che-pos to-cos* (Owl Child)," 7-9/1534; July 11, 1911. DH

270. McWhorter recorded specific questions and answers here:
> "McWhorter: 'How could you get away from so many men without any of them seeing you? You must have had a strong *tah* to be able to do such a daring thing.'
> "*Che-pos to-cos* (Owl Child): 'That was just it. That was my power, to do such things. There is a bird, not the *Why-am-mah* (eagle), but a smaller bird. It comes through the air with sharp, bent wings, like the unseen thunder, on its prey. This was my power, from this bird. I got it when I was young, and it saved me. I was swift, like this bird. My enemies could not see me go. The whites cannot understand these things. It is the Indian way."
> [On Owl Child's specific spirit quest as a youth, he may indeed in a vision aided by lack of sleep and food have been visited by the spirit of the particular hawk of which he spoke. See Sec. III herein.] LVM

271. Begin "Adventure with a Buffalo Cow," 5/1534: told June 1923. DH

272. This was the same knife with which Owl Child killed the Blood Indian who stole his wife from him one night in camp. See Sec. XIII hereafter. DH

273. "Where Owl Child stabbed the buffalo cow to death was a prairie between two mountains in the Sweet-grass Mountains, near the British line north of Fort Benton. 'Very rough and rocky, this mountain.'" LVM

274. Continues 5/1534: June 1923. DH

275. Begin here "Owl Child and the Buffalo Bull," 2-3/1534: no date. DH

276. Begin "Owl Child's Adventure with the Sleeping Buffalo," 45-46/1534: no date. DH

277. Begin here 37/1534: July 13, 1911. DH

278. "He won the title of 'chief' by taking three guns from the Crees in battle on the Red River in Northern Montana. He also took guns while fighting the Crows on the Sun River, Montana. He had distinction as a warrior. He sometimes wore a Cree scalp at his temple." LVM

279. "Was It Custer's Last Stand," 38/1534: July 13, 1911. DH

280. What follows appears to be an eyewitness account of the annihilation of

the forces led by Lt. Col. George A. Custer in the Battle of the Little Bighorn, Montana Territory, 25-26 June 1876. At best this account is a true eyewitness account by Owl Child, particularly as he cites observed details of a large Sioux camp, specific topography, including the confluence of the two small rivers, the flat of the ground, and of the cavalry troop approaching, etc. At the least, if a borrowed narrative, the account which Owl Child gives us may be no less valuable in that it remains an account told widely by Indians who took part in the battle. Of great interest is Owl Child's detailed description of Custer's suicide, seen from a distance. DH

281. McWhorter records specific questions and answers here:
    Q: --"You say the commander was last to fall? Yellow Wolf in the Nez Perce War tells me how, in one battle, he shot first the officer so there would be no one to 'drive the soldiers.'" (See McWhorter's *Yellow Wolf: His Own Story*.)
    A: -- "We recognized him to be commander. The last man; he shot himself. Two shots to himself he made."
    Q: -- "Carbine or pistol?"
    A: -- "Six-shooter."
    Q: -- "Where did he place the gun?"
    A: -- "There was an argument. Some thought the first shot was here (indicating region of the heart), while others said here (placing a finger on the right temple). Myself, I thought he fired first to his breast. He raised on one knee, and then shot to his head. This time he did not get up; did not move."
    Q: -- "Did you afterwards cross over to the battlefield?"
    A: -- "It was a terrible battle we watched from our ridge--hiding. It was not for us to go there. When night came we left that place, returned home without scalps or horses." LVM

282. Begin here 15-18/1534: no date. DH

283. See note 272 above regarding the knife.

284. Owl Child was a superb tale-teller, and we have previously noted the folkloric motifs from his narrated tales. But for his Oral Traditional Historic accounts, we have sought to identify the folkloric motifs which appear in his retelling of his adventures. These motifs have been arranged according to Thompson's *Motif-Index of Folk-Literature*.

INDEX OF MOTIFS

B. ANIMALS

B500 - B599. Services of Helpful Animals

B500. Magic power from animal [otter]. See also D1739.3; and esp. D1811.2. Magic wisdom received from supernatural being.

B513.1. Otter tells man [when a boy] to remember healing powers of water. Cf. B512. Medicine shown by animal.

D. MAGIC

D1240. Magic Waters and Medicines

D1241.1. Magic water.

D1500. Magic Object Controls Disease

D1500.1.18.7. Water from creek as remedy.

D1710. Possession of Magic Powers

D1719.1. Magic power only at night.

D1739.3. Magic power from diving into water.

D1741.10. Magic powers lost by describing/telling of them.

D1752. Voice of Indians' "Spirit Power" calls him, tells him what to do.

D1760. Means of Producing Magic Power.

D1765. Magic results by command.

D1766.9.1. Magic results from singing magic song and dancing.

D1766.9.2 Magic results from performing upon a magical instrument.

D1781. Magic results from singing songs of magic.

D1782. Sympathetic magic. Cf. D1782.1. Magic results obtained by imitating desired action.

D1783.6. Reverse magic--while creating incantation to put enemy asleep, the same magic makes originators more alert.

[D1800 - D2199. Manifestations of Magic Power.]

D1812.3.3. Future revealed in dreams.

D1812.3.3.3.1. Sleepiness induced in enemy through incantation.

D1812.5.1.1.3. Blood (in dream) as omen of killing.

D1825.10. Magic power to "see" spectral fire streaks in the dark.

D1827.3. Magic hearing of the dead talking.

D1827.3. Magic hearing of noises from spirit beings.

D1841.5.1.2. Magic invulnerability to bullets.

D2031. Magic illusions: defender feels lassitude/torpor, lack of will to fight.

D2031.18.1. Person loses "sense"--believes himself in house, but found himself in graveyard.

D2089.11. Canoe paddle magically broken.

K. DECEPTIONS

K710.1. Victim rendered helpless by magic, captured. Cf.
K1872.1. Army appears like forest. Each soldier carries branches. [If the Wasco troops were no "Birnam
Wood," their magic, like a camouflage, apparently
allowed them very close quarter with the enemy.]

---

285. Louis Simpson's "A Personal Narrative of the Paiute War" appears in
Sapir, pp. 204-227.

286. "The Paiute or Snake Indian War spoken of in this personal narrative of
Louis Simpson has been described in detail under the title of "The
Shoshone War" (1866-1868) in H. H. Bancroft's *History of
Oregon*, Vol. II, Chapt. 21, pp. 512-554. The war was conducted
against the Oregon Shoshones of Malheur River and Camp
Warner, the whites being assisted by a considerable body of
Indians from the Warm Spring Reservation." ES

287. "*It!ua'nxayuke*, used to refer to the Paiutes, really means 'Enemies.'"
ES

288. "These names are probably Bancroft's *Panina*, the leader of the Paiutes,
and *Wewawewa* (op. cit., p. 550)." ES

289. The *iqta't* is a piece of hard wood that has a series of semicircular
notches cut into it: . . Another piece of wood was rubbed up and
down over it, a 'thrilling' sound resulting. In the war dance, as
practiced by the Wascos, singing and the simultaneous rubbing of
the *iqta't* accompanied the dancing." [See note 263 above]. ES

290. "That is, 'male cub.'" ES

291. "This sound is broken up into short periods by quickly beating the palm
against the open mouth. The pitch of the vowel is very high, a
shrill effect resulting." ES

292. "As before, but whispered." ES

293. Perhaps a guidon. DH

294. "Literally, 'arrows.'" ES

295. "Indicated by a gesture." ES

296. See note 291 above. ES

297. "With gesture towards the western horizon." ES

298. "Literally,'"birds,' (= 'animals'), somewhat slangy for 'horses.'" ES

299. "It is practically certain that these names are nothing but disguised forms of the English [language] Camp Harney and Malheur River." ES

300 "That is, my companion." ES

301. "As above." [See note 291 above.] ES

302. "Literally, 'Fish-eaters.' This sentence [in Sapir's original text] is in Shoshonean." ES

303. "[In Sapir's original text] this sentence is in Shoshonean." ES

304. "[Again, in Sapir's original notes] this sentence is in Shoshonean." ES

305. "That is, the one near us." ES

306. "As above." [See note 291 above.] ES

307. "As above, in a high pitch." [See note 291 above.] ES

308. "As above." [See note 291 above.] ES

309. "That is, the President of the United States." ES

310. "Sarcastic: 'Don't waste your powder.'" ES

311. "Literally, 'Your bullets will be eaten up, consumed.'" ES

312. "As above." [See note 291 above.] ES

313. "That is,'dreamt when training during the puberty rights for a guardian spirit.'" ES

314. "*Pa'pkEs* is one of Louis Simpson's Indian names. It was said by him to have been borne by a former Wishram chief. His common Indian name today is *Me'nait*." ES

INDEX OF MOTIFS

For each oral narrative in this volume the *motifs* have been noted hereafter. By *motif* we mean that ". . . smallest element in a tale having a power to persist in tradition. . . Most *motifs* fall into three classes. First are the actors in a tale. . .; second come certain items in the background of the action, magic objects, unusual customs, strange beliefs, and the like; . . . in the third place there are single incidents--and these comprise the great majority of *motifs*." (Thompson 1946:415f.). We have employed Thompson's *Motif-Index of Folk-Literature*, also his *Tales of the North American Indians*.

THE TRADITIONAL NARRATIVES OF THE WISHRAMS

I. TALES OF THE ORIGINS OF MAN, ANIMALS AND PLANTS, PHENOMENA

1A. COYOTE AT LAPWAI, IDAHO
A. Mythological Motifs

A522.1.3. Coyote as culture hero

A1263.1.1.Nez Perce created from blood of monster wiped from Coyote's hands [a brave, dangerous race of warriors]

A1263.8. People, villages made of flesh thrown here and there of monster

A1263.9. Wishram people created of monster's tongue--hence their flatheads

F. Marvels

F843.2. Extraordinary rope made of hazel-bushes

F910.1. Monster and Coyote attempt to inhale each other

F911.6. All-swallowing monster

G. Ogres

G106. Mountain monster

G127. Ogre lies on his belly lest he burst, his guts spill out

G155.1. Ogre turns over; his belly bursts--he dies

G155.2. Dead ogre is skinned by Coyote

G332. Sucking monster--swallows that flying overhead or going along underneath

P. Society

P556.3. Verbal challenge to swallow each other

Z. Miscellaneous Groups of Motifs

Z71.2.2.4. Direction: towards the uplands

Z71.3.3. Five [5 taunts/challenges made to monster][5 steps from monster][5
tries to make a rope long enough][5 times Coyote and Monster
attempt to inhale each other]

1B. COYOTE AND *ITC!E'XYAN*
A. Mythological Motifs

A522.1.3. Coyote as culture hero

A1611.1. Origin of Indian tribes--"Soon the people will come into this land."

B. Animals

B142.2.2. Prophetic Coyote

F. Marvels

F911.6. All-Swallowing monster--has many people, many canoes, etc., inside

F911.6.2. Monsters swallows canoes laden with people

F912.2. Coyote kills swallowing monster from within by cutting out its heart;
cf. K952. Animal (Monster) killed from within

F1088.3.3. Coyote and people, etc., at death of monster "float up to the
surface"

G. Ogres

G127. Coyote swallowed, falls through "water" to bottom of Ogre's belly

G332.Sucking [swallowing] monster

G427. Ogre swallows Coyote while he clings to a tree

G513.2. Ogre transformed into harmless being

M. Ordaining the Future

M310.1.1.1. Prophecy: preeminence of "the people" who are "coming soon--
they will note how Coyote transformed Monster into a harmless
being

2. *IS-TAM-MA*, CHIEF OF THE BEAVERS
A. Mythological Motifs

A522.4. Beaver as Chief of all beavers of region--he controls the waters

A934.4.1. Origin of south fork of Satus River, where youth dragged liver of giant Beaver; cf. A901. Topographical features caused by experiences of primitive hero; cf. also A936

A969.10. Origin of gap through which present Satus-Goldendale highway passes

A1263.8. Klamath, Shoshone and other tribes come from pieces of cut-up Giant Beaver thrown to the tribal lands; cf. A1611.1. Origin of American Indian tribes

A1614.6.3. Kittitas and Wenatchee Indians grew from liver of Giant Beaver--thus are short and dark of skin

A1675.1. Shoshonean Indians are strong, mean, always angry--grow from bone of Giant Beaver

B. Animals

B183.2. Magic beaver--changes size

B299.11.*Fish-gills*, sister, requires oil for her painful "dry hair"

B727. Beaver tail very fat--source of oil for sister's hair

B871.2.10. Giant horned Beaver--chief of all the beavers

D. Magic

D411.1.2. Transformation: small beaver, once speared, becomes huge and strong

D965.20. Wonderfully strong, talking reeds [old man bulrush]

D1388.0.7. [Old Men] Bulrushes hold fast, keep youth from being pulled into the ocean

F. Marvels

F614.2.4. Precocious youth pulls up willow, pine trees trying to hold back Giant Beaver

F628.0.1.1. Youth fights, slays chief of Beavers

F834.8. Remarkable bone spear made to kill beaver

F1084.0.3. Continuous fighting. No rest or food.

M. Ordaining the Future

M325.1. Prophecy--coming of a new people to the land

P. Society

P253.11. Sister mourns for brother [for oil for her hair] sunrise to sunrise

P485.2. Hunter, kills game to get oil for sister

P251.9. Brother prepares oil for sister's hair, nurses her

W. Traits of Character

W230.3. A brother and younger sister

Z. Miscellaneous Groups of Motifs

Z357. Place of tale: lake filled with beaver, vicinity of city of Yakima

3. THE VISIT TO THE WORLD OF GHOSTS
B. Animals

B810.3.3. Coyote(s)

C. Tabu

C311.1.5.1. Tabu: observing Eagle as he sings, performs on magical flute; cf. C331. Tabu: looking back

C321. Tabu: looking into box (Pandora) [Eagle carries box lest Coyote open it]

C400. Speaking tabu

C645. Coyote forbidden to open eyes, to look in any direction lest both he and Eagle be drowned

C725.2. Tabu: Chief to defecate on/by path

C833.10. Tabu: traveling too far ahead

C905.3. When Coyote opens magical box, he sees wife and son(s) of self and of Eagle

C953.1. For opening box too soon, Coyote loses chance to bring immortality to life [loses wife and son(s) of self and of Eagle]

C953.1. Wives and sons of Coyote and of Eagle must return to and remain in Other World since Coyote violated tabu

C996.1. Both Eagle and Coyote fall into water--near shore because Coyote opened his eyes [too soon]

D. Magic

D491.2.1.1. Compressible magic box containing many people and objects

D676. Eagle magically transports Coyote [steps] across great river

D1174. Magic box

D1223.1. Magic flute

D1275. Magic song (singing)

D1313.7.1. Magic flute [and singing] reveals Land of the Dead across river

D1520.24. Transportation by magic box [Eagle carries, then Coyote carries box]

D1687.1. As Coyote nears end of his journey, voices talking and laughing are heard from box

E. The Dead

E481.2. Land of the Dead across water [great river]

E481.8.2.1. Moon comes down to the ground at night--lights up Land of Dead

E489.12. Inhabitants of Land of Dead are seen clearly at night (their daytime)-- sleep during the day (their night)

E712.4.1. Soul(s) of wives and of son(s) of Coyote and of Eagle are hidden in box

F. Marvels

F133.6. Land of the Dead across a great river

F137. Long [indeterminate] distance to Land of the Dead

F558.2. Remarkable skin from person of Land of the Dead

F929.3. Man catches, swallows moon; cf. A1174.5. Darkness comes when frog leaps up to swallow moon; cf. F911.6.2. Frog as swallower of moon

F929.4. Coyote catches, swallows moon

G. Ogres

G301. Monster [moon] who devours people, deters spirits from Land of Dead; cf. F150.2. Entrance to Other World guarded by monsters (or animals)

H. Tests

H1114.2. [Eagle's] task: carrying ever-increasing burden up mountain

J. The Wise and the Foolish

J2752.1. Coyote, foolish, is unable to see Land of Dead

K. Deceptions

K684. Coyote spits out moon, throws "her" away

N. Chance and Fate

N339.19.1. Wife and two sons of Coyote die

N339.19.2. Wife and two sons of Eagle die

P. Society

P234.4. Coyote mourns for wife and two sons

S. Unnatural Cruelty

S110. Coyote plans, murders person of Land of the Dead

S114. Murder by flaying; cf. S166. Mutilation: skin cut from back

W. Traits of Character

W230.2.1. Wife [of Coyote]

W230.2.1.1 Wife [of Eagle]

W231.1.2. Boys [2 sons of Eagle]

W231.1.2.1. Boys [2 sons of Coyote]

Z. Miscellaneous Groups of Motifs

Z71.1.1. Three [3 nights Coyote and Eagle remain in Land of Dead]

Z71.1.2. Four [4 nights]

Z71.2.1.1. Trip *homeward*

Z71.3.3. Five [5 days travel]

4. HOW COYOTE DESTROYED THE TRAIL TO THE UPPER WORLD
A. Mythological Motifs

A521. Culture hero is dupe

A1335.16. When trail up to the Spirit World is closed, only spirits of dead Indians may go up

A1541.8. Origin [in early spring] of Feast of the New Foods; cf. A1535. Origin of secular feasts; cf. V70. Religious feasts and fasts

A1700.1. Creation of game [animals, etc.]
A2686.4. Origin of edible roots
A2687.3. Origin of berries

B. Animals

B810.3.1. Fox [Red Fox]
B810.3.3. Coyote

C. Tabu

C650.2. Injunction: Coyote must do everything that he is told to do by Red Fox
C688.1. Injunction: not to dance exceedingly hard
C688.2. Compulsion: to wear buckskins while hunting

D. Magic

D1030.2. Magic banquet--in Spirit Land
D1211. Magic drum
D1245.1. Magic perfume: grass and flowers

E. The Dead

E1.1. From death due to fall from Upper World, Coyote returns to life
E489.5.1. Dancing in Spirit Land

F. Marvels

F10.3. Red Fox leads Coyote to Spirit Land and to feast there
F163.8. In Spirit Land is a great long house, filled with Indians
F499.4. Spirits of Upper World

J. The Wise and the Foolish

J1117.1.1. Coyote, discovered asleep, having sneaked into Upper World--must be evicted
J1959.3. Coyote relates [lies] that he had gone to the Spirit Land "when he was young"

L. Reversal of Fortune

L101.2. Unpromising hero: younger brother

M. Ordaining the Future

M100. Vows and oaths
M119.9. Oath by raising right hand, answering "yes."

P. Society

P251.5. Two brothers
P487. Manager, of hunt
P488. Night watcher [sentry]
P553.2. Bows and arrows
P634. Feasts

V. Religion

V311.4. Upon eating of Feast of the New Food, and then at death--person will see sight of original Feast in the Upper World (from which Coyote was evicted)

W. Traits of Character

W230.2.1. Women [7 women--pick berries, dig roots]

W231.1.1. Men [7 men--hunt all different kinds of game]

W231.1.2. Two brothers

Z. Miscellaneous Groups of Motifs

Z71.0.0. Two [2 brothers]

Z71.1. Three [Coyote dances 3 days and nights] [3 warnings that Coyote shouldn't dance so hard] [3 times walk around house]

Z71.2.2.4. Up [up to the Spirit Land]

Z71.3.3. Five [hunt for 5 days]

Z71.5. Seven [7 men, 7 women]

Z71.5.9. All week [7 days and nights] - people dance "all week"

Z73.0.1. Dawn [*Sapalwit* morning]

Z73.0.2. Sunrise, return home

Z73.1. Night [as the sun was setting]

Z73.1.1. Saturday morning

Z73.2.2.4. Up

5A. COYOTE AND THE FIVE SISTERS
OF THE *N-CHE-WANA*
A. Mythological Motifs

A522.1.4. Coyote as Culture Hero

A935. Origin of falls [cataracts]; cf. A 901. Topographical features caused by experiences of primitive hero [demigod, deity]

A935.2. Origin of *Klah-ti-hut*, falls on Klickitat River

A935.3. Origin of Wenatchee Falls, a prime fishery for all the tribes (the work of Coyote)

A935.4. Origin of Kettle Falls in the Okanogan Country [work of Coyote]

A936.2. Origin of Coyote's clothes hanging place [no fleas there]

A936.3. Origin of netting site (only) for salmon below The Dalles

A936.4. Origin of island fishery [and rites] on Skein Island, above Celilo

A936.5. Origin of place near Umatilla [river mouth?] that salmon can be called ashore

A936.6. Site of Coyote's failure to change channel of Columbia River

A936.7. Origin of "Coyote's Daughter," big rock [work of Coyote]

A989.6. By a stream entering the *n-Che-wana* in the "Upper Country"--place of Coyote's residence

A994. Huge lake near oceanside holding all fish

A1127.1.1.1. Origin of north wind which blows during fishing season that the salmon dry quickly [ordered by Coyote]

A1421. Hoarded game [salmon] released. Fish are kept imprisoned by malevolent creature(s)

A1421.2. Fish are kept imprisoned in pond/lake by malevolent creatures. Released by culture hero

A1429.5. Origin of fish traps for salmon [ordered by Coyote]

A1429.5. Origin of preserving salmon by drying [ordered by Coyote]

A1429.6. Origin of spears and gaff-hooks at a fishery [work of Coyote]; cf. A1527.

A1527.1. Origin of the catching of salmon

A1528.1. Fishing camps must be contiguous, and peaceful

A1528.2. At fishery near Coyote's Daughter, an Indian man or woman always stays longer than planned--"law and ruling of Coyote"

A1543.2. Origin of shouting when catching a large salmon on river near "Coyote's Daughter"

A1549.5. Origin of rite on Skein Island done by one man for one day to assure catching of many fish

A1559.2. Origin of courting site in vicinity of Coyote's Daughter

A2288. Eel's tail is pointed because originally an infant [Coyote transformed] nursed on it

A2482.4.1. Why fish runs extend or no to a region's rivers [the work of Coyote]

A2482.4.2. Why Chinook salmon and eels run up Klickitat River [work of Coyote]

A2484.2. Coyote drives salmon and all [small] fish up the *n-Che-wana*

A2689. Origin of camas and other roots, of serviceberries

B. Animals

B292.14. Wolves pit-bake eggs

B810.3.2. Wolf(s)

B810.3.3. Coyote

D. Magic

D55.2.7. Coyote transforms self into a crying infant in a cradleboard, usually found floating downstream

D55.2.8.1. Coyote transforms self to and from form of infant as he works to dig canal from lake

D151.1.1. Transformation: sisters into the *Chi-Col-lah* [birds] which always herald coming of the salmon

D902. Magic rain

D953.4.1. Coyote makes five digging sticks--to be used to break fish dam

D1177.1. Magic spoons, fitted on head of Coyote

D1312.1.1. Excrements as advisors (twice)

D1317.23. Breaking of digging stick warns of danger

D1811.3.1. "Sisters" tell Coyote what he wishes to know [how to catch salmon--use sand] [what happened to the roasted salmon]

D1964.7. Coyote "wished" asleep by the Wolves

D1964.8. Wolves "wished" asleep by Coyote

D2143.1.1. Rain produced by magic by trickster-hunter

D2151.2.5. Coyote sets out to free impounded waters by digging a canal; cf. A1111. Impounded water

F. Marvels

F634.2. Remarkable hunter of deer

F787.5. Extraordinary cradleboard made by Coyote

F798. Coyote threatens his "sisters" with rain unless they tell him what he wishes to know [twice]

F932.8.5.1. Creeks, swollen by rain, sweep Coyote into *n-Che-wana*, and downstream

J. The Wise and the Foolish

J755.2. Coyote errs--had originally intended only big fish to go upstream--little fish would remain in ocean

J1089. Arrogance of Coyote--"I knew that already." [twice]

J2173.1. Sleeping trickster's feast stolen [feast of Coyote] [feast of Wolves]

K. Deceptions

K2389. Deceptive trick played on trickster Coyote: deer carcass left in woods with defective tumpline [of deer entrails] by which to drag meat in

L. Reversal of Fortune

L434.1.1. Arrogance of Coyote scored [twice]

N. Chance and Fate

N478.1. "Secret" meat-eating betrayed by grease on mouth

N478.1.1. "Secret" egg-eating betrayed by yolks rubbed over mouths

P. Society

P252.1.1. Sisters rescue infant [Coyote] from river; raise, feed and succor it

P252.1.1.1. Oldest sister seeks to rescue the "infant" Coyote

P252.2.2. Five sisters

P415.1. Other labors: sisters set forth daily to dig roots

P486. Hunter

Q. Rewards and Punishments

Q580. Punishment [of Wolves] fitted to crime

R. Captives and Fugitives

R157.1.1. Youngest sister warns others that infant is really Coyote, transformed; cf. P252.8. Youngest sister warns. . .

S. Unnatural Cruelty

S116.4.1. Attempting to kill Coyote, each of sisters clubs him on the head--horn spoons save him

S131.0.1. Attempted murder by drowning

W. Traits of Character

W230.2.2. Sisters

Z. Miscellaneous Groups of Motifs

Z71.2.1.2. Direction: south

Z71.2.1.4. Direction: westward

Z71.3. Five [5 Wolves] [5 "sisters" (excrement)-twice] [5 blows struck at Coyote] [5 days to get things ready] [5 wooden diggers] [5 horn spoons, or bowls] [5 sisters]

5B. THE ORIGIN OF FISH IN THE COLUMBIA
A. Mythological Motifs

A522.1.3. Coyote as Culture Hero

A1421.2. Fish are kept imprisoned in pond/lake by malevolent creatures. Released by culturehero

A2288. Eel's tail is pointed because originally an infant [Coyote transformed] nursed on it.

A2484.2.1. Coyote drives salmon and all fish up the *n-Che-wana* when an outlet from the pond is dug

B. Animals

B810.3.3. Coyote

D. Magic

D55.2.7. Coyote transforms self into crying infant in a cradleboard, usually found floating downstream

D151.1.1. Transformation: two women into the *Chi-col-lah* which always herald coming of the salmon

D217.1. Coyote transforms self into a piece of driftwood that two women might pick him up as he floats past

D631.1.1.1. Coyote transforms self from infant and back to Coyote at will

D956.1. Magic digging sticks, five

D2489.2. Small swallows are ordained by Coyote to be heralds of the coming of the salmon

H. Tests

H251.3.4.1. Coyote, breaking dam, is detected when digging sticks [of women] break

H1229.4. Coyote searches about lake to discover likely place to dig an outlet

K. Deceptions

K321.2. Coyote-infant steals, devours food of two sisters; cf. G610.3. Stealing food from ogre

P. Society

P252.1.1. Two sisters rescue infant from river; raise, feed and succor it

P252.8. Older sister warns other sister(s) against picking up infant [Coyote]

W. Traits of Character

W230.2.1. Two women

Z. Miscellaneous Groups of Motifs

Z71.10. Two [2 women]

Z71.2. Four [4 digging sticks all break]

Z71.3. Five [5 digging sticks]

5C. HOW COYOTE DESTROYED THE FISH DAM
AT THE CASCADES, DISTRIBUTING
SALMON IN THE RIVERS
A. Mythological Motifs

A936.1. Origin of fishing places--created by Coyote: at The Dalles, at "ruined dam of the Cascades;" above Celilo; at *Top-tut* on Yakima River; at the falls of the Satus River; at (mouth of?) the Wenatchee River; at falls of the Spokane River

A993. Great Dam in river bars salmon from migrating upstream

A1421.1. Hoarded fish released. Fish are kept imprisoned by malevolent creatures. Released by culture hero

A1527.1. Origin of the catching of salmon

A2482.4. Why no salmon migrate up Toppenish Creek--the Yakimas refused Coyote a wife

A2484.2. Coyote drives salmon and all fish up the *n-Che-wana* when dam is wrecked

B. Animals

B292.14. Wolves pit-bake eggs [5 times]

B810.3.2. Wolves

D. Magic

D55.2.7. Coyote transforms self into crying infant in a cradleboard [basket], usually found floating downstream

D631.1.1.1. Coyote transforms self from infant and back to Coyote at will

D1002. Magic excrements [5 sisters]

D1067.1.1. Five wooden hats

D1312.1.1. Excrements as advisors [3 times]

D1811.3.1. "Sisters" tell Coyote what he wishes to know: [how to catch salmon--use sand] [what happened to the roasted salmon] [how to call the salmon]

D1964.1. Coyote made to sleep by the wolves [5 times]

D1964.8. Wolves made to sleep by Coyote [5 times]

D2156.12. Salmon are called out of river to be caught by Coyote

F. Marvels

F798. Coyote threatens his "sisters" with rain unless they tell him what he wishes to know 3 times]

F798.1. Coyote blows rain from his mouth [3 times]

G. Ogres

G316.1. Sisters attack Coyote with clubs as he attempts to destroy fish dam

J. The Wise and the Foolish

J1089. Arrogance of Coyote--"I thought so, etc." [3 times]

J2062.4. Wolves quarrel, accuse each other of having eaten the roasted eggs [5 times]

J2173.1. Sleeping tricksters' feast stolen [Coyote's feast-5 times][Wolves' feast]

L. Reversal of Fortune

L61.1. Clever youngest sister

L62.1. Youngest sister suspects impostor

L434.1.1. Arrogance of Coyote scored [3 times]

L436. Thieving wolves are discovered, sneak away ashamed

N. Chance and Fate

N478.1. "Secret" meat-eating betrayed by grease on Coyote's mouth [5 times]

N478.1.1. "Secret" egg-eating betrayed by yolks rubbed over wolves' mouths [5 times]

P. Society

P231.8. Five sisters note infant [Coyote] growing bigger/ stronger each day

P252.1.2. Four sisters rescue infant from river and raise, feed, and succor it

P252.2.2. Five sisters

Q. Rewards and Punishments

Q580. Punishment [of Wolves] fitted to crime

W. Traits of Character

W230.2.2. Five sisters

Z. Miscellaneous Groups of Motifs

Z71.3. Five [5 wooden hats] [5 root-digging sticks] [5sisters] [5 wolves] [5 days digging] [5 wooden hats broken] [5 "sisters"-excrement}

6A. THE RACCOON STORY

A. Mythological Motifs

A2217.2.1. Raccoon's nose, back marked by whip; hence his stripes. When his grandmother whipped him with a stick, welts were left which made marks Raccoons bear today

B. Animals

B143.1.1. Warning crow

B810.3.3. Coyote

B810.3.4. Raccoon(s)

B810.3.5. Grizzly bear

B810.8.3. Crow

C. Tabu

C619.5. Tabu: to go far [great distance] away

D. Magic

D169.5. When no water is given her, choking grandmother is transformed into a bird--pheasant

D981.10.2. Magic balls of berries with thorns sticking out

D1275. Magic song: "I am clean, clean, etc."

F. Marvels

F811.7.1.1.1. Trees bearing all fruits, and fruitful berry bushes

F914.4. Trickster Coyote disgorges grasshopper with black nose

F1011.3. Sitting in top of bushes

F1041.21.8. Young Raccoon cries and wanders forth in grief at grandmother's leaving

G. Ogre

G302. *Wala'lap*, a wicked being

J. The Wise and the Foolish

J2496.2.1. Pretended misunderstanding by Coyote of knowledge of a different language than his own

K. Deceptions

K649.1.Confederate, Coyote, hides fugitive

K649.1.1.1. Coyote swallows grasshopper--look alike to distract pursuer from trickster Raccoon

K721.1. Dupe persuaded to close eyes and open mouth; then, hot stones are thrown down throat, killing him; cf. G512.3.1. Ogre killed by throwing hot stones into his throat

K951.1. Murder by throwing hot stones into mouth

K1013.7. False beauty-doctor. Trickster, Raccoon, pretends to make the dupe beautiful by adding black stripes to his nose. But injures causes him great pain

K1035.1. Berries mixed with thorns thrown into grandmother's mouth

K1871.3. Sham swallowing: into a <u>hollow</u> tree branch which he has placed in his belly, Coyote "swallows" 5 hot rocks, also water which boils in his belly

N. Chance and Fate

N9.2. Shinny, a gambling game

N456.1. Crowd laughs at Raccoon boy, a thief

P. Society

P236.8. Lazy Raccoon scolded by grandmother

P292.2. Grandmother offers food to grandson; cf. S351.1. Abandoned child cared for by grandmother

P292.3. Grandmother punishes youth--he runs away, weeping

P292.4. Grandmother regrets whipping youth, sings a sad song as she searches for him

P292.5. Grandmother calls after grandchild at every noise

P299.2. Grandson refuses to talk to grandmother
P415.2. Nutgatherers, of acorns

S. Unnatural Cruelty
S139.2.2.9. Corpse of grizzly bear flayed, flesh eaten

W. Traits of Character
W111.1.6.1. Young Raccoon is too lazy to pick up many acorns, gathers only wormy ones
W122.19.1. Raccoon deliberately refuses to give water to his grandmother
W125.6. Raccoon eats grandmother's share of acorns as well as his own
W125.6.1. Raccoon and Crow finish eating last of acorns
W230.2.3. A grandmother
W231.1.2. Young Raccoon

Z. Miscellaneous Groups of Motifs
Z71.1.0. Two [Raccoon and Coyote live together] [2 groups of people]
Z71.2. Four [4 caches of acorns eaten]
Z71.3. Five [5 hot rocks] [5 caches uncovered--empty] [5 caches of acorns]
Z73.2.1. Winter, time of hunger
Z73.2.3. Summer

6B. RACCOON AND HIS GRANDMOTHER
A. Mythological Motifs
A2217.2.1.Raccoon's back marked; hence his stripes. When his grandmother whipped him with a stick, welts were left which made the stripes Raccoons have today

B. Animals
B810.3.4. Raccoon(s)

K. Deceptions
K300.2. Acorns stolen by young Raccoon

P. Society
P292. Grandmother

Q. Rewards and Punishments
Q212.5.1. Raccoon's theft is discovered, is punished by grandmother--a severe whipping

W. Traits of Character
W231.1.2.Young Raccoon

II. TALES OF THE LEGENDARY

7. COYOTE ENSLAVES THE WEST WIND

A. Mythological Motifs

A522.1.3. Coyote as Culture Hero
A525.3. Coyote and people fight against each other
A532.1. Coyote fails to capture and tame West Wind
A1128. Regulation of winds
A2305.1.1.1. Origin of Chub's flat body (and many bones?)--was sat on
A2305.1.4. Why flea is flat--was sat on

B. Animals

B810.14.2. Flea
B810.18.3. Chub

D. Magic

D1002. Magic excrements [2 younger sisters]
D1312.1.1. Excrements as advisors
D1602. Self-returning magic object(s); cf. D1686. Magic object(s) depart
    and return at formulaic command
D1610.6.4. Speaking excrements
D1811.3.1. "Sisters" tell Coyote what he wishes to know [What has become
    of/ How to recapture West Wind]

F. Marvels

F110.2. Journey by canoe to home
F989.25. Injured slaves (Chub, etc.) carried indoors
F1041.9.1.4. West Wind becomes ill, assorted swellings
F1088.5. West Wind slave breathes, "loosens" house of Coyote--escapes; cf.
    B210. Escapes

L. Reversal of Fortune

L434.1.1. Arrogance of Coyote scored by Sisters

P. Society

P173.2.1. Child, captured, made a slave
P173.3.1. Captive from battle made a slave

R. Captives and Fugitives

R219.3. West Wind escapes from trap
R356. Escaped West Wind captured in Coyote's trap

W. Traits of Character

W230.4. People

Z. Miscellaneous Groups of Motifs

Z71.1. Two [2 younger "sisters"]

Z71.3. Five [5 swellings on body of slave][5 liklihoods of death][5 escapes at
    night]
Z115.1. West Wind

8. THE EAST WIND AND THE WEST WIND
A. Mythological Motifs
A1127.2.1. West Wind blows today because of Coyote's mistake
A1127.2.2. Origin of strong West Wind

F. Marvels
F617. Mighty wrestlers

H. Tests
H1562.9. Test of strength: wrestling

K. Deceptions
K12.6. Wrestling match won by deception--West Wind pours grease about site

P. Society
P555.4. East Wind defeated in wrestling contest
P557.8. West Wind, victor, addresses loser (East Wind)

Z. Miscellaneous Groups of Motifs
Z71.3. Five [5 times East Wind is thrown]
Z115.1. West Wind

9A. COYOTE AND THE MISCHIEVOUS WOMEN
A. Mythological Motifs
A522.1.3. Coyote as Culture Hero

D. Magic
D169.5. Transformation: two women to birds
D2095.1.1.Two women disappear from sight then reappear; cf. D2188.2.
    Person(s) vanish

F. Marvels
F701.3. A far-distant land

K. Deceptions
K1051.4. Coyote dives into river to have two women

T. Sex
T426. Coyote wishes to seduce two strange women
T475.3. Unknown women declare their wantonness (fondness) across river to
    Coyote

W. Traits of Character
W230.4.Two women

Z. Miscellaneous Groups of Motifs

Z71.0.1. Two [2 women]

Z71.1.1. Three [3 times women vanish--reappear]

Z71.2.2.5.1. Up the river--direction

9B. COYOTE AND THE MISCHIEVOUS
WOMEN (Second Version)
A. Mythological Motifs

A522.1.3. Coyote as Culture Hero

D. Magic

D231.3. Transformation: two women into rocks

D2095.1.1. Two women disappear from sight--then reappear; cf. D2188.2. Person(s) vanish

K. Deceptions

K1051.4. Coyote dives into river to have two women

K1795. Coyote weeps, pretending that his wife has died

Q. Rewards and Punishments

Q551.3.4. Transformation to stone as punishment of women (that they won't "make people crazy")

T. Sex

T420. Coyote wishes to seduce two strange women

T475.3. Unknown women declare their wantonness (fondness) across river to Coyote

W. Traits of Character

W230.4. Two women dancing

Z. Miscellaneous Groups of Motifs

Z71.0.1. Two [2 women]

Z71.1. Three [3 times women vanish]

Z71.2.1.5. Toward "open country"--direction

10. COYOTE EATS DRIED SALMON
A. Mythological Motifs

A522.1.3. Coyote as Culture Hero

A996. Origin of name of White Salmon [Washington]; formerly an Indian fishery, now a Washington town on the Columbia River, approximately across from The Dalles, Oregon

B. Animals

B810.14.2. Flea

B810.3.3. Coyote

D. Magic
D1032.1.1. Magical dried salmon
D2061.1.3.1. Sleep-like death follows eating of dried salmon

F. Marvels
F1005.2. Dried salmon comes out through mouth, nostrils, ears of corpse

S. Unnatural Cruelty
S75. Flea murders Coyote
S139.9. Murder by swallowing flea

Z. Miscellaneous Groups of Motifs
Z71.2.1.5. Coyote "went on"--direction

11. COYOTE MAKES A FISHTRAP
A. Mythological Motifs
A522.1.3. Coyote as Culture Hero
A999.1. Origin of particular place-name
A1429.5. Introduction [to people] of fishing for salmon with a fishtrap; cf.
    A1527. Custom of catching fish with nets

B. Animals
B810.3.3. Coyote
B810.18.1. White salmon

D. Magic
D1209.5.1. Magic fishtrap--cries out when full
D1610.14.4. Speaking fishtrap--is full of fish

F. Marvels
F887.2. Extraordinary implements--fishtrap made by Coyote
F900. Coyote jumps into fishtrap

Z. Miscellaneous Groups of Motifs
Z71.2.1.5. Coyote "went on"--direction

12. COYOTE SPEARS FISH
A. Mythological Motifs
A522.1.3. Coyote as Culture Hero
A526.2.1. Culture hero as mighty fisher
A1457.7. Origin of Salmon-spear
A1422.4. Coyote spears, steams, then eats secretly a salmon
A1527.1. Custom of taking salmon with spears
A2751.2.4. Wild-cherry bark is strong--used as cords on Salmon-spear

B. Animals
B810.33. Coyote
B810.18.1. White salmon

F. Marvels
F1041.21.4.1. Woman cries at loss of bucket

J. The Wise and the Foolish
J1322.3.1. Great thirst

N. Chance and Fate
N777.2. Bucket dropped into river, recovered, leads to adventures

T. Sex
T72. Woman won and then scorned [Coyote refused to take gift wife]

W. Traits of Character
W155.5. Water drunk without knowledge of the people
W230.2.1. An old woman
W230.4. Some people

Z. Miscellaneous Groups of Motifs
Z71.2.1.5. Coyote "went on"--direction

13A. THE WISHOM TRIBE:
A STORY OF THEIR DIVISION AND SEPARATION
B. Animals
B529.2. Ducks tell people of unconscious state of Young Coyote
B569.3. Ducks advise people if Young Coyote is alive by making a unique noise
B810.3.3. Coyote [Old]
B810.3.3.1. Son of Coyote
B810.13.5. Ducks [two or more]

D. Magic
D1500.1.36.1. Young Coyote takes sweatbath to cure his sick eyes, but nearly dies

J. The Wise and the Foolish
J2060.1.1. Quarrel and fight over source of whistling noise made by ducks

N. Chance and Fate
N311.1. Separation of faction from Wishoms caused by quarrel--group travels to Canada

Q. Rewards and Punishments
Q306.1. Quarrelsomeness punished when a people war on each other

13B. A QUARREL OF THE WISHRAM
A. Mythological Motifs
A989.5. Cedar boards mark site where Wishom formerly lived
A1630.1. Tribe seeks new locale because country is too small [four times]

A1675.1. Tribal characteristics: breakaway Wishom band would kill anyone they recognize

B. Animals

B810.13.5. A duck

J. The Wise and the Foolish

J740. Forethought in provision for shelter--group take cedar planks with them.

J2060.1.1. Quarrel and fight over source of noise made by duck

N. Chance and Fate

N311.1. Separation of faction from Wishoms caused by quarrel--group travels to north (?) of Wenatchee.

P. Society

P416. Tribesmen fish: catch varieties of salmon, eels and suckers

P416.1. Tribesmen fish with dipnets: catch salmon

P416.2. Tribesmen fish for salmon, hunt for deer in new country

P716.1 Country of the *Wenatchis*

P716.2. Country of *IxElExtgi'dix* [Yakamas?]

P716.3. Village of *Wa'q'Emap*

P716.4. Village of *Nixlu'idix*

P716.5. Villages [sites] passed (first remove): a) among *Wallawalla*; b) *AcnE'm*; c) *NuL!a'-ik*; d) *NuL!anuL!*; e) *Sts!E'ntsi*; f) *Wisu'm*; g) *Ta'malan*; h) *Txa'iauna*; i) a small river [Yakima River?]; j) *Po'uwankiut*; k) *Xit!a'i;* l) a small dried up river [?]; m) *I!Lu'mEmi*; n) to *Pala'xi* [near Wenatchi]. {14 sites}.

P716.6. Villages [sites] passed (second remove): *Patixkui'ut*, "The Gap"

Q. Rewards and Punishments

Q306.1. Quarrelsomeness punished when a people war on each other

W. Traits of Character

W231. The Wishom (people)

Z. Miscellaneous Groups of Motifs

Z71.1.1. Three (3 yrs. fighting)

Z71.2. Four (4 removes)

14. WHY THE WISHRAM ARE CALLED *ILAXLUIT*
A. Mythological Motifs

A282.0.1.2. Wind-goddess, daughter of East Wind

A991.1. Origin of *Nixlu'idix* (village)

A1191.1. Origin of name of war arrow--from monster, *Akxa'qusa*; cf. Z183. Symbolic name

A1676.2. How the Wishom are called *idaxa'luit* (joined together)

E. The Dead

E13.1. Resuscitation by stepping over piles of remains-- north and south, east and west (5 times)

E30.2. Small bits of bodies gathered into pile(s)

E64.22. Resuscitation by magic paint sprinkled over piles of bits of human remains

E108.2. Resuscitation by magic powder (paint); cf. V68.5. Dead rubbed with red paint

G. Ogres

G11.2.2. Cannibal giant woman--eats people of village

G100.2. Monster woman (*Akxa'qusa*) devours all people of village

P. Society

P716. Village of *Nixlu'idix*

W. Traits of Character

W231. Lots of people

Z. Miscellaneous Groups of Motifs

Z71.3. Five (5 piles)

Z122.4.1. North

Z122.4.2. South

Z122.4.3. East

Z122.4.4. West

15. COYOTE IN *SK!IN*
A. Mythological Motifs

A522.1.3. Coyote as Culture Hero

A1445.1. Origin of dugout canoes manufactured with round-pointed bows and sterns

A1539.2. Origin of shouting [warning?] before crossing over a river

A1602. Naming of the *Ilka'imamt* peoples on the south shores of the *n-Chewana*

B. Animals

B810.3.3. Coyote

D. Magic

D1002.1. Magic urine; cf. D562.2. Transformation by urine

Z. Miscellaneous Groups of Motifs

Z71.2.2.5. Coyote traveled up the river--direction

16. COYOTE AND THE MOUTHLESS MAN
A. Mythological Motifs

A522.1.3. Coyote as culture hero

A1316.7 Coyote cuts open a mouth(s) for man/people who have no mouths

B. Animals

B810.3.3. Coyote
B810.18.3. Sturgeon

D. Magic

D1799.4.1. Magic at counting by pointing at fish
D1817.0.1.7. Magic detection of thief by victim--by pointing a finger about, the hiding place of Coyote is discovered

F. Marvels

F513.0.3. Mouthless people
F561.9. Mouthless people take in nourishment by smelling of the food--then throwing it away [eat by smell]
F639.2.1. Mighty diver. Catches sturgeon in each hand

K. Deceptions

K301.3. Coyote as thief of sturgeon
K341.4.2. While diver dives, Coyote steals one of his fish
K763.1. Coyote and stolen fish apprehended hiding in bushes

P. Society

P634.3. Coyote prepares fire, cooks sturgeon very well

Q. Rewards and Punishments

Q115.4. People offer a woman as reward to Coyote
Q499.9. Coyote severely scolded

R. Captives and Fugitives

R219.3. Coyote refuses to accept woman [to be free?]

W. Traits of Character

W230.1. Man without a mouth

Z. Miscellaneous Groups of Motifs

Z71.0. Two [cooked fish is discarded twice without being eaten]

17. A FAMINE AT THE CASCADES
B. Animals

B810.18.1. Chinook Salmon
B810.18.3. Two fish: suckers

F. Marvels

F969.7. Famine
F969.8. Unseasonable cold and ice about the river

J. The Wise and the Foolish

J1522. Rebuke to the stingy (wife made ashamed)

P. Society

P211.3. Wife sent on errand for food

P213.2. Husband orders wife to hide food that hungry children shall not eat

P213.3. Husband orders wife to cook food, but to feed children but a little lest they become ill

P324.4. Guest gives to sister-in-law a gift: a seashell for a necklace; cf. Q114.2. Gifts made to relative

P416. A man fishes

P416.1. A man fishes: catches Chinook salmon/suckers

P416.5. A fishtrap is built

Q. Rewards and Punishment

Q114.2. Gift as reward for gift: wife given dried salmon and dry fishskin

Q552.3.1. Famine as punishment

S. Unnatural Cruelty

S11.7. Father denies the hungry food

S12.8. Wife feeds badly cooked suckers to slaves--many die

W. Traits of Character

W152. Stinginess

W230.2.1. An elder sister

W230.2.2. Girl, wearing necklace

W230.4. Some children

W231. People; slaves

Z. Miscellaneous Groups of Motifs

Z71.0.1. Two (2 suckers)

Z73.0.1. Morning

Z73.2.2. Springtime

18. A PROPHECY OF THE COMING
OF THE WHITES

A. Mythological Motifs

A1614.9.1.Coming of the white man

B. Animals

B810.3.6. Dog

B810.5.6. Horse(s)

B810.5.7. Cattle

B810.5.7.1. Buffalo

D. Magic

D495. Strange things due

D1275. Magic song

D1731.1. Song(s) learned in dream

D1731.2. Marvels seen in dreams

D1810.8.2. Information received through dream

D1812.3.3. Future revealed in dream
D1814.2. Advice from dream
D2174.1. At prophecy, people dance night and day--are glad (ecstatic)

F. Marvels

F1068. Realistic dream
F1068.1. Advice and information given in dream

J. The Wise and the Foolish

J157. Wisdom (knowledge of future) from dream

M. Ordaining the Future

M302.7. Prophecy through dreams
M340.7. Prophecy of coming of whites (many strange things to happen)
M341.2.0.1. Prophecy: death by a particular weapon (gun)
M369.11.1. Prophecy about the gun
M369.11.2. Prophecy about the steel cooking pot
M369.11.3. Prophecy about matches by which to light fires
M369.11.4. Prophecy about the ax
M369.11.5. Prophecy about the hatchet
M369.11.6. Prophecy about the [metal] knife
M369.11.7. Prophecy about the stove
M369.11.8. Prophecy about white people (wearing mustaches)
M369.11.9. Prophecy about cattle (brought by the whites)

V. Religion

V93. Religious dancing (ecstatic)

W. Traits of Character

W230.1. An old man
W231. People (Indian); people (whites); people (men & women; children, old men--the dancers)

Z. Miscellaneous Groups of Motifs

Z71.1.1. Three (3 Indian songs)
Z71.2. Four (4 Indian songs)
Z72.8. Long ago

19. THE *GY-U-BOO'-KUM* (I)

B. Animals

B16.1.2.2. About to devour a hunter, giant serpent slain by throwing large stones down its throat
B16.5.1.1.1. Giant serpent chases men, giving chirping bleats
B16.5.1.2. Devastating [man-eating] sea-monster (serpent) [devours infant]
B16.5.1.2.2. Noise of great serpent heard as it seizes and swallows infant
B16.5.1.3. Devastating monster serpent leaves print in dust like a log that's been dragged
B16.5.1.3.3. Great serpent slain

B16.5.1.4.5. *Gy-U-Boo'-Kum* monster snake as long as a lodge pole, big around as a man's body, a mouth at the bottom of its head like a sturgeon, has rattles, emits a bad stench

B16.5.1.4.7. Last of giant serpents to be seen

B211. *Gy-U-Boo'-Kum*, monster serpent

B875.1. Giant serpent

B. Marvels

F913.3. Victim [dead infant] removed from dead serpent's belly

F989.15.1. Extraordinary serpent-monster pulled from its cave-lair to mouth of cave

H. Tests

G1161.1. Task: killing ferocious beast [giant serpent]

K. Deceptions

K812.4. Pursuers set large, smoky fire; burn to death giant serpent in its cave-lair

N. Chance and Fate

N271.8.1. Giant serpent traced by trail it leaves

N773.3. Adventure following giant serpent into cave

P. Society

P173.5. Slave boy [from Snake Indians]

P716. Particular places: at Grand Dalles [long stretch of rapids] on Columbia River

R. Captives and Fugitives

R315.1. Deep cave as refuge of great serpent

W. Traits of Character

W230.2.1.2. Mother of infant [wails for lost baby]

W230.2.2. A girl

W230.4. An infant

W231.1.1. Men of village

W231.1.1.1. Some men (hunters)\

W231.1.2. A slave boy

Z. Miscellaneous Groups of Motifs

Z71.1.0. Two [2 bowshots distance]

20. THE *GY-U-BOO'-KUM* (II)
B. Animals

B16.5.1.1.1. Devastating serpent with poisonous body

B16.5.1.2.3. Great serpent pursues hunters

B16.5.1.3. Great serpent slain

B16.5.1.4. Last of giant serpents to be seen

B16.5.1.4.2. *Gy-U-Boo'-Kum* monster snake: has ugly head, a long thick body, makes noise from mouth, accompanied by very loud rattling

B211. *Gy-U-Boo'-Kum*, monster serpent

B810.8.3.1. Many magpies poisoned

B875.1. Giant serpent

D. Magic

D1827.3. Noise, as a voice, heard back on trail--also rattling-bark, barking-scream

F. Marvels

F831.3. Poisoned war-arrows; cf. P5533.1. Poisoned weapons

H. Tests

H1161.1. Task: killing ferocious beast [giant serpent]

P. Society

P716. Particular places: near The Dalles [city] on Columbia River

R. Captives and Fugitives

R169.5.1. Friends save each other from death by serpent

R273. Pursuit by giant serpent

S. Unnatural Cruelty

S111.10. Death of serpent by poisoned arrows

W. Traits of Character

W231.1.1. Two men (warriors hunting)

Z. Miscellaneous Groups of Motifs

Z71.1.0. Two [2 young warriors]

21. THE *GY-U-BOO'-KUM* OF THE WISHOMS
B. Animals

B16.5.1.3. Devastating (man-eating) sea-monster (serpent) [devours many Indians]

B16.5.1.4. Last of giant serpents to be seen

B16.5.1.4.1. *Gy-U-Boo'-Kum* monster snake: has very big mouth, great horns on head, able to overtake running Indians to devour them, makes bleating sound like that of a fawn

B211. *Gy-U-Boo'-Kum*, monster serpent

B875.1. Giant serpent

F. Marvels

F679.5.4. Skillful hunter with a leaf imitates animal calls

F679.5.4.1. Remarkable hunters: kill and skin giant serpent, sleep several days; cf. H1247. Sleep forbidden until quest accomplished

F989.25. Very hard mouth of giant serpent repels arrows

G. Ogres
G165.1.1.2. Devastating serpent dead, stinking and decaying

H. Tests
H1161.7. Task: killing devastating giant serpent

K. Deceptions
K788.2. Giant serpent lured far off when quiver of arrows is thrown down the mountainside

L. Reversal of Fortune
L101.2. Unpromising hero: younger brother
L311.5. Younger brother throws large rock into serpent's mouth--chokes it

P. Society
P206. The people warn two brothers against attempting to slay giant serpent
P553.1. Arrows, made day after day
P716. Particular places: the Klikitat country

Q. Rewards and Punishments
Q412.1. Rolling large rocks into serpent's mouth chokes and kills it

R. Captives and Fugitives
R169.5.1.1. Brothers attempt to save each other from death by serpent
R254. Brothers attempt to flee, to run up or else down the mountain
R273. Pursuit by giant serpent; cf. B16.5.1.2.3. Great serpent pursues hunters
R311.5. Two brothers take refuge in tree

W. Traits of Character
W231.1.1. Two brothers, Wishoms

Z. Miscellaneous Groups of Motifs
Z71.1.0. Two [2 calls] [2 quivers of arrows] [2 brothers]
Z71.1.1. Three [3 calls]

III. TALES OF MAGIC AND THE MARVELOUS

22. STAR HUSBAND
A. Mythological Motifs
A762. Stars descend as human beings

D. Magic
D231.3. Transformation: Star-man to the star-rock
D439.5.2. Transformation: star(s) to person(s)
D1761.1. Wishing by stars

F. Marvels

F809.10. Shining object [stone?] seen in river

P. Society

P716. Particular places: north of Spedis

R. Captives and Fugitives

R227.2.1.1. Flight from star-man husband; cf. J1457. The gray fox

T. Sex

T111.1.1.1. Maiden(s) choose Star-men as husbands

W. Traits of Character

W230.1.3. Stars [as 2 men?]
W230.2.2. Girls [some young girls]

Z. Miscellaneous Groups of Motifs

Z71.1.0. Two [2 sisters: big and a little sister]

23. THE STAR-ROCK OF RICHES
A. Mythological Motifs

A971.1. Origin of Star-Rock, a gift from Great Spirit

C. Tabu

C420. Tabu: uttering secrets
C423.1. Tabu: disclosing source of magic power; cf. C451. Tabu: boasting of wealth

D. Magic

D931.0.5. Mysterious light [as from a star] denotes magical power on rock; cf. D909. Magic light [from star]
D931.0.6.1. Magic stone [star] enables whoever sees it to become wealthy
D956.1. Magic piece of wood [luminescent?]
D1291.2. Star as magic object
D1468.2. Magic star (sparkle) causes wealth to come to finder
D1478.2. Magic light illuminates bottom of lake
D1695. When *sparkle* of a star is wrapped and secretly kept, it will make one rich

L. Reversal of Fortune

L73. Children can best capture magic sparkle of Star-Rock

N. Chance and Fate

N1.2.2. Gambler with supernatural power becomes rich [via racehorses]
N203. Lucky person
N421.2. Lucky bargains: hero acquires fast racehorses
N440. Valuable secret(s) learned from father

P. Society

P716. Particular places: fishing at Wishom

24. COYOTE'S PEOPLE SING
A. Mythological Motifs

A2330.9. Why Bald Eagle has a white head

A2411.2.1.6.1. Origin of color of crow--splashed all over with "black blood"

B. Animals

B810.3.3.1. Son of Coyote

B810.3.3. Coyote

B810.3.4. Raccoon man

B810.3.5. Grizzly bear

B810.8.3. Crow

B810.9.1. Bald Eagle

B810.18.1. Coyote's daughter: "Salmon-Head-Fat;" cf. B810.3.3. Coyote

B810.19.2. Rattlesnake

B810.22.4. Wild potato

B810.22.6. Wild onion

B810.22.8. Wild carrot

B810.22.10. Buttercup

C. Tabu

C875. Tabu: carrying child on one's back into house

D. Magic

D1003. Magic blood

D1261.1. Magic pipe

D1299. Magic tobacco: "dried salmon flesh"

D1541.0.2.1. Magic song brings West Wind and warm weather

D1721.1. Magic power from magician (father)

D1799.7. Magic results from smoking

D2173. Magic singing [Coyote's daughter; Coyote's son]; cf. D2173.2. Magic singers: Wild Potato, Wild Onion, Wild Carrot; also *Amu'lal*, *Aq!o'lawa-itk*; also Buttercup; Grizzly Bear, Crow, Rattlesnake

F. Marvels

F544.0.5. Grease flows out of mouth

F628.1.3.3. Strong victim would kill serpent with bare hands

F911.3. Grizzly would swallow man

F912. Victim would kill swallower from within

F979.23. Wild Onion carries Wild Potato, her daughter, on her back

H. Tests

H507.1.0.3. Grizzly bear defeated in wit combat--backs down

H541.1.1.1. Riddle challenge propounded by Grizzly Bear on pain of death: "Whoever shall have challenged me, his head [only?] shall I eat up"

H541.1.1.2. Riddling challenge A propounded by Rattlesnake: "Where I shoot my arrows, there is the sunflower's shade"

H541.1.1.3. Riddling challenge B further propounded by Rattlesnake: "Whoever has challenged me, himshall I put cheat-grass (*Bromus secalinus*) into"

H543.2. Small (inferior) man answers Grizzly Bear by countering his riddling challenge: "Somewhere it is sung all day long: 'Eat up heads'"

H543.2.1. Raccoon man answers Rattlesnake with countering riddling challenge A: "Somewhere it is sung all day long 'the shade of the sunflowers--there I shall destroy the people'"

H543.2.1. Raccoon man further answers Rattlesnake with countering riddling challenge B: "I have challenged you. Be quick and put the (cheat-grass) into me! Be quick and bite me"

H548. Riddle contest; cf. H507. Wit combat, test in repartee

H843.1. Riddle: "On my back I carry my daughter; We two are dug up" [Wild onion and wild potato]

H843.2. Riddle: "Only by my tail am I dug up" [Wild carrot]

K. Deceptions

K300.2. Theft of salmon by Eagle

P. Society

P459.2. Crow as fisher for Salmon

P556. Challenge to battle: Grizzly Bear; cf. F911.3.

P556.3. Challenge to battle answered: Small man; cf. F912.

P556.3.1. Challenge to battle answered: Raccoon man

U. The Nature of Life

U235.1. Young Coyote is a liar

W. Traits of Character

W230.4. The people

Z. Miscellaneous Groups of Motifs

Z73.2.1. Winter

25. COYOTE AND ANTELOPE
A. Mythological Motifs

A522.1.3. Coyote as Culture Hero

A1727.1. Animal-beings [chiefs] transformed to present forms

A1875.2. Origin of antelope [animal]

B. Animals

B810.3.1. Fox

B810.3.3. Coyote

B810.4.3. Rabbit

B810.5.6. Antelope

B810.9.1. Eagle, a chief

B810.18.1. Salmon, a chief

B810.18.1.1. "Big-Backbone," a son of Coyote
B810.18.1.2. "Big-Fin," a son of Coyote
B810.18.1.3. "Big-Adipose-Fin," son of Coyote
B810.18.1.4. "Head-Fat," daughter of Coyote
B810.18.1.5. "Big-Gristle"

D. Magic

D902.1.1. Magic, dark fog
D931.0.5. Marvelous stove surrounded by "spits," placed in doorway
D935.3. Magic dust
D1256. Marvelous shinny-ball; cf. D1526.2. Magic ball flight
D1312.1.1. Excrements as advisers
D1380.27.1. Magical pieces of shinny-ball protect when rubbed over bodies of
    Antelope and two sons
D1402.7.6. Coyote falls across, is pierced by "spits" about stove
D1402.11.1. Magic music kills person

E. The Dead

E1. Coyote comes to life

F. Marvels

F679.10. Marvelous throwers--sons of Antelope toss ball to and from each
    other, from one mountain summit to another
F681. Marvelous runners [Rabbit and Fox]
F681.0.1. Coyote's daughter a runner
F973.2. Walking on grass-blades without bending them; cf. F681.12. Runner
    runs so swiftly that he does not snap the ears of wheat (bend grass);
    also see E489.9. In land of dead the dead walk on grass without
    bending it and on mud without sinking

H. Tests

H1151.27. Stealing "shinny-ball" from the people

J. The Wise and the Foolish

J1791.5.1. Shooting at enemy's reflection in water
J1791.5.2.1. Throwing stones at enemy's reflection on water
J2665.3. Awkward sons of Antelope [drop ball]

K. Deceptions

K532.1.1. Sons of Antelope escape, steal ball cloaked by heavy fog

L. Reversal of Fortune

L434.1.1. Arrogance of Coyote

N. Chance and Fate

N791.1. Adventures from pursuing foes across a river; but cf. C833.1. Tabu:
    crossing river except at source; also see D1524, F1071.2.1.

P. Society

P233.12. Coyote and four sons
P234.3. Coyote and daughter
P716. Particular places: Goldendale Valley, of Klickitat County, State of
Washington

Q. Rewards and Punishments

Q212.5. Punishment of theft: Rabbit and Fox pursue and slay culprits [all 5]
Q411.13. Death as punishment for thievery [5 instances: Coyote's children]
(Antelope's children?)
Q421.0.9. Beheading as punishment for theft [4 instances]

R. Captives and Fugitives

R351. Fugitives discovered by reflection in water; cf. J1791. Reflection in
water thought to be the original of the thing reflected

S. Unnatural Cruelty

S12.8. Antelope and sons wipe themselves against nose, ears and legs of dead
Coyote [humiliation of the corpse]

W. Traits of Character

W230.4. People
W231.1.2. Sons [4 sons and a daughter of Coyote] [2 sons of Antelope]

Z. Miscellaneous Groups of Motifs

Z71.1.0. Two [2 feces] [2 days and nights]
Z71.1.1. Three [Antelope & sons travel for 3 nights]
Z71.2.1. Four [4 children of Coyote are beheaded]
Z71.2.1.5. Direction: went "that way yonder" [twice]
Z71.3.3. Five [5 children of Coyote] [5 times song sung]
Z71.5.0.1. Seven [Coyote, Antelope and all children]

26. COYOTE AND DEER

A. Mythological Motifs

A2435.3.4.1. Why Coyote is an eater of dead things

B. Animals

B810.3.3. Coyote [and wife]
B810.5.1. Deer

D. Magic

D2105.8. Provisions magically furnished [by Deer]--slice of meat, bucket of
blood [3 times]
D2105.8.3. Deer lops steaks from about his body [3 times]
D2105.9. Deer causes a nosebleed, fills a bucket with blood [3 times]

J. The Wise and the Foolish

J1919.10. Living wife thought to be source of slabs of meat

J2411.3. Unsuccessful imitation of magic production of food
J2425. The bungling host

P. Society

P217. Wife scolds Coyote for his stupid behavior
P320. Hospitality; cf. P321. Salt of hospitality. Eating a man's salt creates mutual obligation
P324.4. Guests are invited to return if ever they become hungry

Z. Miscellaneous Groups of Motifs

Z230.2.1. Wife of Coyote

IV. COYOTE AS TRICKSTER

27A. COYOTE AND *AT!AT!A'LIA*
A. Mythological Motifs

A521.1. Coyote as trickster
A1547.4. Origin of Owl's hoot as a death sign
A1958. Creation of Owl: transformed from former Owl-Chief
A2411.2.4.2. Color of Owl

B. Animals

B147.2.2.4. Owl as bird of ill-omen; cf. E761.7.6. Life token: bird is sent each day to tell of hero's condition; when owl comes it will be to announce death
B810.11.3. Owl

D. Magic

D931.1.2. Magic ashes

F. Marvels

F821.1.4.1. Coyote ties rushes all about himself that he rattles

G. Ogres

G11.6. *At!at!a'lia*; cf. G262.0.1. Lamia: witch who eats children
G11.19. Ogress and Owl steal people

J. The Wise and the Foolish

J2469.6. Ogress has pitch smeared in her eyes, over her body
J2460.2. Literal obedience: ogress follows destructive instructions of Coyote exactly

K. Deceptions

K10.13.2.1.1. Ogress is to gain a lovely rattling [sound] upon painting herself with pitch, standing in a furnace

P. Society
P716. Particular place: site of village of Wishom

Q. Rewards and Punishments
Q414. Punishment: burning alive (children); cf. S112.6. Murder by roasting alive in oven (furnace)
Q414.0.10.1. Burning to death of an ogress

S. Unnatural Cruelty
A112.6. Murder of ogress by roasting in oven (furnace)

W. Traits of Character
W230.4. Children; people

Z. Miscellaneous Groups of Motifs
Z71.0.1. Two [children, by *twos*]

27B. COYOTE AND *TAH-TAH KLE-AH*
B. Animals
B140. Prophetic animal: Coyote
B810.3.3. Coyote

D. Magic
D1002. Magic excrements; cf. D1610.4. Speaking excrements
D1312.1.1. Excrements as advisors

F. Marvels
F817.5. Extraordinary joints of reeds from swamp, cut and fastened as rattles to leggings

G. Ogres
G11.6. *Tah-tah kle-ah*, old woman ogress
G11.6.5. Ogre-woman steals, eats people

K. Deceptions
K199.2. Deceptive bargain--Ogress must allow herself to be covered with pitch, allow it to be burned off, before she can rattle (beautifully) like Coyote
K955.4. Murder by burning after having been smeared with pitch; cf. S112. Burning to death
K1771.10. Sham threat of rain forces advisors [feces] to talk

M. Ordaining the Future
M310.2. Prophecy: Indians, a new people, are coming soon

P. Society
P682.2.1. Traveling along

Z. Miscellaneous Groups of Motifs
Z71.3.3. Five [5 times asks] [5 times taunts by refusing to answer]

28. COYOTE AND HIS DAUGHTER
A. Mythological Motifs
A521.1. Culture hero as trickster
A1552.4. Origin of incestuous conduct of some people

B. Animals
B147.1.2.5. Origin of howl of Coyote as omen of death
B810.3.3. Coyote

D. Magic
D1812.5.0.9. Divination from howling of dog; cf. D1812.5.1.12.1. Howling of dog as bad omen

J. The Wise and the Foolish
J2174.5. Coyote asks that when he dies, his daughter must be given to his look-alike "trading friend"

K. Deceptions
K522. Escape by shamming death. Coyote crawls back into burial site and sleeps when people would verify his death
K522.5.1. Coyote given sham burial in the earth
K1860. Deception by feigned death (sleep); cf. K1352. Death feigned to woo maiden

T. Sex
T110.1. Father given daughter to wife
T410. Incest
T411. Father-daughter incest
T411.1.2. Father, feigning death, returns in disguise and seduces daughter

W. Traits of Character
W230.2.1. Wife [of Coyote]
W230.2.2. Daughter, of Coyote
W230.4.1. People
W230.4.2. Children, of Coyote

Z. Miscellaneous Groups of Motifs
Z71.3.3. Five [5 nights]

29. COYOTE AND THE SUN
A. Mythological Motifs
A220.1. Sun goddess
A521.2. Culture Hero as dupe
A525.3. Inept culture hero would serve as sun's slave
A526.10. Coyote sees all the bad things being done on earth--tells on the

people
A568. Coyote rejected [sent away] as helper to slave of sun

B. Animals

B810.3.3. Coyote

Z. Miscellaneous Groups of Motifs

Z71.0.1. Two [2 times misbehavior told]

30. COYOTE AND SKUNK
A. Mythological Motifs

A1525. Origin of customs: game division--fat meat to Coyote, lean meat to Skunk

B. Animals

B511.6. Raven as healer [medicine-man]: 5 times
B810.2.3. Skunk
B810.3.3. Coyote
B810.5.1. Deer
B810.5.2. Elk
B810.5.4. Mountain sheep
B810.5.6. Antelopes
B810.8.3. Raven

D. Magic

D1211. Magic drum(s)
D1500.1.27.3.Magic drumming [abets healing]: 2 times; cf. E384.1. Ghost summoned by beating drum
D1500.1.27.3.1. Magic drumming refused by all the animals
D1002.1.1. Marvelous urination [2 or more times]; cf. E29.6. Resuscitation by urinating on dead man's bones
D2063.5.1. Marvelous breaking wind kills deer; cf. G93. Cannibal breaks wind as means of attack

F. Marvels

F668.0.1.1. Raven as marvelous doctor [2 or more times]; cf. P424. Physician
F911.8. Skunk has pitch inserted up his rectum [2 or more times]
F950.10. Cure by extracting pitch: then, Skunk discharges "wind"; cf. E21. Resuscitation by withdrawal of wounding instrument [lump of pitch]: 2 or more times

H. Tests

H1199.2. Task: healing sick person [5 times]

Q. Rewards and Punishments

Q141.2. Plentiful game animals as reward [one or more times]

W. Traits of Character

W230.4. People

W231.1.1. Brothers; cf. P251.6. Several brothers

Z. Miscellaneous Groups of Motifs

Z71.0.1. Two [2 brothers] [2 or more cures, extracting pitch] [2 or more marvelous urinations] [2 or more times Raven doctors][2 or more rectal insertions of pitch][2 or more magic drummings]

Z71.3.3. Five [5 times Skunk gets sick][Raven, healer 5 times][5 animal peoples refuse]

31. EAGLE'S SON AND COYOTE'S SON-IN-LAW
B. Animals

B260.2. Two groups of animals prevented from warfare: Coyote's peoples' weapons have been marred by mouse and rat; cf. K632. Mice gnaw enemies' bowstrings and prevent pursuit

B810.3.3. Coyote

B810.4.1. Mouse

B810.4.3. Jack Rabbit

B810.4.4. Rat

B810.9.1. Eagle

B810.9.2. Fish-Hawk

D. Magic

D902. Magic rain

D1410.9. Magic spell [wetted through] prevents Fish-Hawk from running--he falls down;cf. D1837. Magic weakness

D1711.14. Eagle as magician

H. Tests

H1210.3. Quest assigned by Eagle, chief

H1228.3. Quest undertaken by helpers to locate former wife of Chief

H1239.5. Quest accomplished when discovered is sleeping place of former wife of Chief and her new husband

H1385.3. Quest for vanished wife [and her new husband]

K. Deceptions

K620.1. Escape by deceiving the guard--murdered victims made to appear as asleep

K632. Mice gnaw enemies' bowstrings [arrows & bows] and prevent pursuit; cf. Herodotus Bk II,Sect. 141

K632.2. Rats gnaw enemies' bows and arrows and prevent pursuit

K959.2. Murder in one's sleep

L. Reversal of Fortune

L101.2. Unpromising hero: abandoned infant becomes strong, great runner

L111.1.3. Abandoned youth becomes full-grown man

N. Chance and Fate

N731.1.2. Unexpected meeting of father and son

P. Society

P231.8. Mother rejects resemblance of unknown chief to herself [as son]
P414.1. Eagle as hunter
P486.1. Fish-Hawk as marvelous runner
P561.3. Footrace to reveal fastest runner

Q. Rewards and Punishments

Q411.0.3. Ex-husband kills wife and paramour [woman's ex-husband or son?]

R. Captives and Fugitives

R131. Exposed or abandoned child rescued
R153.3.1. Father rescues son abandoned by mother
R227.2. Flight from hated husband; cf. T232.1. Woman deserts husband

S. Unnatural Cruelty

S11.8.3. Murder by cutting neck in two; cf. S139.2. Slain persons dismembered
S62.5. Cruel ex-husband, Eagle
S301. Child abandoned
S322.22. Mother abandons infant son; cf. S12.
S351.1.1. Abandoned child found and reared by father

T. Sex

T100. Eagle marries daughter of Coyote
T232.6. Faithless wife takes another husband
T481. Adultery; cf. T230. Faithlessness in marriage
T494.1. "Somewhat sucked" nipples as sign of a child, abandoned
T580.2. Son of Eagle born

W. Traits of Character

W142. Coyote's daughter as liar
W230.2.1. Daughter, of Coyote; cf. P243. Daughter
W230.4. People [of Eagle]
W231.1.2. Infant son

Z. Miscellaneous Groups of Motifs

Z73.0.1. Dawn [2 times]

32. COYOTE AND THE PREGNANT WOMAN
A. Mythological Motifs

A522. Coyote as Culture Hero
A545. Origin of copulation towards pregnancy
A1352.4. Origin of copulation--demonstrated by Coyote
A1352.5. Formerly pregnancy believed caused by a thorn bringing a pus-filled wound in a digit

A1439.5. Correct manner of carrying a load of firewood demonstrated by Coyote

F. Marvels
F684.2. Man, keeps turning somersaults, stands on his head

J. The Wise and the Foolish
J1849.5. Headstanding man carries load of wood tied between legs

T. Sex
T541.2. Birth from wound or abscess
T570. Pregnancy
T573.1. Woman conceives and bears same day

W. Traits of Character
W230.1. A man
W230.2.1. A woman
W230.4. An infant

33. COYOTE AS MEDICINE MAN
A. Mythological Motifs
A521.1. Coyote as trickster

B. Animals
B511.6. Raven doctors, but cannot find cause of illness of woman
B511.7. Coyote "doctors" sick woman
B517. Large deer [Elk?] as singers of magic
B810.5.1. Large deer
B810.8.3. Raven

D. Magic
D451.5.2. Raven, as "medicine man;" cf. A522.2.2. Raven as culture hero
D1275.1.1. Magic singing
D1766.9.1. Magic results from singing

F. Marvels
F547.3.1. Extraordinary long penis
F547.3.1.1. Long penis joined onto that of Coyote
F547.3.5.1. Man's penis wrapped about him like a rope
F547.3.7. Long penis borrowed from another
F547.3.8. Extraordinary long penis becomes stuck within woman; can only be cut in two
F547.3.9. Extraordinary penis recognizes cut-off section--two pieces join back together

K. Deceptions
K473.1. When Coyote is thrown down, he spits "blood" [juice of alder-bark {alnus}]

K1382. Trickster pretends lameness (sickness) and is taken on woman's back: violates her; cf. K1241. Trickster rides dupe horseback. Usually by feigning sickness he induces the dupe to carry him

K1517.2.1. Coyote poses as doctor, copulates with patient

K1521.5.1.1. Coyote and ill woman hidden behind a screen

K1818. Disguise as a sick man

K1875. Deception by sham blood [Coyote chews alder-bark, pretends to have bleeding "in my breast"]; cf. K473. Sham blood and brains

K2319.4. Coyote demands to be carried upside down lest he bleed to death

Q. Rewards and Punishments

Q451.10.1.1. Punishment: penis cut in two

T. Sex

T135.1. Girl "cured" by Coyote declared his wife (as he had copulated with her)

T178. Coyote refuses to accept woman as his wife--he travels on

T402. Illicit sex--patient complains that Coyote (doctor) had copulated with her

T452.2. Mother tells daughter to accept sexual violation by Coyote--he did cure her

T475.3. With long penis Coyote has intercourse across river, at a distance, and underwater with a young woman

T495. Coyote strokes vagina of [each] woman who carries him

W. Traits of Character

W230.1. An old man

W230.4.1. Some women

W230.4.2. Five women [virgins]

W230.4.3. A mother and daughter

Z. Miscellaneous Groups of Motifs

Z71.2.1.5. Coyote travels "somewheres"

Z71.3.3. Five [5 virgins] [5 times carried] [5 times strokes vaginas] [5 times Coyote thrown down] [5 times Coyote spits "blood"]

34. THE STORY CONCERNING COYOTE
A. Mythological Motifs

A521.1. Coyote as trickster

D. Magic

D444.2.1. Transformation: meat into whole salmon

D1008. Magic human flesh

D1009.2. Magic sores

F. Marvels

F795. Extraordinary clouds

F809.10. Coyote bores holes through some stones

F839.8. Quiver used to transport pieces of woman's flesh
F839.9. Extraordinary bow and quiver are eaten by Coyote

K. Deceptions
K492.2. Woman serves Coyote with plateful of her flesh to eat; but cf. G11.6.3. Old Woman calls beasts together to join her in feast on human flesh; also cf. T215.3. Husband nourishes starving wife with his own flesh and blood
K492.3. Old woman refuses to serve Coyote more of her flesh [he had previously wasted it]
K975.3. Secret of obscene act 'let out' by clouds; cf. B122.1.1. Birds tell a secret; also, cf. D1316.5. Magic speaking reed/tree betrays secret

N. Chance and Fate
N270. Crime inevitably comes to light

Q. Rewards and Punishments
Q253.3. Obscene sex act punished
Q499.4.2. Coyote laughed at--punishment that his obscene secret is discovered
Q499.8. Coyote scolds old woman

T. Sex
T464. Coyote does obscene sexual act upon himself

U. The Nature of Life
U232. No place secret enough for sin; cf. T331.4. No place secret enough for fornication

W. Traits of Character
W230.2.1. An old person, female
W230.4. People, several groups

Z. Miscellaneous Groups of Motifs
Z71.1.0. Two [2 houses where Coyote's secret is known--he is laughed at] [2 visits to old woman] [2 salmon]

V. TALES OF CONFLICTS AND ADVENTURES

35. A CASCADE INDIAN LEGEND
A. Mythological Motifs
A969.10. Origin of Castle Rock: carried by youthful hero to present location

D. Magic
D1067.2. Magic cap
D1381.26.1. Magic cap protects from attack
D2061.2.1. Death-giving glance [at cap]; cf. G264.1. Woman is death of all

who behold her
D2125.1. Big-footed Chief able to walk on water

F. Marvels

F517.1. Person unusual as to his feet; cf. G365. Ogre monstrous as to feet;
also cf. F531.3.7. Giant has feet "three feet long"
F611.3.1.1. Strong hero practices to become strong
F771.0.1. Large *round* lodge

H. Tests

H36.1. Recognition [of son] by footprints as large or larger than Chief's
H919.7. Tasks assigned at instigation of Chief
H931.1.2. Strong sent to capture son [fatal capture]
H1556.6.1.1. Test of fidelity of wives: sand or dirt is spread about house to
show footprints of any intruder

J. The Wise and the Foolish

J1146. Detection by strewing sand. Trespasser [son of Chief] leaves huge
footprints in the sand

K. Deceptions

K601.3. To prevent father killing infant son, mother lies that it's a girl

L. Reversal of Fortune

L311.6. Single youth overcomes two strong attackers, breaks their arms

R. Captives and Fugitives

R227.2.1. Flight from feared husband

S. Unnatural Cruelty

S11. Cruel father
S11.3.3.3. Cruel father kills all sons as soon as they are born
S11.4.7. Father wages war against unknown son
S110.2.1. Woman kills all men who seek to slay son
S322.1.5.3. Chief, fearful of a son as rival, puts all infant sons to death

T. Sex

T52.10. A Hood River [*Nom-i-neet*] wife
T145. Polygamous marriages
T224.1. Wife allowed to return to her home with infant for a visit
T586.2.1.1. Chief has many daughters, but not one son

W. Traits of Character

W138. Falsehood: wife lies to husband to preserve life of infant son
W230.1. A Cascade Indian Chief
W230.4. Many wives
W231.1.1. A boy infant
W231.1.1. Two strong men

Z. Miscellaneous Groups of Motifs

Z71.0.1. Two [2 strong men]

Z16.14.20. Twenty-five [son is 25 years old]

Z71.16.2. Ten [10 years old]

Z71.16.17. *Many* men, *many* canoes

36. HOW YOUNG EAGLE KILLED *PAH-HE-NUXT-TWY*

A. Mythological Motifs

A968.3. Origin of high cliff along *n-Che-wana* [near White Salmon]: Coyote transformed at top of tree as punishment

A968.3.1. Cliff: Coyote forced to climb tall tree--both are then transformed into cliff along Washington side, the Columbia River [near Hood River]

A1535.2.2. Origin of the cessation of killing at the bones game

B. Animals

B291.3.2. Hare (rabbit) as messenger

B810.3.3. Coyote [as deceiver]

B810.3.5. Grizzly Bears

B810.4.3. Cottontail [rabbit]

B810.8.4. Blue Jay

B810.9.1. Eagle

B810.9.1.1. Young Eagle

B810.13.5. Dove, a wife of Eagle

B810.16.3. Cricket, a wife of Eagle

B810.18.2. White-fish

B810.18.3. Small-mouth fish [sucker?]

B810.18.4. Crab

D. Magic

D422.2.4. Transformation: Coyote atop a tree, both into a high cliff

D1021. Magic feather

D1323.16.1. Magic feather on which blood appears, a sign that donor has been killed; cf. D1812.0.1. Foreknowledge of hour of death

D1402.4. Magic fires [2] kill; cf. D1271. Magic fire

D1812.0.2.4. Evil Chief perceives when somebody comes; cf. D1812.0.2.1. Foreknowledge of unwished-for-guests

D1816.4.2. Trail [tracks] of long-dead father located

D2062.2.7. Eagle's magic causes blindness

D2061.2.1.2. Eagle looks at, causes severe burns [to mouth of fish] [to crab]

D2062.5.1. Magic mutilation: mouth of White-fish cut way back

E. The Dead

E30.0.1. Resuscitation by arrangement of members. Parts of a dismembered corpse are brought together and resuscitation follows. (Sometimes combined with other methods.)

E101.0.1. Resuscitation by "paint"; cf. D101. Resuscitation by salve (oil); cf. D1346.8.1. Magic ointment gives immortality

F. Marvels

F621. Strong man: tree-puller. Can uproot and carry off trees; cf. F611.3.1. Strong hero practices uprooting trees

F624.2.0.1. Strong man lifts and throws great rocks, even across the *n-Che-wana*

K. Deceptions

K1213.0.1. Coyote's guise as "helper" of wives of Eagle is seen through

L. Reversal of Fortune

L101. Unpromising hero (male Cinderella). Usually, but not always, the unpromising hero is also the youngest son

N. Chance and Fate

N1.0.2. Young Eagle as gambler

N1.0.2.1. Gambler [the bone game]

N2.3.6. Extraordinary stakes: loser to have throat cut, head taken

N6.0.1. Young Eagle has all the luck--wins at the stick game

N9.1.1. Gambler loses his head [life]

N23.1. Head [throat] wagered in game--lost

N134.0.1. People from Old Women's lodge accompany Eagle to gamble; but cf. N134.1. Persons bring bad luck

N825.3.1. Old women helpers

P. Society

P160.1. Loser at gambling begs for his life

P553.2. Magical fires [2] poised on one side against village

P553.3. Magical grizzly bears [5] poised on one side against village

P555.4.1. All villagers are either killed by bears or by the fires

P632.5.1. Eagle [and later Young Eagle] wears his hair long, dresses in finery to travel; cf. N135.3. the luck-bringing shirt (attire)

Q. Rewards and Punishments

Q421.0.9. Decapitation as punishment for losers at playing the bones game

Q421.1. Head on stake. Punishment by beheading and placing the heads on stakes

S. Unnatural Cruelty

S139.2.2.1.1. Heads of losing gamblers impaled upon stakes; cf. S139.22.1.6. Heads brandished to intimidate foes; cf. H901.1. Heads placed on stakes for failure in performance of tasks

T. Sex

T211.9.1.2. Wife [Dove] mourns that her husband is dead

T231.6. Cricket believes disguised Coyote is indeed her husband, Eagle

T249.3. Coyote disguises himself as Eagle to have his two wives

T320.4.2. Woman escapes lust of Coyote by excessive weeping

W. Traits of Character

W230.1. A Chief
W230.1.2. Two sons, of Eagle
W230.4. Two old women

Z. Miscellaneous Groups of Motifs

Z71.0.1. Two [2 sons] [2 old women]
Z71.3.3. Five [5 suns travel] [5 animal messengers] [5 suns travel] [beg for life
    5 times] [5 grizzly bears] [5 times rub paint] [5 suns follow trail] [5
    times begs]

37A. THE SALMON STORY
A. Mythological Motifs

A522.3.2. Young Salmon as Culture Hero
A969.9. Young Salmon hollows out some rocks, bores a hole, [cavern?] and
    puts his mother(?) therein
A1796. Because youngest wolf escaped death and fled to the woods, wolves are
    extant now
A2426.2.8.1. Origin and meaning of Dove's mourning call: "whenever the
    salmon comes, they kill him at Wishram [i.e., the fishery?], and
    then the Dove cries."
A2491.6. Why Coyote prowls up and down along the river-- directed to do so
    by Young Salmon
A2491.7. Why skunks prowl up and down along rivers--directed to do so by
    Young Salmon

B. Animals

B810.2.3. Skunk
B810.3.2. Wolves
B810.3.3. Coyote
B810.8.3. Ravens, old people
B810.13.5. Dove [wife of Salmon]
B810.18.1. Salmon
B810.18.2. Son of Salmon [Young Salmon]
B810.18.3. Salmon-egg

D. Magic

D192.0.2. Transformation: Maggots crawl about over the sleeping Young
    Salmon; cf. E734.9. Soul of man in form of worms; cf.
    Q551.3.2.5. Punishment: man transformed to a mass of worms
D376.1. Transformation: Young Salmon into an old man
D631.2.1. Young Salmon changes self back to his original form
D651.1. Transformation to kill enemy(s)
D765. Disenchantment by reversing (undoing) enchantment
D766.3. Disenchantment by tears (of woman)
D965.20. Some small trees and bushes magically created by spring of water
D996. Magic hand
D1069.3. When apron is opened and decorated--woman gives information out

of gratitude

D1091.1. Magic bow of father sought [5 times]

D1242.4. Magic oil

D1337.1.2.1.Application of magic oil restores hair, restores physical beauty;
cf. D1338.8. Rejuvenation by magic oil

D1810.14. Magic knowledge of identity of Salmon-youth; cf. F643. Marvelous
presentiment of coming of Salmon-youth

D1835.7. Magic strength (power) given two Ravens

D1847.2. Mother of Young Salmon passes him off as her father, husband's
father-in-law [5 times] but see the curious slip in the story: "stepmother"

D2142.1. Wind produced by magic--to deter two Ravens

D2143.2. Drought produced by magic

D2151.0.4. Level of water made to sink down [5 times]

D2151.2.3. Rivers magically made go dry

D2151.6.3. A single spring of water created in mountains

D2426.2.7.1. Why the Raven cries: he has seen something

E. The Dead

E721.1.1. Sleeper not to be awakened, since soul is absent

F. Marvels

F821.12. Marvelous apron

F982.1.2. Two Ravens transport woman on their backs and interlocked wings

F982.3.1. Ravens interlock wings, carry increasingly heavy stones

F1051.3. Coyote and Skunk weep with fright as Young Salmon comes to them

H. Tests

H1201. Quest: two Ravens assigned to rescue dying woman

H1213.1.3. Quest for woman assigned by Young Salmon to two Ravens

H1228.2. Son goes out to avenge father's death

H1385.13. Quest for lost [marooned] mother

J. The Wise and the Foolish

J1249.2. Parts of body of abandoned woman claimed by two Ravens

J1661.2.1.Wolves detect the "smell of salmon" [5 times]

L. Reversal of Fortune

L42. Youngest Wolf brother escapes, flees to the woods

N. Chance and Fate

N828.1. Woman gives helpful directions

P. Society

P553.2. Bow breaks [5 times]

P553.3. Arrows are made for the Wolf brothers

P661.1. Underground lodge

P683.1. Travel by canoe--the wife to paddle

P716. The *n-Che-Wana*

Q. Rewards and Punishments
Q458.1.1. Beatings given for failing to return magic bow [5 times]

R. Captives and Fugitives
R13.1.5.1. Five Wolf brothers abduct wife of Salmon as their own
R317.1. Refuge: one salmon egg drops into river--escapes

S. Unnatural Cruelty
S110.0.1. Salmon murdered
S112.0.3. Wolf *foeti* are burned to death
S115.4. Murder by shooting with arrows [4 times]
S139.2.3. Corpse(s) are removed and thrown away [4 times]
S139.9. Salmon wife is killed, eaten [but see Salmon-wife again, Tale 37A, also Tale 37B

T. Sex
T572.2.7. Abortion caused when someone steps on "belly" of pregnant woman

W. Traits of Character
W230.1.2. Son [of Salmon]
W230.2.1. A woman [with an apron]

Z. Miscellaneous Groups of Motifs
Z71.0.1. Two [2 Ravens]
Z71.2. Four [4 Wolves killed] [4 queries] [4 corpses discarded] [4 times water level lowers] [4 times Ravens are heard] [4 times Ravens ignore youth] [4 questions and replies]
Z71.2.1.5. Journey "home"
Z71.2.1.5.1. Far Away
Z71.2.1.5.2. Onwards (unknown direction)
Z71.3.3. [5 Wolves] [5 bows] [5 buffetings of Young Salmon][5 arrows] [5 infants aborted] [5 times flying carrying a stone] [5 times oil poured][5 times water level falls]
Z71.16.7. Without number, many
Z73.1. Night
Z73.0.1. Morning

37B. THE SALMON MYTH
A. Mythological Motifs
A969.9.1. Salmon hollows out some rocks, makes a hollow [cave], puts his wife therein
A1796. Because youngest wolf escaped death and fled to the woods, wolves are extant now

B. Animals
B810.3.3. Wolves, five

B810.8.3. Raven(s) [Crows]
B810.18.1. Chinook Salmon

D. Magic

D192.0.2. Transformation: maggots crawl about over the sleeping Salmon; cf.
E734.9. Soul of man in form of worms; cf. Q551.3.2.5. Punish-
ment: man transformed to a mass of worms
D719.3. Disenchantment by pushing
D2143.2. Drought produced by magic
D2151.2.3.1. Rivers (springs) magically made to dry up

E. The Dead

E721.1.1. Sleeper not to be awakened, since soul is absent

F. Marvels

F982.1.2. Crows transport woman on their backs and interlocked wings

H. Tests

H1201. Quest: two Crows assigned to rescue dying woman
H1385.3. Quest for lost [marooned] wife

J. The Wise and the Foolish

J1249.2. Parts of body of abandoned woman claimed by two Ravens
J1661.2.1. Wolves detect the "smell of salmon"

L. Reversal of Fortune

L42. Youngest Wolf brother escapes, flees to woods

P. Society

P211.1. Wife
P486.1. Hunting
P683.1. Travel by canoe--the wife to paddle
P683.2. House

R. Captives and Fugitives

R13.1.5.1. Wolf brothers (5) abduct wife of Salmon as their own

T. Sex

T249.3. Wife stolen away from husband
T298. Reconciliation of separated couple

W. Traits of Character

W230.2.1. Wife, of Chinook Salmon

Z. Miscellaneous Groups of Motifs

Z71.0.1. Two [2 Ravens]
Z71.3.3. Five [5 wolves]

38. THE ADVENTURES OF EAGLE
AND HIS FOUR BROTHERS
A. Mythological Motifs

A2321.3.1. Origin of Blue Jay's crest--his battle-ax

A2376.6. Origin of color and surface-roughness of Crab; cf. A2411.4.

A2433.3.12.1.Why beaver lives along water, eats wood

A2435.4.6.1. Food of Chicken Hawk

A2433.4.7. Why Blue Jay lives where he does

A2433.4.8. Why Sparrow Hawk lives in the woods and "looks on"

A2433.4.9. Why Eagle lives far away in the mountains

A2441.4.2.1. Why Crab is always in the water

A2522.8. Why Eagle is feared--by the deer, the grizzly

B. Animals

B455.3. Helpful Eagle; B500.0.1. Eagle's wings shield, protect others from magic; cf. B172.9. Magic birds cause hosts to sleep by shaking wings

B810.3.5. Black Bear

B810.3.6. Grizzly Bear(s)

B810.4.2. Beaver

B810.4.3. Rabbit, as gambler

B810.4.4. Squirrel

B810.7.2. Seal

B810.8.4. Blue Jay

B810.9.1. Eagle

B810.9.2. Sparrow Hawk

B810.9.3. Chicken Hawk

B810.9.5. Hawk (species uncertain)

B810.13.5. Buzzard

B810.18.3. Crab, as gambler

B900. Huckleberries and nuts

B900. Cottonwood tree; cf.A2721.2.1.3. Cottonwood cursed for serving as cross

B900. Cedar tree; cf. D950.18. Magic cedar tree

D. Magic

D127.1.1. Transformation: Woman as seal

D491.1.3. Grizzly Bears--reduced in size as to tiny dogs (of a maiden)

D921. Magic lake (pond) created by Beaver

D1149.4. Sweat house, made of stones

D1244. Magic [grease] salve/ ointment

D1275. Magic song (of Crab); cf. B505.3. Magic song received from fish

D1778.1. Magic results from somersaults; cf. D1778. Magic results from contact with earth

D1811.3.2. Magic knowledge: Eagle discerns gambling bones are hidden in cracks of "hands" of Crab

D1811.3.1. Magic knowledge: Eagle discerns gambling bones are hidden up rabbit's nose

D1827.3. Brothers hear Eagle's call for help from a far distance--he has been defeated

D2061.2.10. Murder attempted by smokes from burning human bones; cf. M341.2.14. Prophecy: death by means of bone

D2062.6. Beaver's teeth all loosen, fall into water when he bites at spear-line

D2062.7. Sparrow Hawk's claws fall into water when he grabs at spear line [also claws of Eagle][also claws of Chicken Hawk?]

D2074. Attracting by magic--teeth, claws, et al.

D2135.6. Buzzard and Eagle in single combat fight--rise up to the sky

E. The Dead

E1.3. Eagle resuscitates himself

E80.1.2. Resuscitation of *dead* Eagle by dipping body into cold water

E80.1.3. Resuscitation of *dead* Buzzard by dipping body into warm water

E101. Resuscitation by salve (oil); but cf.D1500.1.19.1. Magic healing salve; also cf. D1503.4. Magic balm heals wounds

F. Marvels

F660. Remarkable skill in performance of tasks; cf. H1563. Test of Skill

F713. Extraordinary pond (lake)

F834.8. Hunters spear a seal, are carried on lengthy journey

F911.6.1. Swallower creature [bird?]

F982.9. Buzzard and Eagle clinch, wing and claw, and fight--rise into the air

F986.6. Seal caught with spear--draws boatload of hunters

G. Ogres

G11.6. Man-eating woman

G64. Human flesh (eyeballs, brains) shunned from being eaten by hunters

G94.3. Ogress serves feast consisting of parts of human bodies to travelers

H. Tests

H931. Tasks assigned in order to get rid of hero(s)

H1154.3.2.1. Task: capture "a maiden's tiny little dogs" [5 grizzly bears]

H1546. Contest in enduring the most pain the longest; cf. D1719.1. Contest in magic

J. The Wise and the Foolish

J1115.1. Clever gambler(s)

K. Deceptions

K500.0.1. Escape from death by deception: pebbles tossed into water sound like victims' hearts bursting

K1889.4.1. Grisly body parts are passed off as wholesome food or devices: huckleberries, a stew, etc.

K2294. Treacherous host; cf. P634. Feasts

N. Chance and Fate

N0.1. Gambling game--withstanding greatest pain

N0.2. Gambling at the bones

N0.3. Gambling--wrestling on a rope stretched over water

P. Society

P557.2.1. Upon winning at gambling, Blue Jay will kill the people with his battle-ax

P557.4. Customs concerning single combat

P682.2. Greeting establishes marital relationship

P683.2. Miscellaneous Customs: wrestling

R. Captives and Fugitives

R9.7. While Eagle fights, his four brothers have been captured, blinded--made slaves

R155. Two brothers rescue elder brother(s)

S. Unnatural Cruelty

S110.4.1. Seal-woman resolves to kill Eagle and his brothers

S112.8. Attempted murder by scalding to death in sweat house

S118.3. Buzzard seized and decapitated

W. Traits of Character

W230.4. Some people

Z. Miscellaneous Groups of Motifs

Z10.2. End formulas

Z71.1.1. Three [3 animals maimed while spearfishing]

Z71.2.1. Four [4 grisly offers]

Z71.3.3. Five [5 animal brothers] [5 stones] [5 somersaults] [5 small stones] [5 Grizzly Bears] [5 times pour grease] [people slain 5 times]

39. THE FIVE EAST WIND BROTHERS
AND THE FIVE THUNDER BROTHERS
A. Mythological Motifs

A1142. Origin of thunder due to youngest Thunder brother's escape from death--and survival

B. Animals

B81021.1.1. East Wind brothers

B810.21.2.1. Thunder brothers

B810.3.3. Coyote

B810.8.7. Magpie, as racer

D. Magic

D1275.5. Supernatural dance song; but see esp. D1566.2.3. Magic song quenches fire

D1275.5.1. Magic songs cause increase of warmth--steam and smoke and flames; cf. D1372.7. Song protects from fire; cf. D1566.2.3. Magic song quenches fire

D1275.6. Magic songs cause East-Wind [cold] to blow--everything and everyone freezes

D2144.2. Contest of heat and cold

E. The Dead

E13. Resuscitation by stepping over [five times]

F. Marvels

F497.2. Fire spirits inhabit underground lodge

F692.2. Marvelous singer; cf. F1921.2. Magic singer

F709.4. Place: "where the people are assembled;" cf. A1260. Mankind made from miscellaneous materials

H. Tests

H1221. Quest for adventure

H1233.1. Old person as helper (advisor) on quest; cf. N825. Old person as helper

H1242. Youngest brother alone succeeds on quest

H1248. Quest should be sought--if hero is going to die

H1371.5. Quest to where people are assembled

H1382.3. Quest for unknown wonder [place where people are assembled]

H1511. Heat test. Attempt to kill hero by burning him in fire; cf. D1841.3. Burning magically evaded

H1511. Heat test. Attempt to kill hero by burning him with fire

H1512. Cold test: attempt to freeze adversaries to death; cf. H1541. Contest in enduring cold

K. Deceptions

K149.2. Woven cottonwood leaves passed off as "blankets" in gambling match; cf. K264. Deceptive wager

M. Ordaining the Future

M341.1.2.6. Prophecy: unless hero returns sooner, death within five days

N. Chance and Fate

N0.1. Gambling with "gambling bones"

N1.5. Challenge to gamble

N1.5.1. Challenge to gamble--on two racers

N2.8. All clothing wagered (and lost) at gambling

N2.9. All possessions wagered (and lost) at gambling on fastest runner

N6.4. Coyote and youngest Brother win at gambling

N95. Wager on faster of two runners

P. Society

P251.3.2. Brothers follow, strive to avenge each other

P251.6.2.1. Five brothers

P683.1. Customs, Misc.: House, "smoking"

P683.2. Customs, Misc.: underground lodge

S. Unnatural Cruelty

S112.0.3. Visitors burned to death

W. Traits of Characters

W230.2.1.1. Old woman
W230.2.1.2. An old woman [second visit]
W230.4. The people

Z. Miscellaneous Groups of Motifs

Z10.2. End formulas: characters take their leave
Z71.0.1. Two [Coyote and youngest brother travel] [both bested at gambling]
Z10.2.1.3. Direction: "towards rising sun"
Z71.2.1.4. Direction: "towards the setting sun"
Z71.3.3. Five [5 East Wind brothers] [5 Thunder brothers] [5 overnight camps] [5 days absence--for each brother] [5 times seen in race] [5 songs--by each Thunder brother] [5 songs by East Wind brothers] [5 times stepped over]
Z73.1. Time: evening
Z73.1.1. Time: all night long

40A. THE DESERTED BOY (I)
B. Animals

B81. *Itc!E'xyan's* daughter [a river being]
B531.5. Suckers are caught
B531.5.2. Magpies are trapped
B810.8.3. Magpies
B810.18.4. Suckers

D. Magic

D1316.5.2. Magic speaking reed answers deceptively in place of people; cf.
    D1316. Magic speaking reed betrays secret
D1610.3. Speaking plant (reed)
D1765. Magic results produced by command
D2061.1.6.1. Youth causes a storm to drown villagers as they attempt to cross the river
D2141. Storm produced by magic; cf. D905. Magic storm; cf. D2091.5. Storms magically drawn down on foe

F. Marvels

F403.2.1. Spirit from river helps boy
F420.1.2. Water spirit as woman
F420.1.7. Water spirits give gifts to mortals
F420.5.1.7.5.1. Water spirit gives boy much food
F420.6.1. Marriage or liaison of mortals and water spirits
F679.10. Marvelous fisherman
F771.2.8. Remarkable large house furnished with mountain sheep skins and decorations from water spirit
F789.4. Remarkable blanket(s) [made of magpie skins][mountain sheep fleece

blanket]
F851.1.1. Extraordinary lot of food, great variety of fish from the river--given by water spirit

N. Chance and Fate
N500. Treasure trove. Survival articles left for bad boy include fire, string for bird snare and fishline, some food
N511.1.14. Survival articles buried in ashes of fire
N815.0.2. Helpful water spirit

P. Society
P761. Particular places: the Columbia River

S. Unnatural Cruelty
S301.1. Bad boy abandoned; cf. S144. Abandonment in desert

T. Sex
T615. Supernatural growth: boy becomes full-grown man (overnight?)

W. Traits of Character
W11.0.1. Youth takes pity on two grandmothers, feeds them liberally, allows them to live
W231.1.2. A bad boy; cf. P233.2.1. Father drives away bad son whom the mother prefers
W230.4. The people
W230.2.1. Two grandmothers, provide for youth

Z. Miscellaneous Groups of Motifs
Z10.2. End formulas
Z71.3.3. Five [5 times fishing] [5 nights] [sleeps 5 nights]
Z73.2.1. Winter
Z73.2.2. Spring

40B. THE DESERTED BOY (II)
B. Animals
B81. *Itc!E'xyan's* daughter [a "woman of the river people"]
B531.5. Suckers (chub) are caught
B531.5.2. Many magpies are trapped
B810.8.3. Magpies
B810.18.4. Suckers

D. Magic
D1002. Magic excrements [human feces]
D1610.6.4.1. Speaking excrements; answer in place of people

F. Marvels
F403.2.1. Spirit from river helps boy
F420.1.2. Water spirit as woman

F420.1.7. Water spirits give gifts to mortals
F420.5.1.7.5.1. Water spirit gives boy much food
F420.6.1. Marriage or liaison of mortals and water spirits
F679.10. Marvelous fisherman
F771.2.8. Remarkable nice house furnished with nice blankets
F789.4. Remarkable blanket(s) [a: made of magpie skins][b: produced by water spirit]
F851.1.1. Extraordinary lot of food, great variety of fish from the river--given by water spirit

N. Chance and Fate

N500. Treasure trove. Survival article left for bad boy includes string to make a fishline and bird snare
N815.0.2. Helpful water spirit

P. Society

P292. Grandmother(s)
P683.4. Customs, Misc.: an underground house
P761. Particular places: Spedis
P761. Particular places: the Columbia River

S. Unnatural Cruelty

S301.1.1. Bad boy abandoned across the river; cf. S144. Abandonment in desert

T. Sex

T615. Supernatural growth: boy becomes full-grown man (overnight?)

W. Traits of Character

W11.17.1. Youth and his family cross river to visit grandmothers--bring them back to his house
W230.2.1. Two grandmothers provide for youth
W230.2.4. People, watch youth from afar
W230.4. Two children born, boy and a girl
W231.1.2. A bad boy; cf. P233.2.1. Father drives away bad son whom the mother prefers

Z. Miscellaneous Groups of Motifs

Z10.2. End formulas
Z71.0.1. Two [2 grandmothers]

VI. TALES OF MONSTERS AND OGRES

41. EAGLE AND WEASEL
B. Animals

B11.2.1.1.1. Dragon as modified serpent--flayed when dead

B12.2.1.2. *Gayaba'xe*, alligator-like monster; cf. B16.5.2. Devastating crocodile

B11.11.9. Dragon-like creature is clubbed to death

B16.5.2.1. Crocodile-monster killed by clubbing it to death

B16.5.2.2. Devastating alligator-monster bites at rocks, rattles loudly, makes earth shake

B810.2.2. Weasel

B810.9.1. Eagle

C. Tabu

C32. Tabu: offending supernatural husband

C112. Tabu: sexual intercourse with unearthly beings

D. Magic

D1212.1. Monster's rattles are heard as he pursues

D2069.1.2. Weasel struck to ground by magic power of Eagle

F. Marvels

F821.3.3. Flayed hide of monster worn by both Eagle, then Weasel

J. The Wise and the Foolish

J552.7. Eagle and Weasel quarrel over who shall wear/have the dragon's skin

P. Society

P127.1. Weasel threatens to kill Eagle to gain the monster's skin

Q. Rewards and Punishments

Q429.5. Weasel attempts to kill Eagle with arrows--fails

R. Captives and Fugitives

R315. Cave as refuge from pursuing monster

S. Unnatural Cruelty

S412.2. Weasel taunts Eagle as afraid [hiding from?] monster--now dead

W. Traits of Character

W230.2.2. Two women

Z. Miscellaneous Groups of Motifs

Z10.2. End formula

Z71.0.1. Two [2 women][shoot 2 times]

Z71.3.3. Five [5 times struck monster]

42. *TUH-TAN-NAH*
B. Animals

B463.3. Helpful crane

B810.3.3. Coyote

INDEX OF MOTIFS 307

G. Ogres
G11.6.5.1. Child-stealing and child-eating Ogress; cf. G11.6.5. Ogre-women
steal, eat people
G441. Ogress carries victim(s) in bag (basket)
G552. Rescue from Ogress by helpful animals

H. Tests
H599.7. Ogress ordered to step on Crane's knee [which is slippery]

K. Deceptions
K439.1.1. Ogress discovers not two humans to eat, but only rocks in her basket
K526. Captor's basket holed, filled with rocks while captives escape
K547.5.1. Ferocious animal [Ogress] misunderstands victim's remark: runs off
to look to her children; cf.G572. Ogress overawed by trick
K2320.1.Deception by frightening: Ogress made to believe her children are in
danger

R. Captives and Fugitives
R11. Abduction by monster (Ogress); cf.G334. Ogre keeps human prisoners
R131.1.1. Old fisherman rescues drowning Ogress
R219.4. Brothers escape from Ogress
R246. Crane-bridge. Fugitives are helped across a stream by a crane who lets
them cross on his leg.The pursuer is either refused assistance or
drowned by the crane

W. Traits of Character
W230.1.2. Boys (2)
W231.1.1. An old man

Z. Miscellaneous Groups of Motifs
Z71.0.1. Two [2 little boys]
Z71.2.2.6. Direction: "down the river;" cf. Z71.2.1.4. West
Z71.3.3. Five [5 times Ogress is told] [5 times Ogress refuses]

43. THE BOY THAT WAS STOLEN BY *AT!AT!A'LIYA*
A. Mythological Motifs
A1172.4. Day and night determined. When bundle/box of night is opened,
there will be darkness as long as it remains open--then light will
come
A1174.1. Traveler bearing bundle/box containing night--when opened all
becomes darkness

B. Animals
B463.3. Helpful Crane [fishing with a dip-net]
B810.8.1. Meadowlark
B810.17.2. Lice (people)
B810.17.3. Nits
B810.17.4. Graybacks

C. Tabu

C319.3. Tabu: to look toward Crane

C601. Youth not to step on knee of "crane-bridge"--lest he slip and fall off

C614.1.0.2. Tabu: hunting in certain part of forest; cf. C614.1.0.3. Forbidden direction

C653. Compulsion: particular place. Youth must go into "yonder" mountains, shoot upwards all arrows

D. Magic

D995.2. Magic leg, broken, replaced with one of brushwood, causes Meadowlark to prophesy

D1091. Magic bow

D1092.0.2. Magic arrows--five quivers full

D1154.6. Youth's "babyboard" to be located

D1205.2. Magic digging stick(s)--usually breaks as sign of mishap

F. Marvels

F53. Ascent to upper world on arrow chain. Hero shoots arrows which join one another in the air to form a chain; cf. F52. Ladder to upperworld; see also F831. Extraordinary arrow(s)

F529.1.1. Man has arrow through body--as he passes by, he falls dead; cf. F1096.1. Person lives on after having heart cut free; cf. D997.1. Magic heart--human

F661.7.3. One arrow shot into end of last one to make rope of arrows

F679.5. Skillful hunter: youth gets much small game

G. Ogres

G11.6. Man-eating woman: *At!At!A'lia*, Ogress

G11.6.5. Ogre-woman, steals and eats people

G376.2. Children, of Ogress

K. Deceptions

K874. Deception by pretended lousing; cf. K611.1. Escape by pretended lousing; also cf. K331.2.1.1. Theft after putting owner to sleep by lousing her

N. Chance and Fate

N271.8.1. Monster being traced by trail it leaves

N469. Crane informs youth of his birth--youth has a different mother

P. Society

P201. Inherent enmity between members (brothers) of family

P211.0.1. Chief's wife

P231.8. Ogress raises youth as her youngest son

P251.5.2.1. Brothers are remarkably unlike/dissimilar with each other

Q. Rewards and Punishments

Q414.0.14. Burning of pitchwood in house of Ogress and immolation of her children

R. Captives and Fugitives
R11.1. Youth abducted by Ogress

R49.4. Ogress hold youth captive in her home

R246. Crane-bridge. Fugitive(s) are helped across a stream by a crane who lets them cross on his leg. The pursuer is either refused assistance or drowned by the crane

S. Unnatural Cruelty
S112. Burning to death

S183.2. Ogress and her children eat frogs and snakes

T. Sex
T528.1. Thunder, as husband of meadowlark

V. Religion
V227.2.2.1. Youth disgorges "unclean food," is fed wholesome, "clean food"

W. Traits of Character
W231.1.2. Young boy

Z. Miscellaneous Groups of Motifs
Z71.3.3. Five [5 times turns back] [makes 5 tracks] [5 times tracked] [5 quivers of arrows and a bow]

44. THE CANNIBAL WOMAN
A. Mythological Motifs
A969.10. Origin of huge rock close by river: transformed into great rock is Ogress, her basket on her back, her monster children

B. Animals
B463.3. Helpful crane

F. Marvels
F841. Extraordinary boat [note abrupt change in story: from crane-bridge to a boat]; cf. R246. Crane-bridge

G. Ogres
G11.6.5. *At!At!A'lia*, child-stealing and child-eating monster

G441.Ogress carries victim(s) in bag [basket]

G442. Child-stealing demon

G552. Rescue from Ogress by helpful animals

K. Deceptions
K526. Captor's basket filled with animals or objects [stones and dirt] while captives escape

K547.5.1. Ferocious animal [Ogress] misunderstands victim's remark: runs off

to look to *her* children; cf. G572. Ogress overawed by trick
K2320.1. Deception by frightening: Ogress made to believe her children are
in danger

P. Society
P253.11.1. Sister injures brother, causes him to cry out
P716. Particular places: Spedis
P716. Particular places: Celilo

Q. Rewards and Punishments
Q428. Ogress drowned

R. Captives and Fugitives
R11. Abduction by monster (Ogress); cf. G334. Ogre keeps human prisoners
R219.3. Brother and sister escape from Ogress

U. The Nature of Life
U43. Task: Children sent to gather flint (arrowheads)

W. Traits of Character
W230.4. A boy and a girl

Z. Miscellaneous Motifs
Z71.0.1. Two [2 children]

VII. TALES COMPARABLE WITH
EUROPEAN *MÄRCHEN*

45. A WISHOM LEGEND
B. Animals
B531.6. Great number of game animals available near lodge

F. Marvels
F679.5.3.2. Skillful hunter slays and cooks huge amount of game that cannibal
will no longer feast on people

G. Ogres
G532. Hero hidden and ogre deceived by his wife [daughter] when he says that
he smells humans (blood); cf. G84. *Fee-fi-fo-fum*. Cannibal
returning home smells human flesh and makes exclamation.
Particularly A-T 327 contains this motif

J. The Wise and the Foolish
J765. Mark the way one is going in an unfamiliar country: arrows used as
ground markers; cf. J1922. Marking the place

INDEX OF MOTIFS

K. Deceptions

K515. Escape by hiding; Cf. R318.1. Boy hidden under skin(s) in order not to be seen and prophesied about; also cf. P322. Guest given refuge. Murderer of a man's father takes refuge in his house and is saved by him

P. Society

P486.2. Extraordinary hunter; F679.5. Skillful hunter
P716. The place "where the sun comes up"

Q. Rewards and Punishments

Q114.1.1. Gifts of suits of buckskin, of land given to daughter and son-in-law

T. Sex

T103. Marriage: youth and cannibal's daughter
T294.1. Husband of cannibal's daughter longs for home, to visit relatives

W. Traits of Character

W230.2.2. A girl
W230.4. Parents
W231.1.1. Evil father, eats people
W231.1.2. A boy

Z. Miscellaneous Groups of Motifs

Z71.2.1.3. Direction: "towards the sunrise"
Z71.3.3. Five [5 quivers of arrows][5 queries of daughter][5 denials to father] talked 5 times] [repeated 5 times]

COMPARATIVE NOTES TO OTHER PLATEAU INDIAN TALES COLLECTIONS

The comparative notes hereafter cite similar narratives related by tribes residing over the Plateau Region. The tribes and the authors and titles of printed collections of traditional narratives cited hereafter follow.

COEUR d'ALENE
Reichard, Gladys A. 1947. *An Analysis of Coeur d'Alene Indian Myths*, MAFS 41. New York: American Folklore Society.

Teit, James A. 1917. "Coeur d'Alene Tales," in *Folk-Tales of Salishan and Sahaptin Tribes*, MAFS 11. New York: American Folk-Lore Society.

KLIKITAT
Jacobs, Melville 1929. *Northwest Sahaptin Texts, I*, UWPA 2, No. 5. Seattle, WA: University of Washington Press.

Jacobs, Melville 1969. *Northwest Sahaptin Texts*, CUCA 19, Part I. New York: AMS Press.

KUTENAI
Boas, Franz 1918. *Kutenai Tales*, BAE 59. Washington, D.C.: U.S. Government Printing Office.

LILLOOET
Hill-Tout, Charles 1978. *The Squamish and the Lillooet II, The Salish People*. Vancouver, B.C.: Talonbooks.

NEZ PERCE
Farrand, Livingston (ed. Theresa Meyer) 1917. "Folk-tales of Sahaptin Tribes," in *Folk-Tales of Salishan and Sahaptin Tribes*, MAFS 11. New York: American Folk-Lore Society.

Hines, Donald M. 1984. *Tales of the Nez Perce*. Fairfield, WA: Ye Galleon Press.

Slickpoo Sr., Allen P. 1977. *Nu Mee Poom Tit Wah Tit (Nez Perce Legends)*. NP: Nez Perce Tribe of Idaho.

Spinden, Herbert J. 1917. "Nez Perce' Tales" in *Folk-Tales of Salishan and Sahaptin Tribes*, MAFS 11. New York: American Folk-Lore Society.

OKANOGAN
(Northern Okanogan)
Gould, Marian K. 1917. "Okanagon Tales," in *Folk-Tales of Salishan and Sahaptin Tribes*, MAFS 11. New York: American Folk-Lore Society.

Hill-Tout, Charles 1978. *The Thompson and the Okanagan I, The Salish People*. Vancouver, B.C.: Talonbooks.

Teit, James A. 1917. "Okanogan Tales," in *Folk-Tales of Salishan and Sahaptin Tribes*, MAFS 11. New York: American Folk-Lore Society.

(Southern Okanogan)
Hines, Donald M. 1976. *Tales of the Okanogans*. Fairfield, WA.: Ye Galleon Press.

Spier, Leslie ed. [with others], 1938. *'Tales,"* in *The Sinkaietk or Southern Okanogon of Washington*, GSA 6. Menasha WI: George Banta Publishing Co.:195-249.

PEND d'OREILLE
Teit, James A. 1917. "Pend d'Oreille Tales," in *Folk-Tales of Salishan and Sahaptin Tribes*, MAFS 11. New York: American Folk-Lore Society.

SANPOIL
Ray, Verne F. 1933. "Sanpoil Folk Tales," in *Journal of American Folklore*, 46: 129-187.

THOMPSON
Hill-Tout, Charles 1978. *The Thompson and the Okanagan I, The Salish People*. Vancouver, B.C.: Talonbooks.

Teit, James A. 1898. *Traditions of the Thompson River Indians of British Columbia*, MAFS 6. New York: American Folk-Lore Society.

Teit, James A. 1917. "Thompson Tales," in *Folk-Tales of Salishan and Sahaptin Tribes*, MAFS 11. New York: American Folk-Lore Society.

WASCO
Hines, Donald M. 1996. *Celilo Tales: Wasco Myths, Legends, Tales of Conflicts and Adventures.* Issaquah, WA: Great Eagle Publishing, Inc.

WISHOM (WISHRAM)
Hines, Donald M. 1998. *Where the River Roared: The Wishom Tales.* Issaquah: Great Eagle Publishing, Inc.

YAKAMA
Beavert, Virginia ed. 1974. *The Way It Was; Yakima Legends.* Yakima: Consortium of Johnson O'Malley Committees, Region IV.

Hines, Donald M. 1992. *Ghost Voices: Yakima Indian Myths, Legends, Humor and Hunting Stories.* Issaquah, WA: Great Eagle Publishing, Inc.

PART TWO.
THE TRADITIONAL TALES OF THE WISHOMS

I. TALES OF THE ORIGIN OF MAN,
OF ANIMALS, PLANTS, PHENOMENA

1A. COYOTE AT LAPWAI, IDAHO
In his *Tales of the North American Indians* (Bloomington: Indiana University Press, 1966), Stith Thompson includes invaluable comparative notes of representative motifs in Indian tales from across the U.S. on pp. 269-370. And see his bibliography of Indian tales in print, pp. 371-386.
COEUR D'ALENE Reichard 1947:68-72;Teit 1917:121-122, 122; **KLIKITAT** Jacobs 1969:esp. 65-66; **NEZ PERCE** Hines 1984:43-46; Slickpoo 1977:201-206; Farrand 1917:148-151 (2 texts); Spinden 1917:200-201; **OKANOGAN** Hines 1976:116-117; **PEND D'OREILLE** Teit 1917:115-116,117 ; **WASCO** Hines 1996: 19-21; **WISHOM** Hines 1998:#1B below; **YAKAMA** Beavert 1974:28-31; Hines 1992:19-22.

1B. COYOTE AND *ITCIE'XYAN*
COEUR D'ALENE Reichard 1947:68-72; Teit 1917:121-122, 122; **KLIKITAT** Jacobs 1969: esp. 65-66; **NEZ PERCE** Hines 1984:43-46, Slickpoo 1977:201-205, Farrand 1917:148-151 (2 texts), Spinden 1917:200-201; **OKANOGAN** Hines 1976:116-117; **PEND D'ORIELLE** Teit 1917:115-116, 117; **WASCO** Hines 1996: 19-21; **WISHOM** Hines 1998:#1A above; **YAKAMA** Beavert 1974:28-31; Hines 1992:19-22.

2. *IS-TAM-MA*, CHIEF OF THE BEAVERS
COEUR D'ALENE Reichard 1947:83-86; **KLIKITAT** Jacobs 1929:234-236; **KUTENAI** Boas 1918:130-133; **OKANOGAN** Hines 1976:50-53; **THOMPSON** Hill-Tout 1978:116-117.

3. THE VISIT TO THE WORLD OF GHOSTS

At least two independent varieties of narratives concern visits to the land of the dead: a) a visit to the land (on earth) of the shadow people; b) a visit to a world apart containing a moon-frog which swallows the moon.
COEUR D'ALENE Teit 1917:125; **KLIKITAT** Jacobs 1969:55-57, 190-191; Jacobs 1929:227-231; **KUTENAI** Boas 1918:213; **LILLOOET** cf. Hill-Tout 1978:146-147; **NEZ PERCE** Hines 1984:82-85, 85-88; Mayer 1917:178-179; Slickpoo 1977:65-69; **OKANOGAN** Gould 1917:106; **THOMPSON** Teit 1917:1; **WASCO** Hines 1996:46-49, 49-51; **WISHOM** Hines 1998:#4; **YAKAMA** Hines 1992:190-191.

4. HOW COYOTE DESTROYED THE TRAIL TO THE UPPER WORLD

At least two independent varieties of narratives concern visits to the land of the dead: a) a visit to the land (on earth) of the shadow people; b) a visit to a world apart containing a moon-frog which swallows the moon.
COEUR D'ALENE Teit 1917:125; **KLIKITAT** Jacobs 1969:55-57, 190-191; Jacobs 1929:227-231; **KUTENAI** Boas 1918:213; **LILLOOET** Hill-Tout 1978:146-147; **NEZ PERCE** Hines 1984:82-85, 85-88; Mayer 1917:178-179; Slickpoo 1977:65-69; **OKANOGAN** Gould 1917:106; **THOMPSON** Teit 1898:68-69, Teit 1917:1; **WASCO** Hines 1996:46-49, 49-51; **WISHOM** Hines 1998:#3; **YAKAMA** Hines 1992:190-191.

5A. COYOTE AND THE FIVE SISTERS OF THE *N-CHE-WANA*

Commonly included in this narrative are segments which are often told separately: a) Origination of the salmon runs; b) Selection of particular fishing sites and spawning streams; c) Distribution of salmon into streams, past fishing sites; d) Origination of means of taking salmon; e) Meat stolen from sleeper [A-T 15 {cf. #7. "Coyote and His Anus" in *Tales of the Nez Perce*}].
COEUR D'ALENE Reichard 1947:98-109; Teit 1917:121; **KLIKITAT** Jacobs 1969:74-76, 79-91, 91-93; **KUTENAI** Boas 1918:esp.171-179; **NEZ PERCE** Farrand 1917:139-144 (3 versions); Hines 1984:esp.64-65; Slickpoo 1977:17, 99-101, 123-124; **OKANOGAN** Gould 1917:101-103; Hill-Tout 1978:87-100, 143; Hines 1976:23-28; Teit 1917:67-72 (3 versions) ; Spier 1938:214-217; **SANPOIL** Ray 1933:173-175; **THOMPSON** Teit 1898:21-29; **WASCO** Hines 1996:51-53, 53-56; **WISHOM** Hines 1998:#5B, # 5C; **YAKAMA** Beavert 1974:34-37, 42-44; Hines 1984:45, 121-126, 126-131, 131-139--esp. 131-134.

5B.THE ORIGIN OF FISH IN THE COLUMBIA

Commonly included in this narrative are segments which are often told separately: a) Origination of the salmon runs; b) Selection of particular fishing sites and spawning streams; c) Distribution of salmon into streams, past fishing sites; d) Origination of the salmon runs; e) Meat stolen from sleeper. [A-T 15 {cf #7 "Coyote and His Anus" in *Tales of the Nez Perce*.}]
COEUR D'ALENE Reichard 1947:98-109; Teit 1917:121; **KLIKITAT** Jacobs 1969:74-76, 79-91, 91-93; **KUTENAI** Boas 1918: (see esp.Versions e-

g) 171-179; **NEZ PERCE** Farrand 1917:139-144 (3 versions); Hines 1984:esp.64-65; Slickpoo 1977:17 , 99-101, 123-124; **OKANOGAN** Gould 1917:101-103; Hill-Tout 1978:87-100, 143; Hines 1976: 23-28; Teit 1917:67-72 (3 versions) Spier 1938:214-217; **SANPOIL** Ray 1933:173-175; **THOMP-SON** Teit 1898:21-29; **WASCO** Hines 1996:51-53, 53-56; **WISHOM** Hines 1998:# 5A, #5C; **YAKAMA** Beavert 1974:34-37, 42-44; Hines 1992:45, 121-126, 126-131,131-139--esp.131-134.

5C. HOW COYOTE DESTROYED THE FISH DAM AT THE CASCADES, DISTRIBUTING SALMON IN THE RIVERS

Included often in this narrative are segments which otherwise occur separate-ly: a) Origination of the salmon runs; b) Selection of particular fishing sites and spawning streams; c) Distribution of salmon into streams, past fishing sites; d) Origination of means of taking salmon; e) meat stolen from sleeper (A-T 15 [cf. 7 "Coyote and His Anus" in *Tales of the Nez Perce*] are often recounted separately.
COEUR D'ALENE Reichard 1947:98-109; Teit 1917:121; **KLIKITAT** Jacobs 1969:74-76, 79-91, 91-93; **KUTENAI** Boas 1918:(see esp.Versions e-g) 171-179; **NEZ PERCE** Farrand 1917:139-144 (3 versions); Hines 1984:esp. 64-65; Slickpoo 1977:17, 99-101, 123-124; **OKANOGAN** Gould 1917:101-103; Hill-Tout 1978:87-100, 143; Hines 1976:23-28; Spier 1938:214-217; Teit 1917:67-72 (3 versions); **SANPOIL** Ray 1933:173-175; **THOMPSON** Teit 1898: 21-29 esp. 27-29; **WASCO** Hines 1996:51-53, 53-56; **WISHOM** Hines 1998:#5A, #5B; **YAKAMA** Beavert 1974:34-37, 42-44; Hines 1992:45,121-126, 126-131, 131-139--exp. 131-134.

6A. THE RACCOON STORY

NEZ PERCE Hines 1984:105-107; Slickpoo 1977:147-150; Spinden 1917:196-197; **WASCO** Hines 1996:56, 57; **WISHOM** Hines 1998:#6B; **YAKAMA** Beavert 1974:116-120, 194; Hines 1992:173-178.

6B. RACCOON AND HIS GRANDMOTHER

NEZ PERCE Hines 1984:105-107; Slickpoo 1977:147-150; Spinden 1917:196-197; **WASCO** Hines 1996:56, 57; **WISHOM** Hines 1998:#6A; **YAKAMA** Beavert 1974:116-120, 194; Hines 1992:173-178.

II. TALES OF THE LEGENDARY

7. HOW COYOTE ENSLAVED THE WEST WIND

COEUR D'ALENE Reichard 1947:146-147; Teit 1917:124; **THOMPSON** Teit 1898:87-88; **WISHOM** Hines 1998:#8.

8. THE EAST WIND AND THE WEST WIND

The Wishoms and other Plateau tribes recount of contests between varying animal beings, of a struggle to set the limits of cold vs. warm weather.
COEUR D'ALENE Reichard 1947:146-147; Teit 1917:124 (2 texts);

KLIKITAT cf. Jacobs 1969:30-32, 32-33; **KUTENAI** Boas 1918:178-183; **LILOOEET** Hill-Tout 1978:154-155; **NEZ PERCE** Farrand 1917:144-148, esp. 147-148; Hines 1984:120-127; Slickpoo 1977:10-16; **OKANOGAN** Gould 1917:104-105; Hines 1976:42-47; Teit 1917:74; **THOMPSON** Teit 1898:55-56; Teit 1917:21; **WASCO** Hines 65-78,79-84; **WISHOM** Hines 1998:#9, #39; cf.#36; **YAKAMA** Beavert 1974:10-22.

9A. COYOTE AND THE MISCHIEVOUS WOMEN

An interesting group of narratives finds Coyote at a stream across from which are enticing women with whom he would dally. He is frustrated as often as he succeeds in amour; often he transforms the forward women into birds. **COWLITZ** Jacobs 1929:102-103, see also 243-246; **NEZ PERCE** Hines 1984:76-77; **OKANOGAN** Teit 1917:70-71; **PEND ORIELLE** cf. Teit 1917:116-117; **THOMPSON** Teit 1917:25; **WISHOM** Hines 1998:#9B below.

9B. COYOTE AND THE MISCHIEVOUS WOMEN (SECOND VERSION)

An interesting group of narratives finds Coyote at a stream, across from which are enticing women with whom he would dally. He is frustrated as often as he succeeds in amour; often he transforms the women into birds. **COWLITZ** Jacobs 1929:102-103, see also 243-246; **NEZ PERCE** Hines 1984:76-77; **OKANOGAN** Teit 1917:70-71; **PEND D'ORIELLE** cf. Teit 1917:116-117; **THOMPSON** Teit 1917:25;**WISHOM** Hines 1998:#9A above.

10. COYOTE EATS DRIED SALMON

WASCO Hines 1996:63-64.

11. COYOTE MAKES A FISHTRAP

KLIKITAT Jacobs 1969:74-76, 79-91--esp. 86-88, 91-93; **KUTENAI** Boas 1918:176-179; **OKANOGAN** Hill-Tout 1978:143; Hines 1976:23-28; Teit 1917:67-70; **WISHOM** Hines 1998:#12; And see episodes wherein Coyote "calls" salmon up to a beach, employs sand to hold tight, to capture the fish; **YAKAMA** Beavert 1974:42-44; Hines 1992:95-98, 98-99, 99-100, 131-139-- esp. 131-134; cf. also tales 7D, 44, 45;

12. COYOTE SPEARS FISH

KLIKITAT Jacobs 1969:74-76, 79-91--esp. 86-88, 91-93; **KUTENAI** Boas 1918:176-179; **OKANOGAN** Hines 1976:23-28; Teit 1917:67-70; **WISH-OM** Hines 1998: #11; and see episodes wherein Coyote "calls" salmon to shore and employs sand to hold tight , to capture the fish; **YAKAMA** Beavert 1974:42-44; Hines 1992:95-98, 98-99, 99-100, 131-139--esp. 131-134; cf. also texts 7D, 44, 45;

13A. THE WISHOM TRIBE:
A STORY OF THEIR DIVISION AND SEPARATION

This narrative resembles a marvelous account of war between air and land/or water creatures. See esp. A-T 222 *War of Birds and Quadrupeds*. Very many problems of narrative form and culture deter us from declaring this and the following texts as "historical." Under the motif A1620. *Wandering of Tribes*, Stith Thompson lists a number of European parallels with the story. And he also lists versions from other North American Indians: Thompson, Gros Ventre, Sarcee, Blackfoot, Cheyenne, Creek. According to to Leslie Spier, *Wishram Ethnography*, similar Indian versions, which occur closer in location to the Wishrams, include texts from among the Moses-Columbia, Thompson, Shoshone, Havasupai, Northern Paiute, and others.
WISHOM Hines: 1998:#13B hereafter.

13B. A QUARREL OF THE WISHRAM

As with the previous narrative, 13A above, this narrative account reflects more the marvelous, the fanciful, than the historical. Under motif A1620. *Wandering of Tribes*, in *The Motif Index*, Stith Thompson cites many versions of similar accounts of wandering tribes from over Europe. And he cites versions from North American Indian tribes including the Thompson, Gros Ventre, Sarcee, Blackfoot, Cheyenne, and Creek. Similarly, in *Wishram Ethnography*, Leslie Spier cites Plateau Indian accounts from the Moses-Columbia, Thompson, Shoshone, Havasupai, Northern Paiute and others.

14. WHY THE WISHRAM ARE CALLED *ILAXLUIT*
NONE

15. COYOTE IN *SK!IN*
NONE

16. COYOTE AND THE MOUTHLESS MAN

WASCO Hines 1996:51-53 contains an episode concerning "people without mouths," 84; **YAKAMA** Hines 1992:69-80--esp.73-76.

17. A FAMINE AT THE CASCADES

A severe winter might quickly exhaust food supplies. And with game animals hunted out and summer vegetation still snow-covered, great hunger, as reflect-
ed here, was probably not uncommon. Thus, an extended delay in the annual spring-time salmon runs up the Columbia River spelled disaster for the area's Indian nations. **WASCO** Hines 1996:104-105 relates of a severe winter and allied suffering in tale 25 "A Hard Winter Near the Dalles."

18. A PROPHECY OF THE COMING OF THE WHITES

Employing a traditional oral format, this vision narrative reflects the tribe's revelatory mode of worship (visions by the old man and also the group; ecstatic dancing), the ecstasy of "gladness" found or associated with the Shaker religion practiced by the Indians, a more recent mode of worship.

19. THE *GY-U-BOO'-KUM (I)*

NEZ PERCE Slickpoo 1977:178-182; Spinden 1917:200-201; **WASCO** Hines 1996:88-89, 89-90; **WISHOM** Hines 1998: #20, #21, #41; **YAKAMA** Hines 1992:80-81, 82-83, 83-84.

20. THE *GY-U-BOO'-KUM* (II)

NEZ PERCE Slickpoo 1977:178-182; Spinden 1917:200-201; **WASCO** Hines 1996:88-89, 89-90; **WISHOM** Hines 1998: #19, #21, #41; **YAKAMA** Hines 1992:80-81, 82-83, 83-84.

21. THE *GY-U-BOO'-KUM* OF THE WISHOMS

NEZ PERCE Slickpoo 1977:178-182; Spinden 1917:200-201; **WASCO** Hines 1996:88-89, 89-90; **WISHOM** Hines 1998:#19, #20, #41; **YAKAMA** Hines 1992:80-81, 82-83, 83-84.

III. TALES OF MAGIC AND THE MARVELOUS

22. STAR HUSBAND

See especially Stith Thompson's "The Star Husband Tale," in *The Study of Folklore*, ed. Alan Dundes (Englewood Cliffs, N.J.: Prentice-Hall, Inc., 1965), pp. 414-474.
KUTENAI Boas 1918:246-249; **WASCO** Hines 1996:91-92, cf. 21-26; **YAKAMA** Beavert 1974:188-193; Hines 1992:141-146.

23. THE STAR-ROCK OF RICHES

WASCO Hines 1996:41-46; **WISHOM** Hines 1998:#22 [see mention of "shining object" in river].

24. COYOTE'S PEOPLE SING

WASCO Hines 1996:99-101.

25. COYOTE AND ANTELOPE

An interesting group of narratives pits one father and his sons (usually five in number) against another father and all his sons within magical circumstances. At last one group of sons is slain in this recounting of intratribal bad relations and mayhem. And see Tale 35, *Tales of the Nez Perce*, pp. 151-158. In this narrative appears a comparable episode wherein Skunk attempts to slay his wives and foe, mere images of which are reflected in water.
KLIKITAT Jacobs 1969:16-17; **NEZ PERCE** Slickpoo 1977:87-90; **OKANOGAN** Hill-Tout 1978:147-149; Hines 1976:50-53, 66-68; Teit 1917:79-80; **THOMPSON** Teit 1898:32-34.

26. COYOTE AND DEER

KUTENAI Boas 1918:8-11; **NEZ PERCE** Farrand 1917:164-168 (2 versions); Hines 1984:95-97; Slickpoo 1977:113-115; Spinden 1917:181-184; **OKANOGAN** Ray (Sanpoil) 1933:177-178; Spier 1938:233-234; **THOMPSON** Teit 1917:6; **WASCO** Hines 1996:92-95; 96-98; **YAKAMA** Hines

1992:109-110, 111-112.

IV. COYOTE AS TRICKSTER

27A. COYOTE AND *AT!AT!A'LIA*

The *At!at!a'lia* is related of in numerous Wasco narratives. See especially where the ogress is immolated: #37 "An *At!at!a'lia* Has Her Arm Pulled Off." See also Wasco versions #33 "The *At!at!a'lia* Who Was Deceived By Her Two Sons;" [the ogress here is really a Spirit-Bear]; #38 "A Jack Rabbit Boy Tricks and *At!at!a'lia*;" #39 "The Five *At!at!a'lia* Sisters Steal a Boy;" #40 "Two Children Escape from an *At!at!a'lia*." Note that at least three names for the monster occur hereafter and apparently point to a similar creature.
KUTENAI Boas 1918:42-45, 44-47, 112-113, 272, 273-279; **NEZ PERCE** Farrand 1917:176-177; Spinden 1917:192-194; **OKANOGAN** Hines 1976:98-103; Spier 1938:228; **THOMPSON** Teit 1898:63-64; Teit 1917:26-30; **WASCO** Hines 1996:138-139, 139-141, 141-144, 144-146; **WISHOM** Hines 1998:#27B, #42, 43, #44; **YAKAMA** Beavert 1974:78-82; Hines 1992:63-65, 188-189, cf.196-206--esp.196-202.

27B. COYOTE AND *TAH-TAH KLE-AH*

McWhorter notes that the *Tah-tah kle-ah* narrative varies among the different tribes, but it is told by the Yakimas as given in Hines, *Yakima*, 18 "*Tah-tah Kle-ah*." McWhorter said, "I have seen disobedient Indian children frightened into submission by the mere threat,'*Tah-tah Kle-ah* will carry you off in her basket! She will take you to her cave-house, roast you, and eat you!'"
KUTENAI Boas 1918:42-45, 44-47, 112-113, 272, 273-279; **NEZ PERCE** Farrand 1917:176-177; Spinden 1917:192-194; **OKANOGAN** Hines 1976:98-103; Spier 1938:228; **THOMPSON** Teit 1898:63-64; Teit 1917:26-30; **WASCO** Hines 1996:138-139, 139-141, 141-144, 144-146; **WISHOM** Hines 1998: #27A, #42, #43, #44; **YAKAMA** Beavert 1974:78-82; Hines 1992:63-65, 188-189, cf. 196-206--esp. 196-202.

28. COYOTE AND HIS DAUGHTER

Coyote's role as an incestor, marked by derisive humor as he violates a major tribal tabu, poses a fascinating counter to his role as a demigod or transformer in American Indian mythology.
COWLITZ Jacobs 1969:146-147; **NEZ PERCE** Slickpoo 1977:119-122; **OKANOGAN** Hines 1976:96-97; Teit 1917:72-74;

29. COYOTE AND THE SUN

COEUR D'ALENE cf. Teit 1917:123; **KUTENAI** Boas 1918:cf. 66-69, 116-117; **NEZ PERCE** cf. Slickpoo 1977:187-190; **OKANOGAN** Hill-Tout 1978:141; Hines 1976:54-57.

30. COYOTE AND SKUNK

COWLITZ Jacobs 1969:177-179; **KLIKITAT** Jacobs 1969:98-100.

31. EAGLE'S SON AND COYOTE'S SON-IN-LAW

An ancient parallel to the episode herein of mice eating the bowstrings of an enemy army and the defeat of Senacherib's invasion are mentioned by Herodotus, Bk II, Sect. 141. But see also the Old Testament account of the same battle in II Kings 19:35 ff.
OKANOGAN Spier 1938:239-240; **THOMPSON** Hill-Tout 1978:122-125.

32. COYOTE AND THE PREGNANT WOMAN
NONE

33. COYOTE AS MEDICINE MAN

An interesting group of narratives finds Coyote at a stream, across from which are enticing women with whom he would dally. He is frustrated as often as he succeeds in amour.
COWLITZ Jacobs 1969:102-103, 243-246; **NEZ PERCE** Hines 1984:76-77; **OKANOGAN** Spier 1938:237-238; Teit 1917:70-71; **THOMPSON** cf. Teit 1917:25; **WISHOM** Hines 1998: #9A, #9B.

34. THE STORY CONCERNING COYOTE

Several modern versions of this legendary narrative have been collected in recent times at the former Grande Ronde reservation of Western Oregon, far removed from a Wasco-Wishom setting. In his "Comments," to Karl Kroeber's "Scarface Vs. Scar-face: The Problem of Versions," *Journal of the Folklore Institute*, 18 (1981), esp. 145-150, Dell Hymes notes of a version told in Santiam Kalapuya by Mr. John B. Hudson which appears in Melville Jacobs' *Kalapuya Texts*, UWPA, no. 11 (Seattle, 1945), p. 91. Also, a Clacka-mas Chinook version told by Victoria Howard appears in Melville Jacobs' *Clackamas Chinook Texts, Part I*, Indiana University Research Center in Anthropology, Folklore, and Linguistics, Publication 8 (Bloomington, 1958), pp. 95-96. Still other versions told by Louis Simpson and by Hiram Smith appear in Dell Hymes *'In Vain I Tried to Tell You': Essays in Native American Ethnopoetics* (Philadelphia: University of Philadelphia Press,1981), Ch.6. [Hymes' investigations are bothersome for he overlooks that Louis Simpson related the narrative not in Wasco, but in the Wishom tongue. (According to Sapir's "Introduction," *Wishram Texts*, Simpson ". . . has a command of Wishram, Klickitat, and the Chinook jargon; but his English is extremely broken, hardly intelligible at times." [p. xi]). And Hymes also fails to consider Sapir's footnote #4 that the narrative explained the configurations of a mount-ain across the river from the modern town of Mosier, [i.e., Eastern] Oregon. **KLIKITAT** Jacobs 1969:59-62, esp. 61.

V. TALES OF CONFLICTS AND ADVENTURES

35. A CASCADE INDIAN LEGEND
COWLITZ Jacobs 1969:123-124; **KUTENAI** Boas 1917:28-33; **WASCO** Hines 1996:120-124.

36. HOW YOUNG EAGLE KILLED *PAH-HE-NUXT-TWY*

Portions of at least two separate tales appear in this narrative. In *Tales of the Nez Perce*, cf. "Coyote Causes His Son to Be Lost," pp. 61-65; but also cf. Wasco tale 42 "Eagle, A Klamath Man, Goes to the Columbia River to Gamble," pp. 150-151.

COEUR D'ALENE Reichard 1947:128-129; **KLIKITAT** Jacobs 1969:10-11; **KUTENAI** Boas 1918:150-153; **LILLOOET** Hill-Tout 1978:147-149; **NEZ PERCE** Slickpoo 1977:26; **WASCO** Hines 1996:150-151; **YAKIMA** Hines 1992:49.

37A. THE SALMON STORY

Versions of this narrative detail the magical struggle between forces wishing long and extremely cold winters, and others who wish for short and mild winters in the vicinity of the Wasco, Wishom and other nearby tribes. Cf. Wasco tale 15A "Battle of the *At-te-yi-yi* and *To-Que-nut*," pp. 65-78; but see also the Wasco tale 32 "Battle Between Eagle and Chinook, Origin of the Horn Spoon," pp.125-128. And for another account of the dead transformed who exude maggots, see Wasco tale 13 "The Dead Canoeman of the n-Che-wana," pp. 63-64; also Wishram tale 10 "Coyote Eats Dried Salmon" above.

COEUR D'ALENE Reichard 1947:189-190; Teit 1917:124 (2 versions); **KLIKITAT** Jacobs 1969:30-32, 32-33; **KUTENAI** Boas 1918:178-183; **LILLOOET** Hill-Tout 1978:154-155; **NEZ PERCE** Farrand 1917:144-148, esp 147-148; Hines 1984:120-127, esp. 124-127; Slickpoo 1977:3-6, 10-16; **OKANOGAN** Gould 1917:104-105; Hines 1976:42-47; cf. Spier 1938:225-226; Teit 1917:74; **SANPOIL** cf. Ray 1933:142-145; **THOMPSON** Teit 1898:55-56; Teit 1917:21; **WASCO** Hines 1996:65-78, 79-84; **WISHOM** Hines 1998:#8; **YAKAMA** Beavert 1974:10-24.

37B. SALMON MYTH

Versions of this narrative detail the magical struggle between forces wishing long and extremely cold winters, and others who wish for short and mild winters in the vicinity of the Wasco, Wishom and other tribes. Cf. Wasco tale 15A "Battle of the *At-te-yi-yi* and *To-Que-nut*," 65-78; also Wasco tale 15B "Battle of Cold-Wind and Chinook-Wind," pp. 79-84. But see also Wasco tale 32 "Battle Between Eagle and Chinook, Origin Of the Horn Spoon," pp. 125-128. And see the Wishram tale 37A "The Salmon Story" above. And for another account of the dead transformed who exude maggots, see Wasco tale 13 "The Dead Canoeman of the *n-Che-wana*," pp. 63-64; also Wishram tale 10 "Coyote Eats Dried Salmon" above.

COEUR D'ALENE Reichard 1947:189-190; Teit 1917:124 (2 versions); **KLIKITAT** Jacobs 1969:30-32, 32-33; **KUTENAI** Boas 1918: 178-183; **LILLOOET** Hill-Tout 1978:154-155; **NEZ PERCE** Farrand 1917:144-148, esp. 147-148; Hines 1984:120-127, esp. 124-127; Slickpoo 1977:3-6, 10-16; **OKANOGAN** Gould 1917:104-105; Hines 1976:42-47; cf. Spier 1938:225-226; Teit 1917:74; **SANPOIL** cf. Ray 1933:142-145; **THOMPSON** Teit 1898:55-56; Teit 1917:21; **WASCO** Hines 1996:65-78, 79-84; **WISHOM** Hines 1998:#8 #37A; **YAKAMA** Beavert 1974:10-24.

38. THE ADVENTURES OF EAGLE
AND HIS FOUR BROTHERS
COEUR D'ALENE Reichard 1947:128-129; **KLIKITAT** Jacobs 1969:10-11; **KUTENAI** Boas 1918:150-153; **LILLOOET** Hill-Tout 1978:147-149; **NEZ PERCE** Slickpoo 1977:26; **WASCO** Hines 1996:150-151; **WISHOM** Hines 1998:#36 above; **YAKAMA** Beavert 1974:145-147; Hines 1992:49.

39. THE FIVE EAST WIND BROTHERS
AND THE FIVE THUNDER BROTHERS
This narrative details the magical contest, the struggle between forces wishing long and extremely cold winters, and others who wish for milder winters in the vicinity of the Wishom, Wasco, and other tribes.
COEUR D'ALENE Reichard 1947:189-190; Teit 1917:124 (2 versions); **KLIKITAT** Jacobs 1969:30-32, 32-33; **KUTENAI** Boas 1918:178-183; **LILLOOET** Hill-Tout 1978:154-155; **NEZ PERCE** Farrand 1917:144-148, esp. 147-148; Hines 1984:120-127, esp. 124-127; Slickpoo 1977:3-6, 10-16; **OKANOGAN** Gould 1917:104-105; Hines 1976:42-47; Teit 1917:74; **THOMPSON** Teit 1898:55-56; Teit 1917:21; **WASCO** Hines 1996:65-78; 79-84, see also the magical contest 99-101; **WISHOM** Hines 1998:#8, also #37A; **YAKAMA** Beavert 1974:10-24.

40A. THE DESERTED BOY (I)
LILLOOET Hill-Tout 1978:150-153; **NEZ PERCE** Hines 1984:100-103; Slickpoo 1977:53-58; **OKANOGAN** Hill-Tout 1978:150-152; **SANPOIL** cf. Ray 1933:138-142; **THOMPSON** Teit 1898:51-52; Teit 1917:34-35;**WAS-CO** Hines 1996:135-138; **WISHOM** Hines 1998:#40B below.

40B. THE DESERTED BOY (II)
LILLOOET Hill-Tout 1978:150-153; **NEZ PERCE** Hines 1984:100-103; Slickpoo 1977:53-58; **OKANOGAN** Hill-Tout 1978:150-152; **SANPOIL** cf. Ray 1933:138-142; **THOMPSON** Teit 1898:51-52; Teit 1917:34-35; **WASCO** Hines 1996:135-138; **WISHOM** Hines 1998:#40A above.

VI. TALES OF MONSTERS AND OGRES

41. EAGLE AND WEASEL
NEZ PERCE Slickpoo 1977 :178-182; Spinden 1917:200-201; **WASCO** Hines 1996:88-89, 89-90; **WISHOM** Hines 1998:#19, #20, #21 (3 versions).

42. *TUH-TAN-NAH*
KUTENAI Boas 1918:42-45, 44-47, 112-113, 272, 273-279; **NEZ PERCE** Farrand 1917:176-177; Spinden 1917:192-194; **OKANOGAN** Hines 1976:98-103; Spier 1938:228; **THOMPSON** Teit 1898:63-64; Teit 1917:26-30; **WASCO** Hines 1996:138-139, 139-141, 141-144, 144-146; **WISHOM** Hines 1998:#27A, 27B, #43, #44; **YAKAMA** Beavert 1974:78-82; Hines 1992:63-65, 188-189, 215-216.

43. THE BOY THAT WAS STOLEN BY *AT!AT!A'LIYA*
KUTENAI Boas 1918:42-45, 44-47, 112-113, 272, 273-279; **NEZ PERCE** Farrand 1917:176-177; Spinden 1917:192-194; **OKANOGAN** Hines 1976:98-103; **THOMPSON** Teit 1898:63-64; Teit 1917:26-30; **WASCO** Hines 1996:138-139, 139-141, 141-144, 144-146; **WISHOM** Hines 1998: #27A, 27B, #42, #44; **YAKAMA** Beavert 1974:78-82; Hines 1992: 63-65, 188-189, 215-216..

44. THE CANNIBAL WOMAN
KUTENAI Boas 1918:42-45, 44-47, 112-113, 272, 273-279; **NEZ PERCE** Farrand 1917:176-177; Spinden 1917:192-194; **OKANOGAN** Hines 1976:98-103; **THOMPSON** Teit 1898:63-64; Teit 1917:26-30; **WASCO** Hines 1996:138-139, 139-141, 141-144, 144-146; **WISHOM** Hines 1998:#27A, #27B, #42, #43; **YAKAMA** Beavert 1974:78-82; Hines 1992:63-65, 188-189, 215-216.

VII. TALES COMPARABLE WITH EUROPEAN *MÄRCHEN*

45. A WISHOM LEGEND
The version of "Jack and the Beanstalk" recorded by Franz Boas, *Chinook Texts*, RBAE 20 (Washington, D.C., 1894), seems apparently that recorded previously the closest geographically to Wishom territory.
KLIKITAT Jacobs 1929:236-240; Jacobs 1969:11-14--esp. 12; **THOMPSON** Teit 1898:93-94.

LIST OF INFORMANTS

Listed below are the informants from whom this collection of oral traditional narratives of the Wishoms was obtained together with the date (if known) and the source in which they were published or else discovered.

I. EDWARD SAPIR

1. Pete McGuff, as informant (he also served Sapir as translator). Sapir notes that "Pete McGuff, . . . may serve as a type of the younger generation of Indian, though only a half-blood (his father was a Negro, his mother is a full-blood Indian). Having lived much of his life with the Wishrams, he speaks their language fluently, though long contact in early life with the Cascades Indians on the Columbia is responsible for a number of un-Wishram phonetic peculiarities that the linguistic material obtained from him exhibits. He has not of course that feeling for the old Indian life, and faith in the truth of the myths, that a man like Louis Simpson has; nevertheless, in spite of his white man's rationalism, he is not at all disposed to dismiss as idle the ideas of the Indians in regard to medicine-men and guardian spirits. He has been trained in the Agency school, reads and writes English well, and in general displayed throughout remarkable intelligence; he has been of the greatest help to me, both in the field and in correspondence, and I take this opportunity of thanking him" (Sapir, *Wishram Texts.* . . , Intro., p. xii.)--July-August 1905: 39.

2. Louis Simpson (Indian name *Me-nait)*, with Pete McGuff as the stated or presumed translator. Sapir notes, "Louis Simpson is a fair example of the older type of Wishram Indian, now passing away. Of short and stocky build, bow-legged from constant riding on horseback, he is about seventy or seventy-five years of age, of an impatient and somewhat self-willed temperament, dramatically talkative, with a good deal of the love of gain and bargain-driving proclivities with which many of the early Western travelers charged the Indians about The Dalles; yet, despite this, he proved to be a lovable personality, owing chiefly to his keen sense of humor. He has a command of Wishram, Klickitat, and the Chinook jargon; but his English is extremely broken, hardly intelligible at times. Superficially, Louis is a convert to the ways of the whites; in other words, he is a "civilized" Indian,-- lives in a frame house, raises and sells wheat and hay, is dressed in white man's clothes, is theoretically a Methodist. Judging by the contents of his mind, however, he is to all intents and purposes an unadulterated Indian. He implicitly believes in the truth of all the myths he narrated, no matter how puerile or

as worthy of the highest respect, despite the ridiculous and lascivious sides of his character; and with him he is strongly inclined to identify the Christ of the whites, for both he and Coyote lived many generations ago, and appeared in this world in order to better the lot of mankind. On one point Louis always insisted with great emphasis -- the myths as he told them were not invented by himself, but have been handed down from time immemorial, and hence have good claims to being considered truth" (Sapir, Wishram Texts, Intro., p. xi-xii)--July-August 1905: 1A, 1B, 3, 5B, 6B, 7, 8, 9B, 10, 11, 12, 13B, 15, 16, 24, 25, 26, 27A, 28, 30, 31, 32, 33, 34, 37A, 38, 40A, 41. And see Louis Simpson's Oral Traditional History account, "A Personal Narrative of the Paiute War, above.

3. Narrator unknown, told to Pete McGuff (Sapir)--July-August 1905: 6A, 29.

4. An old woman ("This account of a famine at the Cascades was taken down in Indian from an old woman [not identified] by my interpreter, Peter McGuff, who supplied also an interlinear translator. The events took place about 1835" p. 226)(Sapir)--July-August 1905: 17 [but see below].

5. Sophie Klickitat. "A Prophecy of the Coming of the Whites,"(and perhaps also "A Famine At The Cascades") ". . .was taken down in Indian and provided with an interlinear translation by my interpreter, Peter McGuff, the source being an old woman named Sophie Klickitat. Of the latter text the events are supposed to have taken place at the Cascades long before the coming of the whites" (Sapir, *Wishram Texts*. . ., p.228f.)--July-August 1905: 17, 18.

6. Tom Simpson, Indian name *Ta'xcani*, was brother of Louis Simpson and was also head of the Shaker Church on the Yakama Reservation, according to Sapir--July-August 1905: 9B, 10.

7. *AnEwi'kus* ("an old Indian woman, interpreted with interlinear translation by Pete McGuff who took down the phonetic Wishram," Sapir, *Wishram Texts...* p. 164)--July-August 1905: 43.

II. LUCULLUS V. MCWHORTER
1. Chief Menineck. McWhorter states, "Chief Meninock (originally *Menine-okt*) belonged to the *Skein-tla-ma* tribe, residing on the *n-Che-wana* opposite the mouth of the Deschutes River." According to Spier, *Wishram Ethnography*, "the peoples residing opposite the mouth of the Deschutes River were the *Sk!in* Indians." (L.V. McWhorter:)--August 1922: 2, 23.

2. *Ye-mow-wit* [Jobe Charley, also known as Jobe Colwash--a Yakama] (L.V. McWhorter)--18 Sept. 1925: 4, 13A.

3. *An-nee-Shiat* (L.V. McWhorter)--May 1918: 5A.

4. *Che-pos to-cos* (Owl Child). According to McWhorter *Che-pos to cos* was also known as *Shat-Taw-Wee* (Leader in Battle), whose English name was Alec McCoy. In his autobiography found herein, Owl Child recalls: "I was born at

the Dalles, Oregon; we call the place Wasco. I was born on the site of the old Wishom village which was burned by the soldiers during the Yakima War, 1855-56. My father, *Pul-Kus*, was of the Wishom tribe, while my mother *Annee-swolla* was a Wasco woman." An accomplished raconteur, he had lived, hunted, and fought alongside the Piegans of the Montana Country for a number of years. Upon returning to the Yakama Reservation, he served as a tribal policeman under four different Indian Agents at Fort Simcoe. He eventually became Chief of Police, and served one term as Judge of the Yakama Nation Tribal Court. Owl Child died on June 13, 1939 at the age of 104 years. (L.V. McWhorter):5C (October 1916), 27B (June 1923), 35, 36 (October 1923), 42 (October 1923), 45(7 June 1926). And see Owl Child's Autobiographical, Oral Traditional History account, "Autobiography," above.

5. Narrator unknown (L.V. McWhorter): 19 (1909), 21.

6. *Salatsze* (L.V. McWhorter)--1911: 20.

III. LESLIE SPIER

Mrs. Mabel Teio. "An elderly Wishram, she wasn't disposed to volunteer information" (Spier and Sapir, *Wishram Ethnography*, Intro, p. 154): 22, 37B, 40B, 44.

SELECTED LIST OF READINGS ABOUT THE WISHOM INDIAN NATION

A. GENERAL STUDIES

Alvord, B. 1857. "Report Concerning the Indians in the Territories of Oregon and Washington." *H.R. Exec. Doc.* 75 (Serial No. 906). 34th Congress, 3rd Session, I:10-22.

Alvord, B. 1855. "Concerning the Manners and Customs, the Superstitions, . . . of the Indians of Oregon," *Information Respecting the History, Condition, and Prospects of the Indian Tribes of the United States.* Henry Rowe Schoolcraft, ed. V:651-657. Philadelphia.

Attwell, Jim 1974. *Columbia River Gorge History*. Skamania WA: Tahlkie Books.

Cox, Ross 1832. *Adventures on the Columbia River*, 2d ed. New York, NY, 335 pp.

Cobb, John N. 1921. *Pacific Salmon Fisheries* [Report of U.S. Commissioner of Fisheries for 1921, Appendix 1]--Bureau of Fisheries, Doc. 902. Washington D.C..

Curtis, Edward S. 1911. *The North American Indian*. See esp. vol. 8:86-154, 172-181, 185-191, 198-205. Norwood, Mass.: Plimpton Press. [Reprinted, New York: Johnson, 1970].

Eells, M. 1892. "Aboriginal Geographic Names in the State of Washington," *American Anthropologist* 5:27-35.

Franchere, Gabriel 1904. *Narrative of a Voyage to the Northwest Coast of America in the Years 1811, 1812, 1813, and 1814. . .*, VI in *Early Western Travels, 1748-1846*, ed. Reuben G. Thwaites. Cleveland OH.

Hunn, Eugene 1981. *Nch'i Wana, 'The Big River:' Mid-Columbia River Indians and Their Land*. Seattle: University of Washington Press.

Kane, Paul 1925. *Wanderings of an Artist Among the Indians of North America, from Canada to Vancouver's Island and Oregon...* Toronto: The Radisson Society of Canada Ltd., 329 pp.

Lee, Daniel and J.H. Frost 1844. *Ten Years in Oregon.* New York: J. Collord, 344 pp.

Lockley, Fred 1928. *History of the Columbia River Valley from the Dalles to the Sea.* Chicago: S.J. Clarke, 3 vols.

McArthur, Lewis L. 1974. *Oregon Geographic Names*, 4th ed. Portland: Oregon Historical Society, 835 pp.

McWhorter, Lucullus V. 1913. *The Crime Against the Yakimas*. N. Yakima WA.

_____; ed. Donald M. Hines 1995. *Tragedy of the Wahk-Shum: The Death of Andrew J. Bolon, Yakima Indian Agent As Told by Su-el-lil, Eye-witness; Also, The Suicide of General George A. Custer, as Told by Owl Child, Eyewitness.* Issaquah: Great Eagle Publishing Inc.

Meany, E.S. 1923. *Origin of Washington Geographic Names*. Seattle WA, 357pp.

Meinig, D.W. 1968. *The Great Columbia Plain: A Historical Geography, 1805-1910.* Seattle: University of Washington Press.

Moorhouse, Lee 1906. *Souvenir Album of Noted Indian Photographs*. Pendleton OR: East Oregonian Print, 25 pp.

Quaife, Milo M. 1916. *The Journals of Captain Meriwether Lewis and . . . Sergeant John Ordway Kept on the Expedition of Western Exploration, 1803-1806*, Collections 22. Madison: State Historical Society of Wisconsin.

Roe, Frank G. 1955. *The Indian and the Horse*. Norman OK: University of Oklahoma Press.

Schafer, Joseph ed. 1940. *Memoirs of Jeremiah Curtin*. Madison: State Historical Society of Wisconsin.

Stewart, Edgar I. and Jane R. Stewart, eds. 1957. *The Columbia River.* Norman OK: University of Oklahoma Press. [For original edition of Ross Cox, see above].

Strong, Thomas N. 1906. *Cathlamet on the Columbia*. Portland OR.

Thwaites, Reuben G. ed. 1904-1905. *Original Journals of the Lewis and Clark Expedition.* New York NY:7 vols.

Vaughn, Thomas ed. 1971. *Paul Kane, The Columbia Wanderer, 1846-47; Sketches and Paintings of the Indians and His Lecture, "The Chinooks."* Portland: Oregon Historical Society, 154 pp.

Wallace, W.S. 1952. "The Intermontane Corridor," *SWL* 18:38-46.

Wyeth, Nathaniel J. 1899. "The Correspondence and Journals of Captain Nathaniel J. Wyeth, 1831-1836: A Record of Two Expeditions for the Occupation of the Oregon Country, with Maps, Introduction and Index. . . ," edited by F.G. Young, in *Sources of the History of Oregon*:1, parts 3-4. Eugene OR: University Press.

B. RELIGION, SHAMANISM, MAGIC, THE MISSIONARIES

Barnett, Homer G. 1957. *Indian Shakers; A Messianic Cult of the Pacific Northwest.* Carbondale: Southern Illinois University Press, 378 pp.

Boas, Franz 1893. "The Doctrine of Souls and of Disease Among the Chinook Indians," *Journal of American Folklore* 6:39-43.

Cominsky, Sheila 1964. *An Analysis of Wasco-Wishram Mythology.* Pullman: WSU, M.A. Thesis, 108 pp.

Crowder, Stella I. 1913. "The Dreamers," *Overland Monthly* 62:607-609.

Dixon, Roland B. 1904. "Shamans of Northern California," *Journal of American Folklore* 17:23-27.

_____ 1908. "Some Aspects of the American Shaman," *Journal of American Folklore* 21:1-23.

DuBois, Cora 1938. *The Feather Cult of the Middle Columbia*, GSA 7. Menasha: George Banta, 1-45.

Gatschet, A.S. 1893. "Medicine Arrows of the Oregon Indians," *Journal of American Folklore* 6:111-112.

Gunther, Erna 1928. *A Further Analysis of the First Salmon Ceremony*, UWPA 2(5). Seattle: University of Washington Press, 129-173.

_____ 1926. "An Analysis of the First Salmon Ceremony," *American Anthropologist* 28:605-617.

Harmon, Ray 1971. "Indian Shaker Church: The Dalles," *Oregon Historical Quarterly* 72:148-158.

Hines, Donald M. 1993. *Magic in the Mountains, The Yakima Shaman: Power & Practice*. Issaquah: Great Eagle Publishing, Inc.

Huggins, E.L 1891. "Smohalla, The Prophet of Priest Rapids," *Overland Monthly* 17:208-215.

The Last Salmon Feast of the Celilo Indians--Mid-Columbia, 1956]. Portland: Oregon Historical Society [Motion Picture, 18 min., sd., b&w, 16mm].

Larsell, Orloff 1947. "Medicine Among the Indians," in *The Doctor in Oregon, A Medical History*. Portland: Binfords & Mort (The Oregon Historical Society).

MacMurray, J.W. 1887. "The 'Dreamers' of the Columbia River Valley in Washington Territory," *Transactions of the Albany Institute* 11:241-248.

Mooney, James 1896. *The Ghost-Dance Religion and the Sioux Outbreak of 1890*, ARBAE 14(2). Washington DC:641-1110.

Murdock, George P. 1965. "Tenino Shamanism," *Ethnology* 4:165-171.

Park, W.Z. 1938. *Shamanism in Western North America*, NUSSS 2. Evanston IL:1-166.

Radin, Paul 1914. *Some Aspects of Puberty Fasting Among the Ojibwa*, BGSC 2(4). Ottawa, Canada.

Ray, Verne F. 1937. "The Blue Jay Character in the Plateau Spirit Dance," *American Anthropologist* 39:593-601.

Ruby, Robert H. 1966. "A Healing Service in the Shaker Church," *Oregon Historical Quarterly* 67:347-355.

_____ 1989. *Dreamer-Prophets of the Columbia Plateau: Smohalla and Skolaskin*. Norman: U of OK Press.

Smith, M.W. 1954. "Shamanism in the Shaker Religion of Northwest America," *Man* 54:119-122.

Spier, Leslie 1927. *The Ghost Dance of 1870 Among the Klamath of Oregon*, UWPA 2(2). Seattle WA.

_____, 1935. "The Prophet Dance of the Northwest and Its Derivatives . . . ," *General Series in Anthropology* 1. Menasha: George Banta Publishing Co., 1-74.

_____, 1921. *The Sun Dance of the Plains Indians: Its Development and Diffusion*, AP-AM 16(7). New York NY.

Strong, William D. 1945. "The Occurrence and Wider Implications of a 'Ghost Cult' on the Columbia River, Suggested by Carvings in Wood, Bone and Stone," *American Anthropologist* 47:244-261.

C. TRIBAL ECONOMIC STUDIES, CONTEMPORARY ACCOUNTS

Griswold, Gillett G. 1970. "Aboriginal Patterns of Trade Between the Columbia Basin and the Northern Plains," *Archaeology in Montana* 11:1-96.

The Indian Dip Net Fishery at Celilo Falls on the Columbia River, 17. Salem: Oregon Fish Commission.

Michael, Elva Olson 1980. *Governmental Policies and the Preservation and Display of Native American Cultural Resources in the Middle Columbia Basin*. Corvallis: OSU M.A. Thesis, 201 pp.

Norton, Helen and Robert Boyd and Eugene Hann 1983. "The Klickitat Trail of South Central Washington: A Reconstruction of Seasonally-Used Resource Sites, in *Prehistoric Places on the Southern Northwest Coast*, ed. Robert Greengo, 121-152. Seattle: Thomas Burke Memorial Washington State Museum Research Report 4.

Toepel, Kathryn Ann, et al 1980. *Cultural Resource Overview of BLM Lands in North-Central Oregon: Archaeology, Ethnography, History*, UOAP 17. Eugene OR, 215 pp.

D. INDIAN TRIBAL HISTORY, WARS, REGIONAL RELATIONS

Bancroft, Hubert Howe. *The Works of Hubert Howe Bancroft: I, The Native Races*. San Francisco, 1886.

Brown, Joseph H. 1892. *Political History of Oregon. Provisional Government, Treaties, Conventions, and Diplomatic correspondence on the Boundary Question;. . . History of the Cayuse War. . .*, I. Portland: W.B. Allen, 462 pp.

Browne, J. Ross 1857. "Indian War in Oregon and Washington Territories," *Special Report to the Secretary of War and the Secretary of the Interior* (Dated December 4, 1857). 35th Cong., 1st Sess., House Exec. Doc. No. 38, pp. 1-66 (Serial set 955). Also in Sen. Exec. Doc. No. 40, Serial set 929.

Clark, Robert C. 1935. "Military History of Oregon, 1849-1859," *Oregon Historical Quarterly* 36:14-59.

Curry, George C. 1855. "Expeditions Against the Indians," in *Correspondence and Official Proceedings, Governor of Oregon Territory, George C. Curry, to the Citizens*. Salem: Asahel Bush, Territorial Printer.

Deutsch, Herman J. 1956. "Indian and White in the Inland Empire: The Conquest for the Land, 1880-1912," *Pacific Northwest Quarterly* 47:44-51.

Doty, James 1855. "A True Copy of the Record of the Official Proceedings at the Council in the Walla Walla Valley, Held Jointly by Isaac L. Stevens Govn. & Supt., W.T., and Joel Palmer, Supt. Indian Affairs, O.T. on the part of the United States with the Tribes of Indians Named in the Treaties Made at That Council June 9th and 11th, 1855: National Archives, Record Group 75. Washington, D.C.: Records of the Bureau of Indian Affairs [See Microcopy T-494, roll 5, item 3].

Gunther, Erna 1950. "The Indian Background of Washington History," *Pacific Northwest Quarterly* 41:189-202.

Indian Hostilities in Oregon and Washington Territories. Message from the President of the United States, Transmitting the Correspondence on the Subject of Indian Hostilities in Oregon and Washington Territories. (U.S. 34th Congress. House 1st sess. Ex. Doc. No. 118). Washington DC 1856:58 pp.

Indian Hostilities in Oregon and Washington; Message from the President of the United States (U.S. 34th Congress, 1st sess., House Ex. Doc. No. 93). Washington DC 1856:144 pp.

Memorial of the Legislative Assembly of Oregon Territory, August 10, 1848 [repr. 1972]Fairfield, WA: Ye Galleon Press, 1972, 26 pp.

Reese, J.W. 1965. "OMV's Fort Henrietta: On Winter Duty, 1855-56," *Oregon Historical Quarterly* 66:132-160.

Ruby, Robert H. And John A. Brown 1976. *The Chinook Indians: Traders of the Lower Columbia River.* Norman: University of Oklahoma Press.

Thompson, Flora Cushinway n.d.. "Interviews of Flora (Cushinway) Thompson, Wife of the late Tommy Thompson, Chief of the Celilo Indians." n.p., Oregon Historical Society:3 tapes/cassette.

Victor, Frances F. 1894. *The Early Indian Wars of Oregon.* Salem, OE: Frank C. Baker.

E. FOLK ART, DECORATION, AND COSTUME

Boas, Franz 1927. *Primitive Art.* Oslo, Norway.

Cornhusk Bags of the Plateau Indians, 1974. Spokane: Cheney Cowles Memorial Museum, Eastern Washington State Historical Society: 12 pp.

Gogol, J.M. 1979. "Columbia River Indian Basketry," *American Indian Basketry Magazine* 1:4-9.

_____, 1980. "Cornhusk Bags and Hats of the Columbia Plateau Indians," *American Indian Basketry Magazine* 1:4-11.

Haeberlin, H.K., James A. Teit and Helen H. Roberts 1928. *Coiled Basketry in British Columbia and Surrounding Region,* BAE 41. Washington DC, 119-484.

Kuneki, Nettie, et al., 1882. *The Heritage of Klickitat Basketry; A History and Art Preserved.* Portland: Oregon Historical Society, 54 pp. [Biblio. pp. 53-54].

Schlick, Mary D. 1980. "Art Treasures of the Columbia Plateau," *American Indian Basketry Magazine* 1:12-21.

_____, 1979. "A Columbia River Indian Basket Collected by Lewis and Clark in 1805," *American Indian Basketry Magazine* 1:10-13.

Spier, Leslie 1925. *An Analysis of Plains Indian Parfleche Decoration,* UWPA 1. Seattle: University of Washington Press, 89-112.

_____ 1931. *Plains Indian Parfleche Designs,* UWPA 4. Seattle: University of Washington Press, 293-322.

F. FOLKTALES, LEGENDS
AND MYTHS

An extensive listing of collections of American Indian tales from over the Plateau Region appears in "Comparative Notes to Other Plateau Indian Tales Collections" above.

Boas, Franz 1894. *Chinook Texts*, BAE 20. Washington DC.

_____ 1910. *Kwakiutl Tales*. Columbia University Contributions to Anthropology, 20. New York: Columbia University.

Clark, Ella 1952. "The Bridge of the Gods in Fact and Fancy," *Oregon Historical Quarterly* 53:29-38.

_____1955-56. "George Gibbs' Account of Indian Mythology in Oregon and Washington Territories," *Oregon Historical Quarterly* [Part I] 56: 293-325; [Part II] 57:125-167.

_____1953. *Indian Legends of the Pacific Northwest*. Berkeley: University of California Press.

Cornelison, J.M. 1911. *Weyekin Stories: Titwatit Weyekishnim*. San Francisco: E.L. Mackey & Co., 30 pp.

Curtin, Jeremiah 1940. *Memoirs of Jeremiah Curtin*, WBS 11, ed. Joseph Schafer. Madison WI. [See especially Curtin's recounting of his collecting traditional texts among the Wascos at Warm Springs, Oregon, during the winter of 1885, pp. 351-361.]

Hines, Donald M. 1995. "Of Big Foot, The Oedipal Tale Told along the Columbia River," *Fabula, Journal of Folktale Studies* 36:98-104.

_____ 1991. *The Forgotten Tribes, Oral Tales of the Teninos and Adjacent Mid-Columbia River Indian Nations*. Issaquah: Great Eagle Publishing, Inc.

_____ 1992. *Ghost Voices: Yakima Indian Myths, Legends, Humor and Hunting Stories*. Issaquah: Great Eagle Publishing, Inc.

Hymes, Dell H. 1953. "Two Wasco Motifs," *Journal of American Folklore* 66:69-70.

_____ 1984. Bungling Host, Benevolent Host: Louis Simpson's 'Deer and Coyote.' *American Indian Quarterly* 8, 171-198.

Lowie, Robert H. 1924. "Shoshonean Tales," *Journal of American Folklore* 37:1-242.

Lyman, W.D. 1915. "Indian Myths of the Northwest," *PAAS* 25:375-395.

Randall, B. U. 1949. "The Cinderella Theme in Northwest Coast Folklore, *CUCA* 36:243-286.

Sapir, Edward J. 1909. *Wishram Texts by Edward Sapir Together with Wasco Tales and Myths, Collected by Jeremiah Curtin. . .*, PAES II. Leyden: E.J. Brill:314 pp. [See Wasco tales, pp. 239-311]. A recent reprinting has been done of the collected works of Edward Sapir-- with no updating or scholarly emendation.

Thompson, Stith. *Tales of the North American Indians*. Bloomington IN: Indiana University Press. [See esp. "Sources," pp. 368 ff; also "Bibliography," pp. 373-386].

G. SOCIOLOGICAL, ANTHROPOLOGICAL, ARCHAEOLOGICAL STUDIES

Aikens, C. Melvin 1986. *Archaeology of Oregon*, 2d ed. Portland: U.S. Department of Interior, Bureau of Land Management, Oregon State Office, 133 pp. [Biblio. pp. 129-133].

Barrett, S. A. 1910. *The Material Culture of the Klamath Lake and Modoc Indians of Northeastern California and Southern Oregon*, UCPAE 5(4). Berkeley CA.

Barry, J.N. 1927. "The Indians of Oregon," *Oregon Historical Quarterly* 28:49-61.

Berreman, J.V. 1937. *Tribal Distribution in Oregon*, MAAA 47. Menasha: American Anthropological Association, 7-65.

Biddle, H.J. 1926. "Wishram," *Oregon Historical Quarterly* 27:113-130.

Boas, Franz 1911. "Chinook," BAE 40. Washington DC:638-645, 650-654.

_____ 1894. *Chinook Texts*, BAE 20. Washington DC.

_____ 1901. *Kathlamet Texts*, BAE 26. Washington DC.

_____ 1897. *The Social Organization and the Secret Societies of the Kwakiutl Indians*, Report: U.S. National Museum-1895. Washington DC, 311-737.

Boyd, Robert 1996. *People of the Dalles, The Indians of Wascopam Mission; A Historical Ethnography Based on the Papers of the Methodist Missionaries*. Lincoln: University of Nebraska Press.

Browman, David L. and David A. Munsell 1969. "Columbia Plateau Pre-History: Cultural Development and Impinging Influences," *American Antiquity* 34:249-264.

Brunton, Bill B. 1968. "Ceremonial Integration in the Plateau of Northwestern North America," *Northwest Anthropological Research Notes* 2:1-28.

Cain, H. Thomas 1950. *Petroglyphs of Central Washington.* Seattle: University of Washington Press.

Cook, Sherburne F. 1955. "The Epidemic of 1830-1833 in California and Oregon," *University of California Publications in American Archaeology and Ethnology* 43:303-326.

Cope, Leona 1919. *Calendar of the Indians North of Mexico,* in *University of California Publications in American Archaeology and Ethnology* 16(4). Berkeley CA: University of California Press, 119-176 .

Cressman, Luther, et al. 1960. *Cultural Sequences at the Dalles Oregon; A Contribution to Pacific Northwest Prehistory.* Philadelphia: American Philosophical Society, 108 pp.

_____ 1937. *Petroglyphs of Oregon,"* UOPA 2:1-78. Eugene: University of Oregon.

_____ 1981. *The Sandal and the Cave; the Indians of Oregon.* Corvallis: OSU Press, 81 pp.

Daugherty, Richard D. 1956. *Early Man in the Columbia Intermontane Province,* University of Utah Anthropological Papers, No. 24. Salt Lake City: University of Utah Press.

Driver, Harold E. 1961. *Indians of North America.* Chicago: University of Chicago Press, 667 pp. [Biblio. pp. 613-633.]

French, David 1961. "The Wishram-Wasco." in *Perspectives in American Indian Culture Change,* ed. Edward H. Spicer. Chicago: University of Chicago Press, 340-430.

French, Kathryn and David 1955. "The Warm Springs Indian Community," *AMI* 7:3-16.

Gatschet, Albert S. 1890. *The Klamath Indians of Southwestern Oregon,* CNAE 2, 2 Pts. Washington DC.

Gibbs, George 1967. *Indian Tribes of Washington Territory* [repr]. Fairfield WA: Ye Galleon Press, 56 pp.

Goddard, Pliny Earl 1903. *Life and Culture of the Hupa*, UCPAAE 1(1). Berkeley, CA

Gunther, Erna 1927. *Klallam Ethnography*, University of Washington Publications in Anthropology 1(5). Seattle, WA 1927).

_____ 1950. "The Westward Movement of some Plains Traits," *American Anthropologist* 52:174-180.

Hodge, Frederick Webb, ed. 1907. *Handbook of American Indians North of Mexico*, BAE 30 [repr. 1959]. New York: Pageant Books, Inc. See "Wasco:" 917-918.

Jorgensen, Joseph G. 1980. *Western Indians; Comparative Environments, Languages and Cultures of 172 Western American Indian Tribes*. San Francisco CA: W.H. Freemason & Co., 673 pp.

Keyser, James D. 1992. *Indian Rock Art of the Columbia Plateau*. Seattle: University of Washington Press.

Krieger, H.W. 1927. "Archeological Investigations in the Columbia River Valley," *Smithsonian Institution Miscellaneous Collections* 38:187-200.

_____ 1928 . "A Prehistoric Pit House Village Site on the Columbia River at Wahluke, Grant County, Washington," *Proceedings of the U.S. National Museum* 73:1-29.

Kroeber, A.L. 1925. *Handbook of the Indians of California*, BBAE 78. Washington D.C.

Lewis, Albert B. 1906. *Tribes of the Columbia Valley and the Coast of Washington and Oregon*, MAAA I:147-209.

Loring, J. Malcolm and Louise 1982-1983. *Pictographs and Petroglyphs of the Oregon Country: Pt I. Columbia River & Northern Oregon; Pt II. Southern Oregon*. Los Angeles: Institute of Archaeology, University of California, 2 vols. [Biblio., Vol. 1:306-313; Vol. 2:334-341.]

Loud, Llewellyn L. and M.R. Harrington 1929. *Lovelock Cave*, UCPAE 25(1). Berkeley, CA.

Mason, Otis. T. 1894. *North American Bows, Arrows, and Quivers*, Report: Smithsonian Institution 1893. Washington DC:631-679.

_____ 1896. *Primitive Travel and Transportation* Report: U.S. National Museum-1894. Washington DC:235-593.

Minto, John 1900. "The Number and Condition of the Native Race in Ore--
      gon. . . ," *Oregon Historical Quarterly* 1:296-315.

Mooney, James 1928. *The Aboriginal Population of America North of Mexico,*
      Smithsonian Misc. Coll. 80, no. 7 [Publ. 2955]. Washington DC.

Olson, Ronald L. 1927. *Adze, Canoe, and House Types of the Northwest
      Coast,* UWPA 2(1). Seattle WA.

Ray, Verne F. 1939. *Cultural Relations in the Plateau of Northwestern Ameri-
      ca,* Publications of the Frederick Webb Hodge Anniversary Publi-
      cation Fund, No. 3. Los Angeles: Southwest Museum, 154 pp.

_____ 1941. "Historic Backgrounds of the Conjuring Complex in the Pla-
      teau and the Plains," in *Language, Culture, Personality, Essays in
      Memory of Edward Sapir.* Menasha WI:204-216.

_____ 1936. "The Kolaskin Cult," *American Anthropologist* 38:67-75.

_____ 1936. "Native Villages and Groupings of the Columbia Basin," *Pacific
      Northwest Quarterly* 27:99-152.

_____ 1938. "Tribal Distribution in Eastern Oregon and Adjacent Regions,"
      American Anthropologist 40:384-415.

Sapir, Edward 1907. "Notes on the Takelma Indians of Southwestern Oregon,"
      American Anthropologist 9:251-275.

Schuster, Helen 1975. *Yakima Indian Traditionalism: A Study in Continuity and
      Change,.* Seattle: U of WA Ph.D. diss.

Smith, A.H. 1953. *The Indians of Washington,* RSSCW 21:85-113.

Spier, Leslie 1928. *Havasupai Ethnography,* PaAM 29(3). New York NY.

_____ 1936. *Tribal Distribution in Washington,* General Series in Anthro-
      pology 3. Menasha WI: George Banta, 1-43

_____ & Edward Sapir 1930. *Wishram Ethnography,* UWPA 3. Seattle, Uni-
      versity of Washington Press, 151-300.

Spinden, Herbert J. 1908. *The Nez Perce Indians,* MAAA 2, pt. 3. Lancaster
      PA: The New Era Publ. Co.

Steward, Julian H. 1928. "A Peculiar Type of Stone Implement," *American
      Anthropologist* 30:314-316.

Strong, Emory 1959. *Stone Age on the Columbia River.* Portland OR: Binsfords and Mort

Strong, W.D., W.E. Schenck and J.H. Steward 1930. *Archaeology of the Dalles-Deschutes Region,* UCPAAE 29:1-154. Berkeley: University of California Press.

Strong, W.D. and W. E. Schenck 1925. "Petroglyphs Near the Dalles of the Columbia River, *American Anthropologist* 27:76-90.

Sturtevant, William C. ed. 1978. *Handbook of North American Indians.* Washington DC: Smithsonian Institution. See esp. Vol. 7.

Suphan, Robert J. 1974. *Oregon Indians II: Ethnological Report on the Wasco and Tenino Indians; Ethnological Report on the Umatilla, Walla Walla, and Cayuse Indians: Commission Findings,* American Indian Ethnohistory Series: Indians of the Northwest. New York: Garland Publishing Co., 534 pp.

Swanson, Earl H. Jr. 1962. *The Emergence of Plateau Culture,* Occasional Papers 8. Pocatello: Idaho State University Museum.

_____1970. "Sources for Plateau Prehistory," *American Antiquity* 35: 495-496.

_____ C. Melvin Aikens, David G. Rice, and Donald H. Mitchell 1970. "Cultural Relations Between the Plateau and Great Basin," *Northwest Anthropological Research Notes* 4:65-125.

Swanton, John R. 1952. *The Indian Tribes of North America,* BAE 145. Washington DC 1952:762 pp. [Biblio. pp. 643-682. See "Wasco," p. 475; also "Wishram," pp. 449-450.]

_____ 1968. *Indian Tribes of Washington, Oregon and Idaho.* Fairfield WA: Ye Galleon Press, 80 pp.

Teit, James H. 1928. *The Middle Columbia Salish,* UWPA 2(4). Seattle WA.

_____ 1900. *The Thompson Indians of British Columbia,* M-AMNH 2(4). New York NY.

Wight, E.L., Mary Mitchell and Marie Schmidt, comps. 1960. *Indian Reservations of the Northwest; the People, Their Land, Their Life.* Portland: U.S. Bureau of Indian Affairs (Portland Area Office), 97 pp.

Wissler, Clark 1910. *Material Culture of the Blackfoot Indians,* PaAM 5(1). New York NY.

Zucker, Jeff, et al. 1983. *Oregon Indians: Culture, History, and Current Affairs, An Atlas and Introduction*. Portland, OR: Western Imprints, Press of the Oregon Historical Society, 229 pp. [Biblio. pp. 193-221].

H. FOLK SPEECH, LANGUAGE

Boas, Franz 1904. "The Vocabulary of the Chinook Language," *American Anthropologist* 6:118-147.

Gatschet, A.S. 1877. "Indian Languages of the Pacific States and Territories," *MAH* 1:145-171.

Dyk, W. and Dell H. Hymes 1956. "Stress Accent in Wishram Chinook," *International Journal of Anthropological Linguistics* 22:238-241.

Jacobs, Melville 1937. "Historic Perspectives in Indian Languages of Oregon and Washington," *Pacific Northwest Quarterly* 28:55-74.

Sapir, Edward 1926. "A Chinookan Phonetic Law," *International Journal of Anthropological Linguistics* 4: 105-110.

_____ 1907. "Preliminary Report on the Language and Mythology of the Upper Chinook," *American Anthropologist* 9:533-544.

_____ 1916. "Terms of Relationship and the Levirate," *American Anthropologist* 18:327-337.

_____ 1909. *Wishram Texts, Together with Wasco Tales and Myths*, PAES II. Leyden: E.J. Brill. [Sapir's Wishram language versions of tales appear here alongside English translations.]

Swanton, John R. 1900. "Morphology of the Chinook Verb," *American Anthropologist* 2:199-232.

I. GAMES

Butler, B.R. 1958. The Prehistory of the Dice Game in the Southern Plateau," *TEBIWA* 2:65-71.

K. BIBLIOGRAPHIES

Ault, Nelson A. 1959. *The Papers of Lucullus Virgil McWhorter*. Pullman WA: Friends of the Library, State College of Washington [WSU], 144 pp.

Bjoring, Bob and Susan Cunningham 1982. *Explorers' and Travellers' Journals Documenting Early Contacts with Native Americans in the Pacific Northwest, 1741-1900*, Bibliographic Series, UW Libraries 3. Seattle WA, 15 pp.

Bonnerjea, Biren, comp. 1963. *Index to Bulletins 1-100 of the Bureau of American Ethnology; With Index to Contributions to North American Ethnology, Introductions, and Miscellaneous Publications* BAE 178. Washington DC: U.S. Gov't Printing Office, 726 pp.

Butler, Ruth Lapham comp. 1937. *A Check List of Manuscripts in the Edward E. Ayer Collection, The Newberry Library.* Chicago: The Newberry Library, 295 pp.

Carriker, Robert C. and Eleanor R. 1987. *Guide to the Microfilm Edition of the Pacific Northwest Tribes Missions Collection of the Oregon Province Archives of the Society of Jesus.* Wilmington DE: Scholarly Resources, 97 pp.

Field, Thomas W. repr. 1951. *An Essay Towards an Indian Bibliography. Being a Catalogue of Books, Relating to the History, Antiquities, Languages, Customs, Religion, Wars, Literature, and Origin of the American Indians, in the Library of Thomas W. Field.* [New York: Scribner, Armstrong & Co. 1873]. Columbus: Long's College Book Co., 430 pp.

Freeman, John F. comp. 1966. *A Guide to Manuscripts Relating to the American Indian in the Library of the American Philosophical Society*, MAPS 65. Philadelphia PA: American Philosophical Society, 491 pp. {But see "Kendall" below}.

Hewlett, Leroy, comp. 1969. *Indians of Oregon; A Bibliography of Materials in the Oregon State Library.* Salem OR, 125 pp.

Index to Literature on the American Indian, 1970. [Published for the American Indian Historical Society] San Francisco CA: Indian Historian Press.

Kendall, Daythal comp. 1982. *A Guide to Manuscripts Relating to the American Indian in the Library of the American Philosophical Society*, MAPS 65s [supplemental]. Philadelphia PA: American Philosophical Society, 168 pp. {See "Freeman" above}.

Larner, John W. comp. 1987. *Guide to the Scholarly Resources, Microfilm Edition, of the Papers of the Society of American Indians.* Wilmington DE: Scholarly Resources, 74 pp.

Murdock, George P. and Timothy J. O'Leary 1975. *Ethnographic Bibliography of North America*, 4th ed. New Haven CT: Human Relations Area

Files Press, 5 vols.

Schuster, Helen H. 1982. *The Yakimas, A Critical Bibliography*. Bloomington IN: Indiana University Press, 158 pp.

Seaburg, William R. 1982. *Guide to Pacific Northwest Native American Materials in the Melville Jacobs Collection and in Other Archival Collections in the University of Washington Libraries*, Communications in Librarianship 2. Seattle WA: University of Washington Libraries, 113 pp.

Young, Frederick G. ed. 1897-1899. *Sources of the History of Oregon*. Eugene OR: University Press.

ACKNOWLEDGMENTS

This manuscript was prepared in WordPerfect 7. Printing of the manuscript was done by Patterson Printing, Benton Harbor, MI. I am grateful for their expertise.

For the cover design and its preparation for press I am grateful to Mrs. Kathleen S. McAffrey of Starr Design, 7123 W. Weaver Pl., Littleton, Colorado 80123. The front cover features a petroglyph from the vicinity of Spedis, Washington--likely a representation of the Water Monster of Tale 1B, or the "Walalap" Monster of Tale 6A herein. For his computer expertise in preparation of the volume's photo pages, my thanks go to Mark Todd, of Mark Todd Graphics, 1311 NE Ravenna Blvd, Seattle WA 98105

I am indebted to the following individuals for publication permissions. First, Prof. John Guido, Head, Manuscripts, Archives and Special Collections, and his staff at Holland Library, Washington State University, gave permissions to publish materials from the "Lucullus McWhorter Papers." Second, I am especially grateful to Mrs. Judy McWhorter Goodwin for allowing me to publish from the papers originally compiled by her grandfather, Lucullus V. McWhorter. Finally, for providing photographs used herein, I am grateful to the Special Collections and Preservation Division, the University of Washington, especially Librarian for Photographs Prof. Richard H. Engeman.

For their sharp-eyed proofreading I am grateful to Alan Hines and to Silke Wendt. All remaining errors are mine alone.

ORDER FORM

GREAT EAGLE PUBLISHING, INC.
3020 Issaquah-Pine LK Rd. SE   Ste 481
Issaquah WA 98029 7255
☎ 425 392 9136
FAX 425 391 7812

Please Send:
_____copies of **WHERE THE RIVER ROARED: THE WISHOM TALES** at $23.95 per copy.

_____ copies of **CELILO TALES: WASCO MYTHS, LEGENDS, TALES OF MAGIC AND THE MARVELOUS** at $21.95 per copy.

_____ copies of **TRAGEDY OF THE WAHK-SHUM: THE DEATH OF ANDREW J. BOLON, AS TOLD BY SU-EL-LIL, EYEWITNESS; ALSO, THE SUICIDE OF GENERAL GEORGE A. CUSTER AS TOLD BY OWL CHILD, EYEWITNESS** at $10.95 per copy.

_____ copies of **MAGIC IN THE MOUNTAINS, THE YAKIMA SHAMAN: POWER & PRACTICE** at $17.95 per copy.

_____ copies of **GHOST VOICES, YAKIMA INDIAN MYTHS, LEGENDS, HUMOR AND HUNTING STORIES** at $23.95 per copy.

Please turn over

_____ copies of **THE FORGOTTEN TRIBES, ORAL TALES OF THE TENINOS AND ADJACENT MID-COLUMBIA RIVER INDIAN NATIONS** at $12.95 per copy.

I understand that I may return any book for a full refund--for any reason, no questions asked.

Name _____

Address _____

City _____ State _____ ZIP+4_____

Sales Tax
Please add 8.2% for books shipped
to Washington State addresses

Shipping and Handling
Book rate: $2.00 for the first book
and $0.75 for each additional book
(Surface shipping may take 3 or 4 weeks

(Please pass this order form to your librarian.)